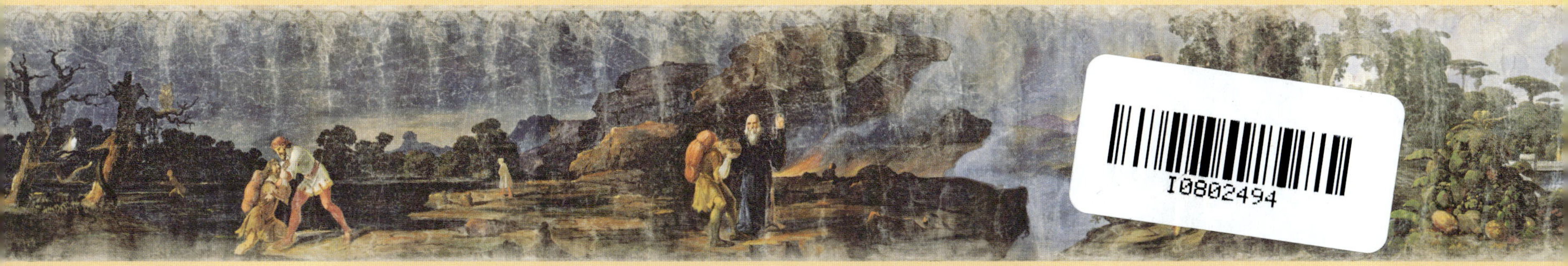

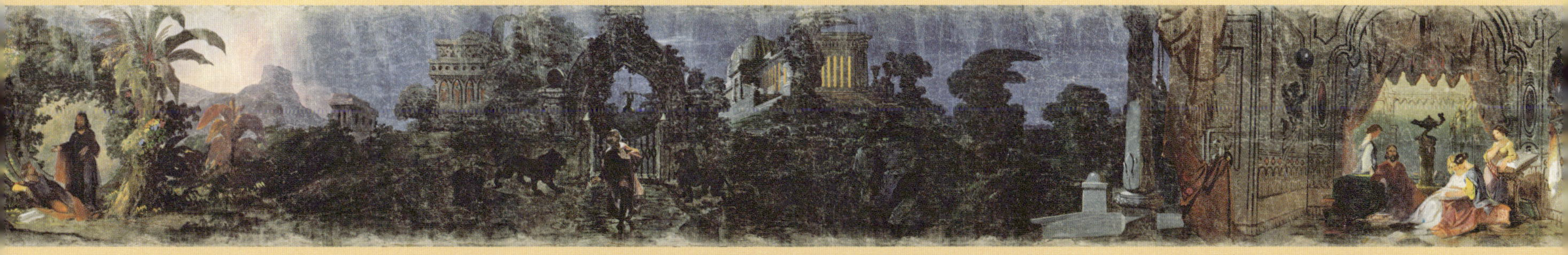

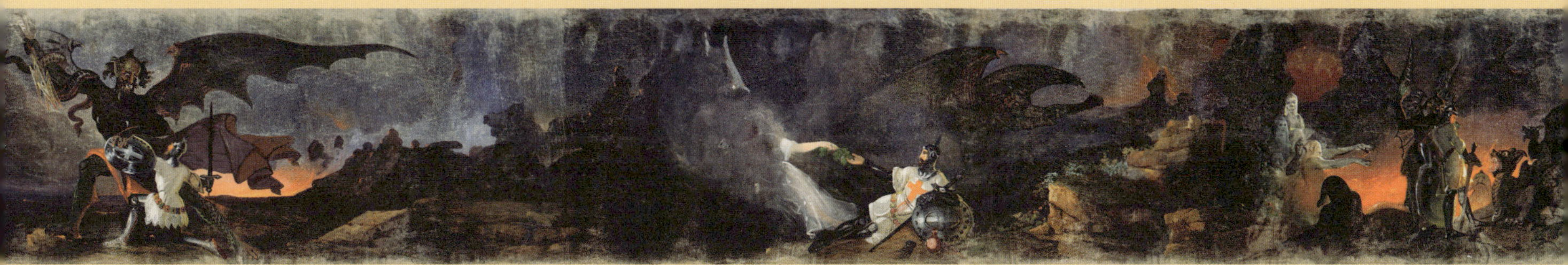

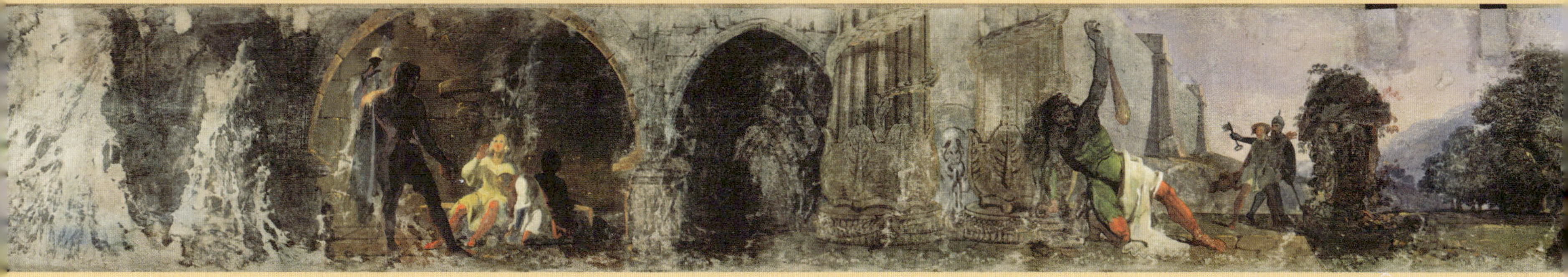

THE PAINTERS' PANORAMA

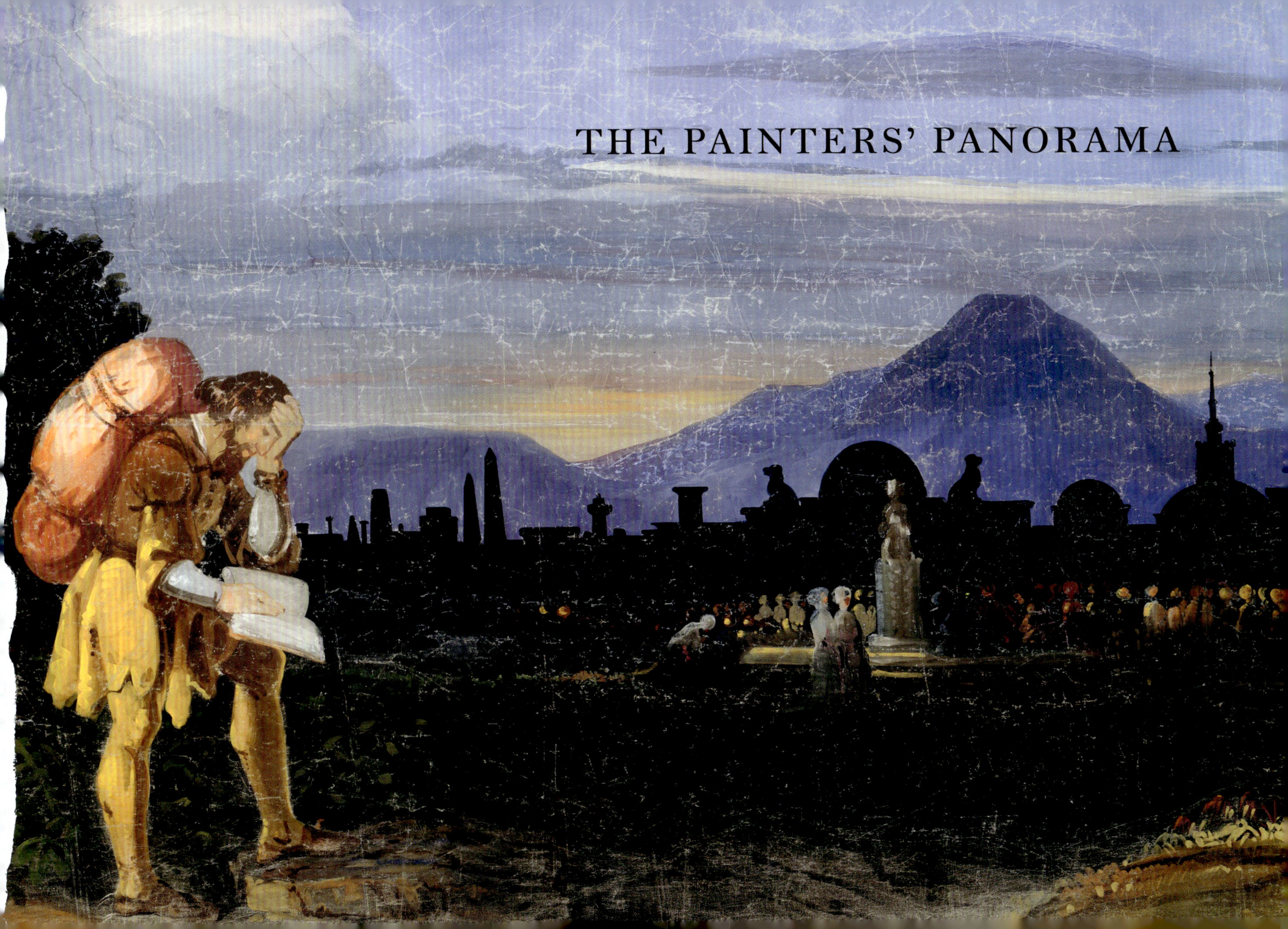

JESSICA SKWIRE ROUTHIER, KEVIN J. AVERY, AND THOMAS HARDIMAN JR.

THE PAINTERS'

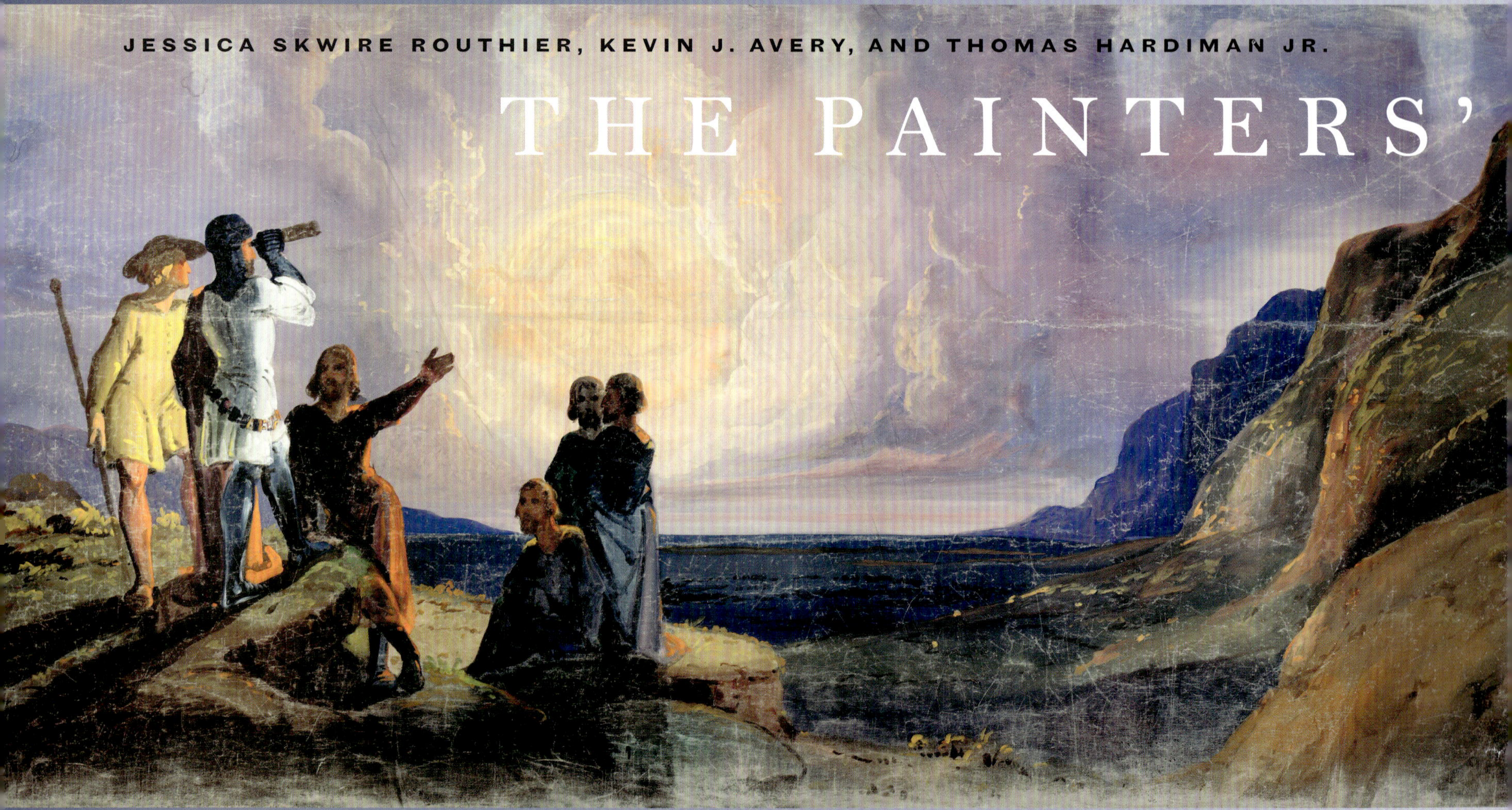

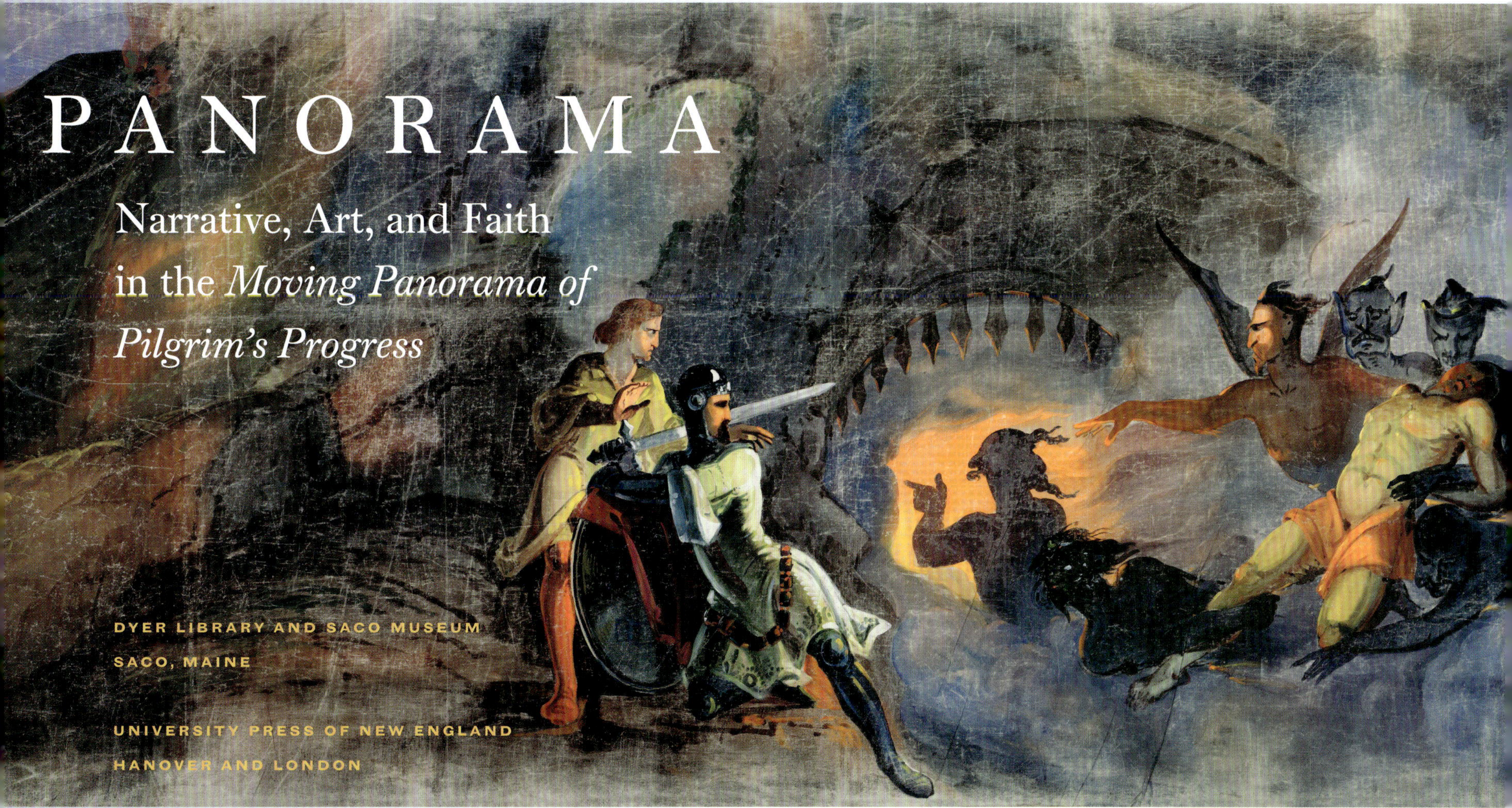

PANORAMA

Narrative, Art, and Faith in the *Moving Panorama of Pilgrim's Progress*

DYER LIBRARY AND SACO MUSEUM
SACO, MAINE

UNIVERSITY PRESS OF NEW ENGLAND
HANOVER AND LONDON

University Press of New England
www.upne.com

Manufactured in China
Designed and typeset in Monticello by Eric M. Brooks

Production of this publication has been supported by generous grants from the Wyeth Foundation for American Art and the Maine Arts Commission.

The Painters' Panorama: Art, Faith, and Narrative in the Moving Panorama of Pilgrim's Progress represents the final phase in a larger project, organized by the Dyer Library and Saco Museum, to preserve and reinterpret the *Moving Panorama of Pilgrim's Progress* and to make it accessible to a global audience. That project was made possible by grants from Save America's Treasures through a partnership between the National Endowment for the Arts and the National Park Service, Department of the Interior; the Wyeth Foundation for American Art; the Maine Arts Commission; the Davis Family Foundation; the Maine Humanities Council; Saco & Biddeford Savings Institution; and the Gateway Foundation.

All photography of the *Moving Panorama of Pilgrim's Progress* is by Matthew Hamilton of the Williamstown Art Conservation Center, unless otherwise noted.

All color plates are from Jacob Dallas, Joseph Kyle, and Edward Harrison May, *The Moving Panorama of Pilgrim's Progress*, 1851, distemper on muslin. Saco Museum, Saco, Maine. Gift of the heirs of Luther Bryant, 1896. Photography by Matthew Hamilton, Williamstown Art Conservation Center; photo splicing by Portland Color.

Library of Congress Cataloging-in-Publication Data
Routhier, Jessica Skwire.
The painters' panorama: narrative, art, and faith in the *Moving Panorama of Pilgrim's Progress* / Jessica Skwire Routhier, Kevin J. Avery, and Thomas Hardiman Jr., Dyer Library and Saco Museum, Saco, Maine.
pages cm
Includes bibliographical references and index.
ISBN 978-1-61168-663-0 (cloth: alk. paper)
1. Bunyan, John, 1628–1688. Pilgrim's progress. 2. Christianity and literature. 3. Art in literature. I. Avery, Kevin J. II. Hardiman, Thomas, Jr. III. Title.
PR3330.A9R76 2014 828'.407—dc23 2014025346

5 4 3 2 1

FOR MAINE'S MUSEUMS

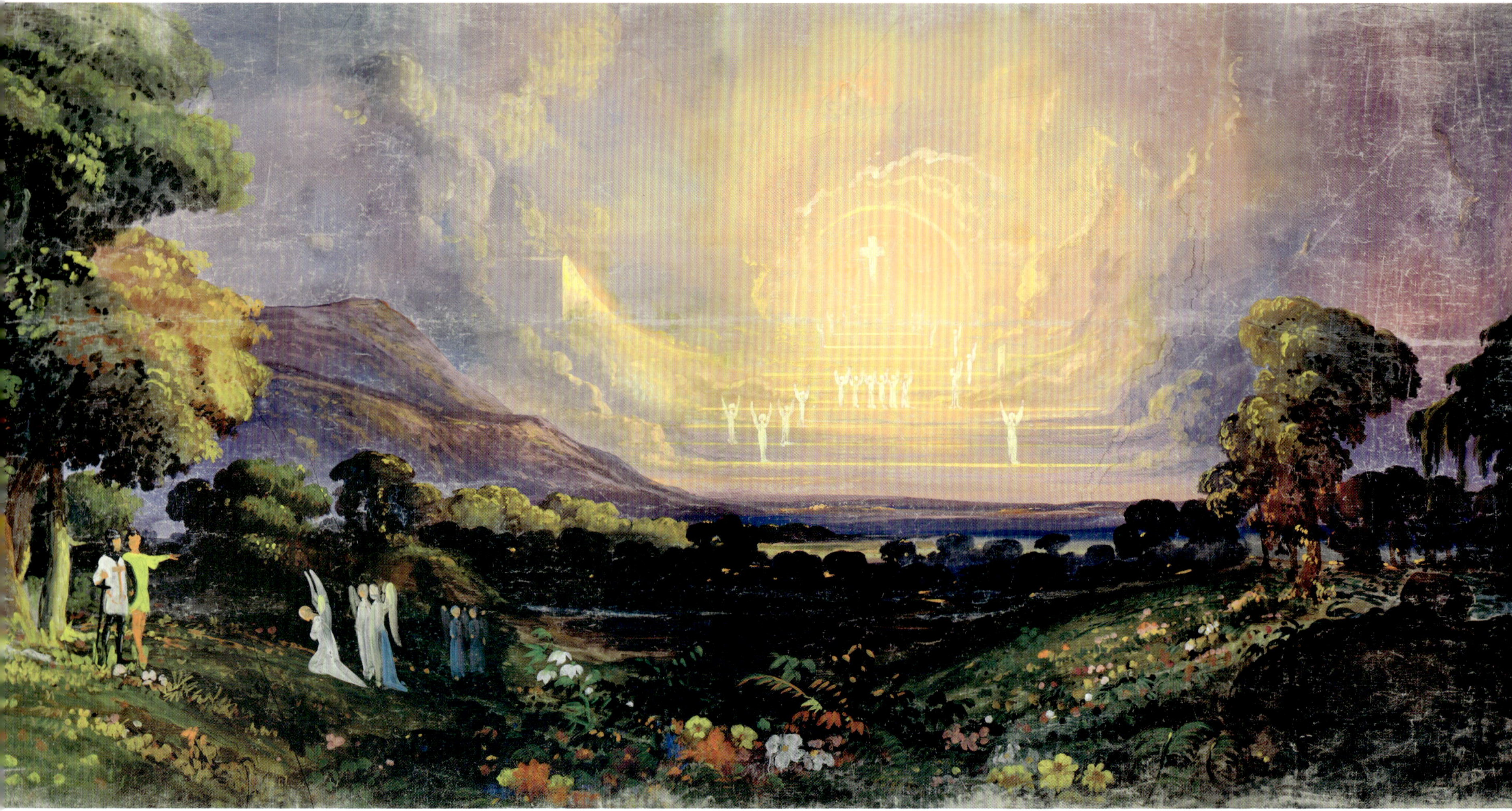

CONTENTS

Foldout appears after page 46.

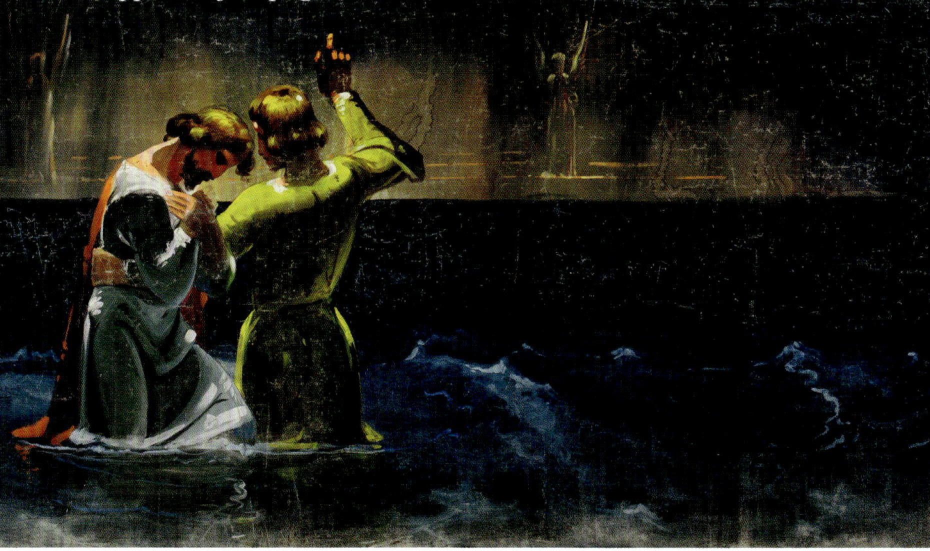

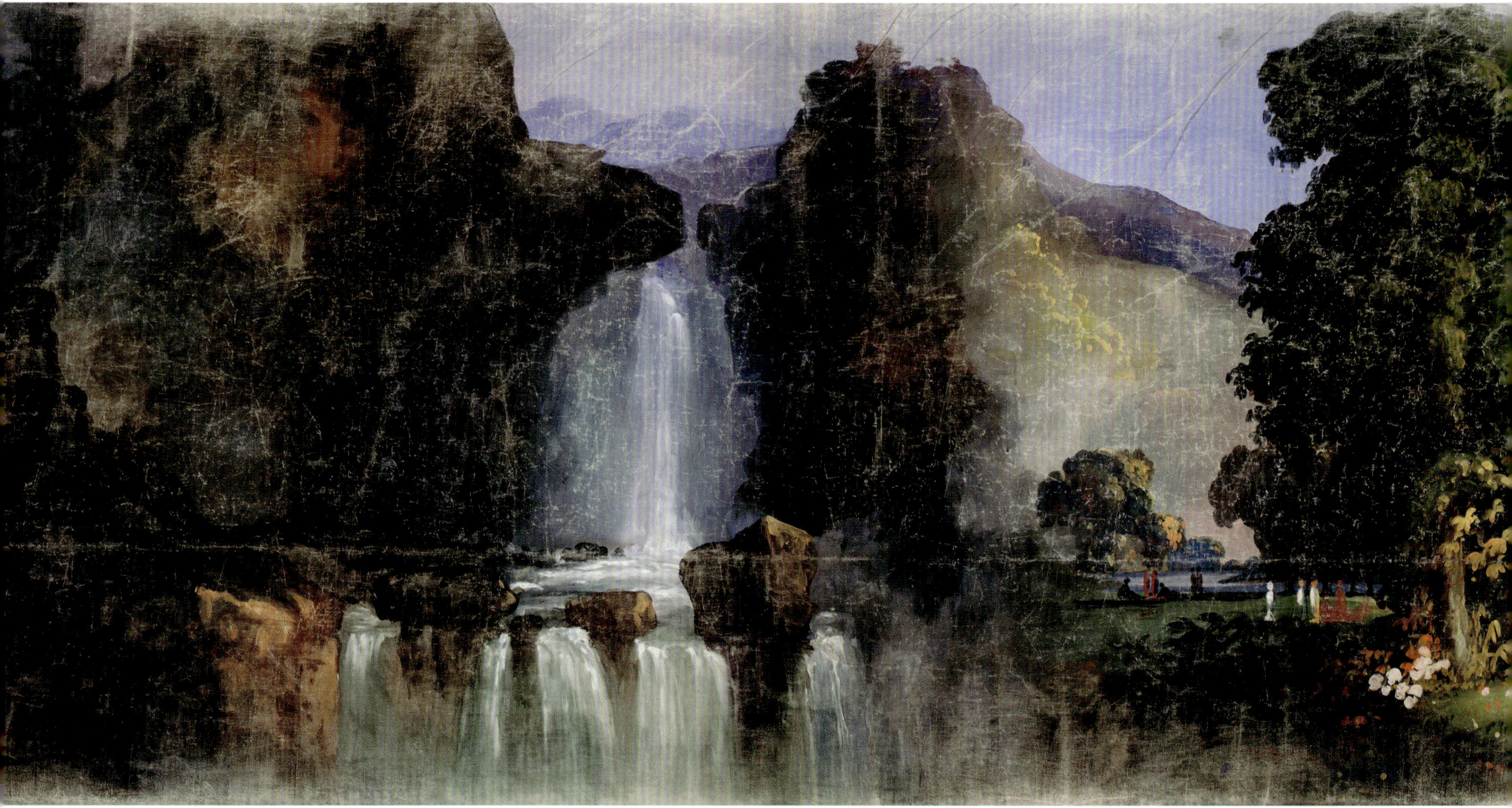

INTRODUCTION & ACKNOWLEDGMENTS

When people talk about the *Moving Panorama of Pilgrim's Progress*, they often talk about the numbers: measuring eight feet high and eight hundred feet long, it cost $10,000 to create, generated $100,000 in admissions in its first six months, and was the focus of a $170,000-plus restoration project in 2012. After its 1851 debut, it toured the country for some fifteen years and then was lost for one hundred years. It was created in 1851, donated in 1896, rediscovered in 1996, and finally completely conserved in 2012, when it was seen by thousands of people in a historic textile mill in downtown Biddeford, Maine. But the numbers do little to quantify what a truly monumental undertaking this book and the project that preceded it have been for the Dyer Library and Saco Museum, and how many people contributed to its success.

It is pure happenstance that this remarkable object came to be in the collections of the Saco Museum, a small but important historical museum on the southern Maine coast. Designed by leading American artists Frederic Edwin Church, Jasper Cropsey, and Daniel Huntington, among others, the panorama was the toast of the town in 1850s New York—a unique combination of artistic masterpiece and theatrical performance that absolutely could not be missed. It was reviewed and written about endlessly during its time, providing fodder for everything from sermons to poetry. Later, twentieth-century art historians referred to it frequently when they wrote about the Hudson River School painters who had contributed to its production; but by then, no one had seen it in decades, and so they wrote about it without ever knowing what it looked like or where it was.

That all changed in 1996, when the panorama, tightly rolled with the images concealed from sight, was rediscovered in the storage vault of the Saco Museum, and an old newspaper clipping confirmed that the *Moving Panorama of Pilgrim's Progress* had indeed been given to the museum (then known as the York Institute) in 1896. (The panorama's complicated provenance, detailed in the essays in this book, identifies the New York-Maine point of connection as Charles E. Shaw, a Biddeford entrepreneur who was also a theater owner and friend to P. T. Barnum.) For the first time in a hundred years, scholars could talk not only about the panorama's importance but also about its appearance; its significance as a work of art as well as a rare existing example of this strange and wonderful phenomenon known as a moving panorama could be discussed in tandem.

Efforts to preserve the panorama and make it accessible to a broad audience began shortly after its rediscovery; a late-1990s conservation campaign culminated in an exhibition tour, organized by the Montclair Art Museum in New Jersey, of about half the panorama. Ten years later, a transformative grant from Save America's Treasures gave the Dyer Library and Saco Museum the tools needed to complete what they had begun: full conservation and photography of every inch of the panorama, front and back; creation of a full-size replica on modern fabric that can be performed in motion, as the original was meant to be seen (and which delighted hundreds of viewers in five performances in 2012); a web-based film that is both a treat to watch and an invaluable digital record of the panorama in motion; a major museum exhibition with accompanying programs; and finally, rewardingly, and lastingly, this book.

Thanks must first go to Jessica Skwire Routhier, former Saco Museum director, who shepherded this most recent phase of the panorama project from beginning to end. Even after Jessica no longer worked for the Saco Museum, she remained devoted to completing the project with this book in a way that will be of lasting benefit to both the panorama and the museum. Jessica's scholarship, both inside and outside of these pages, was influenced greatly by those involved in the panorama's initial discovery and accompanying research: Kevin J. Avery and Thomas Hardiman Jr., both of whom also have contributed essays to this book and advised Jessica on the content of hers, and Peter Morelli, a long-standing Dyer Library/Saco Museum trustee, who presented what would become an outline of the project at the International Panorama Council's 2004 New York City conference and who has actively studied, promoted, and literally wrangled with the panorama for nearly twenty years.

This book is the culminating achievement of the larger project to preserve and interpret the *Moving Panorama of Pilgrim's Progress*, and as such, thanks are due here to all who participated. These individuals and institutions include

Save America's Treasures (a partnership between the National Endowment for the Arts and the National Park Service), the Wyeth Foundation for American Art, the Maine Arts Commission, the Davis Family Foundation, the Maine Humanities Council, Saco & Biddeford Savings Institution, and the Gateway Foundation, all of whom provided crucial funding; Tom Branchick, Gabriel Dunn, and Matthew Hamilton at Williamstown Art Conservation Center, who conserved the panorama and took the incredible photographs that are used in this book; Andy Graham, Paul Glynn, and Mark Marchesi at Portland Color (now a division of Designtex), who created the fabric replica; Joshua Hurd, Jeff Fleming, Mark Thompson, and John Eaton, who with substantial help from Bob Flint, Ed Profenno, Marcel Desrosiers, and David Lawlor created the machine to make the replica "go"; panorama showmen Scott Marcoux, Will Rankin, Dean Smalley, and Terry Borton of the American Magic Lantern Theater; performance pianist Jeff Rapsis; panorama backstage crew and turners Bob Hamblen, Dick Lambert, Janet Morelli, Gil Poirier, Nancy Tripp, and David Twomey; Bill Millios of Back Lot Films, along with Michael Howard and Jeff Rapsis, who provided direction and talent for the panorama film; Doug Sanford and Scott Joslin from the Pepperell Mill Campus, who furnished the awe-inspiring space in which three-quarters of the panorama was exhibited; Carolyn Gosselin and others from the Biddeford Mills Museum, Carolyn's students at Biddeford High School, and the University of New England's Trailblazer volunteers, who offered indispensable on-site support; the City of Saco, Saco Spirit, and the Saco Sesquibicentennial Committee for embracing the project as their own; collectors Jonathan Gestetner and Richard Balzer, and many others, who lent valuable objects for the exhibition; Suzanne Wray, Erkki Huhtamo, and Ralph Hyde, who provided key research and counsel over many years; and most important, eternally hardworking Saco Museum staff, volunteers, and trustees Anna Kelley, Jim Macos, Marie O'Brien, Linsey Pilon, Tara Vose Raiselis, John Morrill Read, Camille Smalley, Dean Smalley, Martha Taylor, and countless others.

Finally, thanks to those who believed in this project enough to make this book its final, satisfying chapter: Michael P. Burton and the University Press of New England for giving it the green light and all the support that followed; Lora Urbanelli and Gail Stavitsky at the Montclair Art Museum, who graciously paved the way for Kevin Avery and Tom Hardiman's essays to be reprinted here; and the Wyeth Foundation for American Art, which remained a steadfast supporter of this book and provided additional and essential funds through various twists and turns in the publication process. Special thanks are due to Wanda M. Corn, the Robert and Ruth Halperin Professor Emerita in Art History at Stanford University and a member of the Wyeth Foundation's board, who provided the support and encouragement without which this book would never have become a reality.

LESLIE L. ROUNDS
Executive Director
Dyer Library & Saco Museum

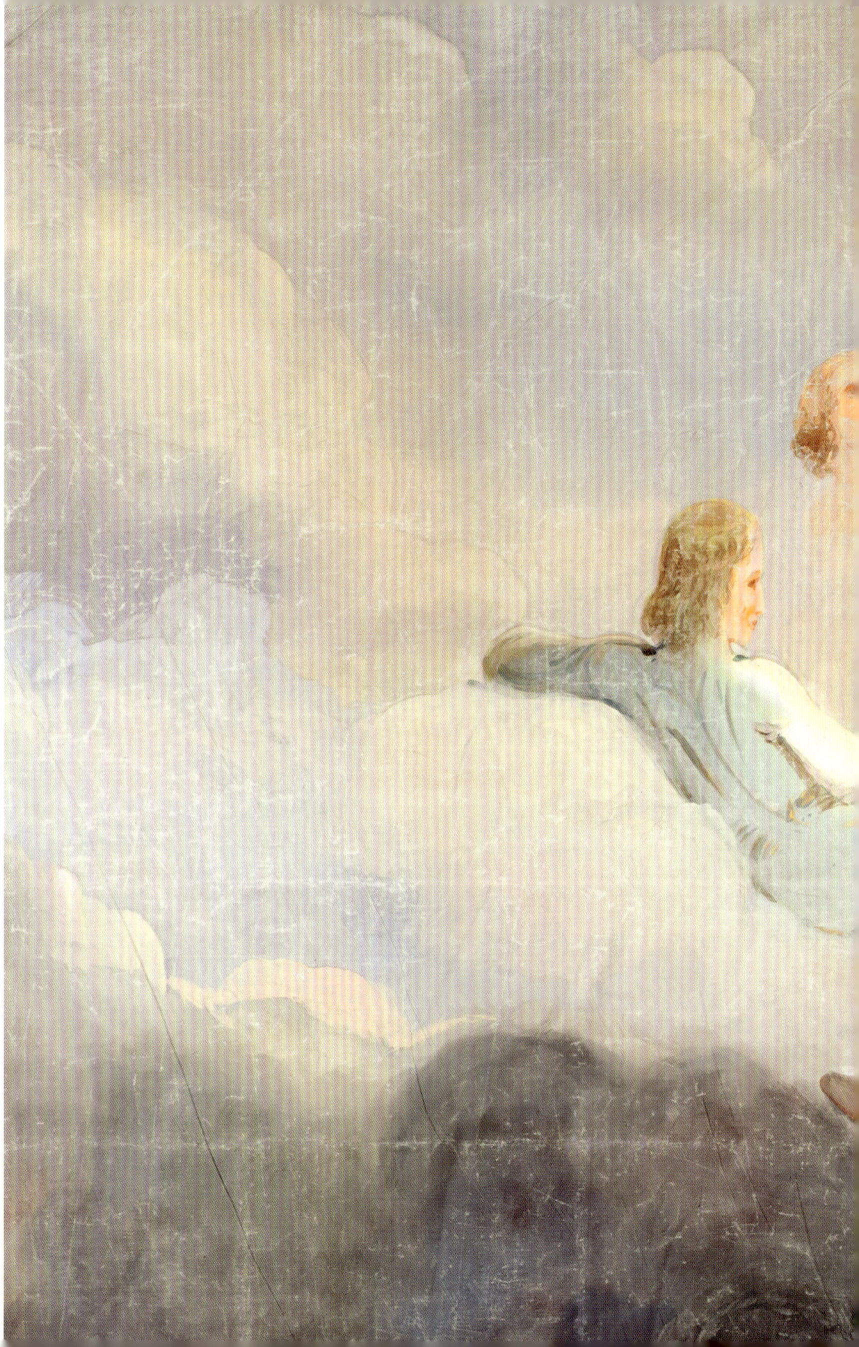

THE PAINTERS' PANORAMA

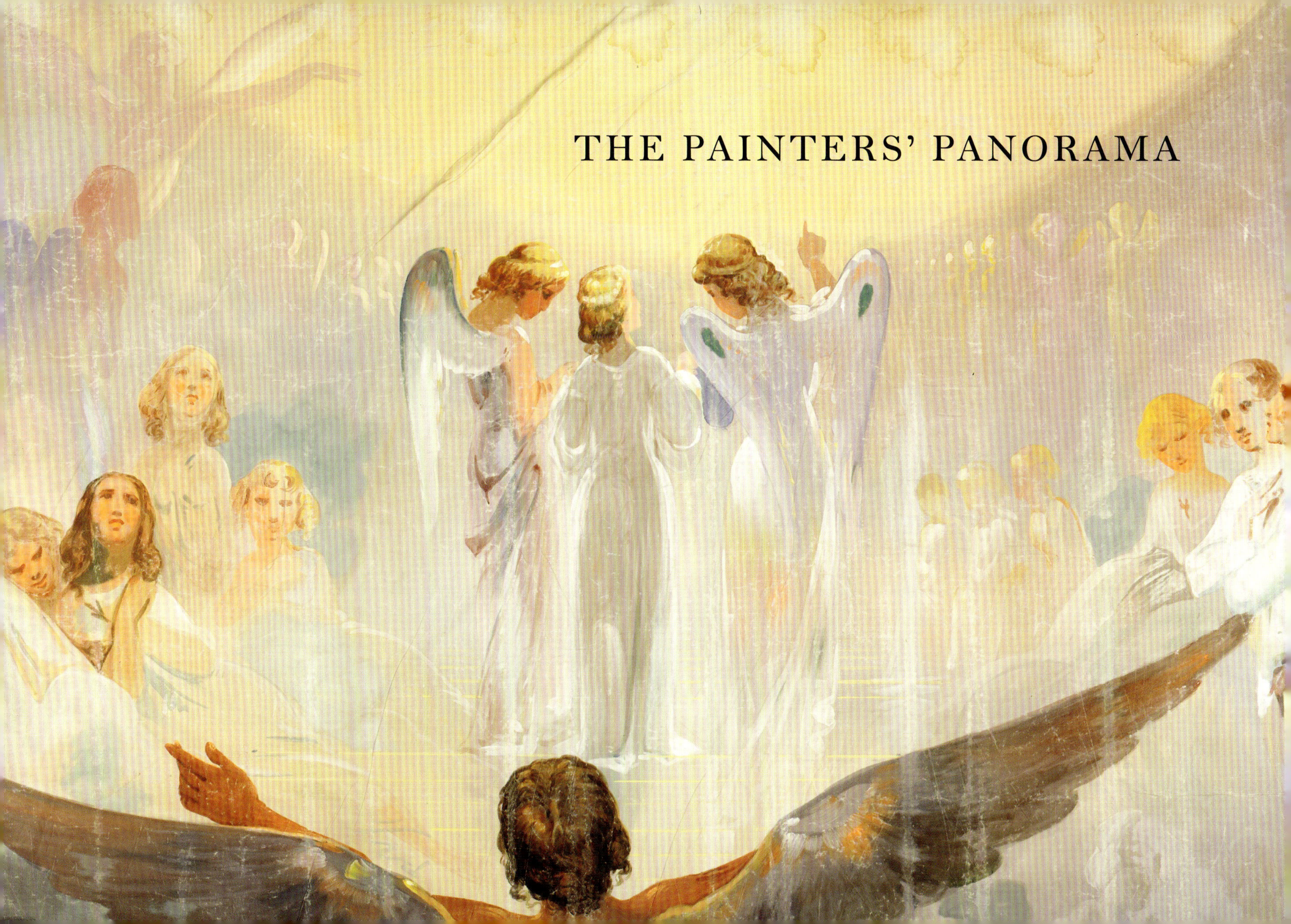

JESSICA SKWIRE ROUTHIER

"A MORE PERFECT VIEW THEREOF"

Landscape, Religion, and the Artistic Underpinnings of the Panorama

Now as they walked in this land, they had more rejoicing than in parts more remote from the kingdom to which they were bound; and drawing near to the city, they had yet a more perfect view thereof.

John Bunyan, *The Pilgrim's Progress*

"WE KNEW THIS THING WAS DOWN THERE," explained Tom Hardiman, curator of what was then known as the York Institute Museum in Saco, Maine.[1] "It was that rolled-up thing we had to work around all the time." Gesturing to the colossal scenes of monsters, demons, armored men, and virtuous maidens blanketing the wall behind him, he added, "We were not expecting what we found."[2] Speaking in the galleries of the museum

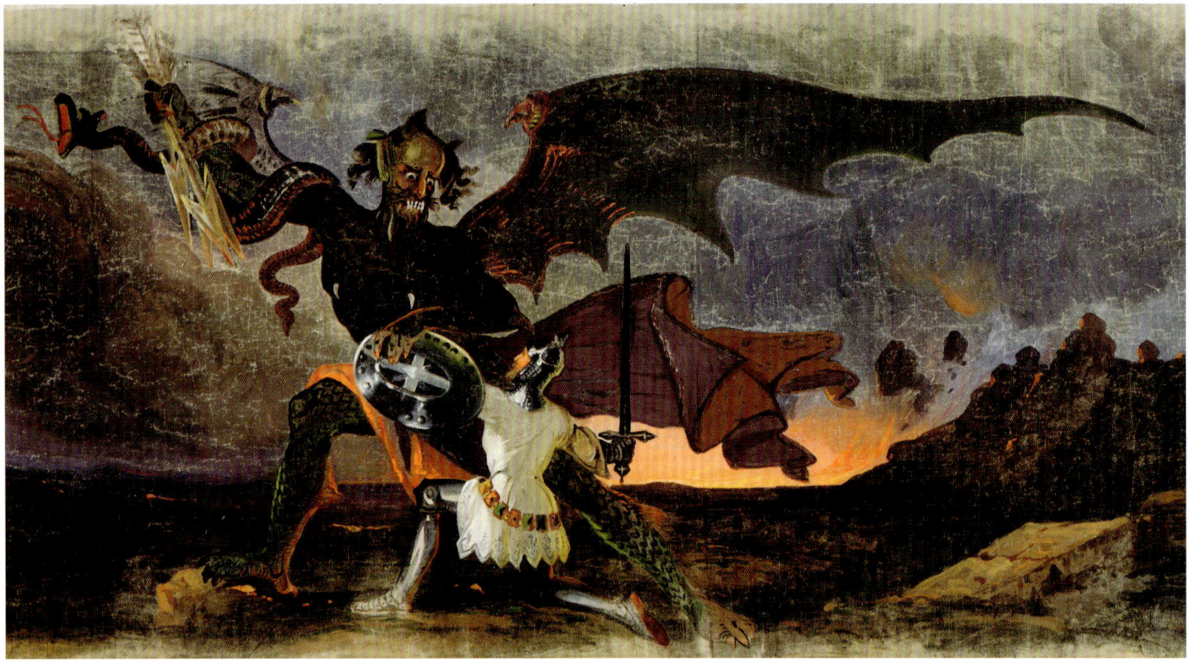

FIGURE I.I.
Fight with Apollyon, design attributed to Edward Harrison May, from the *Moving Panorama of Pilgrim's Progress*, 1851, distemper on muslin. Saco Museum, Saco, Maine. Gift of the heirs of Luther Bryant, 1896. Photo by Matthew Hamilton, courtesy Williamstown Art Conservation Center.

(now the Saco Museum), Hardiman was recalling one of those mythical moments of discovery that all curators dream about. While cleaning out the museum's storage basement in 1996, he was compelled to take a peek at two vast rolls of fabric that had been tucked away in a dark corner long ago. Unrolling just a few feet of colorful painted scenes, he could tell that this was something special, but he still was not certain what, in fact, he had discovered. Volunteer Keith Sherburne, a retired English teacher, recognized the subject as *The Pilgrim's Progress*, the iconic Christian allegory written by English preacher John Bunyan in 1678. And through diligent research (in the years when the Internet was still in its infancy), trustee Peter Morelli soon identified the museum's rolls as none other than the once-famous masterpiece of American art known as the *Moving Panorama of Pilgrim's Progress* or "The Bunyan Tableaux," created in the 1850s and thought lost for nearly a century.[3]

As Hardiman, Sherburne, and Morelli came to discover, the *Moving Panorama of Pilgrim's Progress* is not only one of the most significant objects in the collection of the Saco Museum, but it is also a remarkable, distinctive, and rare work of art by any standard. Eight feet high and nearly eight hundred feet long in its current state, it is a surviving example of a visual entertainment medium that thrived before motion pictures. Moving panoramas, which peaked in popularity in the third quarter of the nineteenth century, were meant to be displayed theatrically in front of a seated audience, with dramatic lighting, music, and narration. As the audience watched, the panorama was continuously unrolled from one gigantic spool onto another, creating the illusion that the painted scenes were progressing before the spectators' eyes. Other moving panoramas of the day included John Banvard's "three-mile picture" of the Mississippi River and a panorama based on the search for Arctic explorer Sir John Franklin,[4] but few received anything like the attention paid to the Bunyan Tableaux. Few of the others, too, have survived past their initial moment of popularity in so complete and intact a state.[5]

In 1848 American artists Edward Harrison May and Joseph Kyle conceived the idea of a moving panorama depicting the story of *The Pilgrim's Progress*,[6] the seventeenth-century Christian allegory that had become (especially in the early 1800s) a staple of literature, religious instruction, and domestic life in England and America. Kyle and May were both affiliated with the National Academy of Design in New York, an art school, membership organization, and exhibition venue for professional artists. There May studied with renowned figure painter Daniel Huntington, and in emulation of his teacher he exhibited portraits and religious and historical scenes stylistically influenced by European artistic traditions, including an 1847 painting inspired by *The Pilgrim's Progress*.[7] The panorama's sly quotations from Renaissance art — Evangelist's upward-pointing gesture, so like Plato's in Raphael's *School of Athens* (see plate 6); the allusion to Michelangelo's *The Creation of Adam* in the panorama's *Christian Reposing after the Battle* (plate 18); and the baptismal tone of Christian and Hopeful's passage through the River of Death (plate 31), so like scenes of the Baptism of Christ by Andrea Mantegna and others — may be attributable to May's interest in these traditions and easily explained by readily available print versions of the paintings in nineteenth-century America. Philadelphia-trained Kyle, for his part, had some panorama experience, having worked on one of the Mississippi in 1848.[8] He specialized in the landscape portions of the panoramas he produced,[9] a skill that dovetailed well with May's talents as a painter of portraits and figures.

Together, Kyle and May recruited Huntington and many of their other National Academy colleagues — several of whom became some of the most recognized names in nineteenth-century American art — to contribute designs for the *Moving Panorama of Pilgrim's Progress*. In addition to Huntington, Frederic Edwin Church, Jasper Cropsey, Felix Octavius Carr Darley, Paul Duggan, and Henry Courtney Selous were all participants, a fact that was hyped enthusiastically by advance publicity in the *Bulletin of the American Art-Union*[10] and no doubt contributed to the panorama's early, astonishing success after its 1850 debut at New York's Washington Hall.[11] Because the panorama was so popular and such a huge financial triumph, Kyle and May decided to create a second version that could travel the country at the same time as the first, allowing them to cover more ground and make even more money. But before the actual execution began, May left for Paris, and Kyle soon found a new partner in Jacob Dallas, a colleague from his Philadelphia days.[12] Dallas took over the figural work for the panorama's second version, and together they added some new scenes, omitted a few old ones, and corrected several imperfections from the first version.[13] The premiere of the second version took place in New York in 1851, and its success and critical reception rivaled that of the first.[14] Thomas Hardiman's essay in this book outlines a detailed history of this second version of the *Moving Panorama of Pilgrim's Progress*, which had its own travels before reaching its permanent home at the Saco Museum in 1896. There it lay mostly forgotten — even though it must have been relocated during museum building campaigns in 1926 and 1969 — until that serendipitous day one hundred years later. The fate of the original version of the panorama is not known.

So what was it about the *Moving Panorama of Pilgrim's Progress* that made it so remarkable? To modern eyes, a moving, eight-hundred-foot-long painting on fabric is indeed an unusual thing, but in its time the panorama and its twin were only two of many such curiosities touring the nation.[15] What was it that set it above its competitors, drew in thousands of viewers and their fifty-cent admissions, and caused one reviewer to praise it as "a master-piece of art, which words fail to describe"?[16] In addition to the panorama's unusually large size, the prestige of the artists who contributed to it, and the celebrated expense of its production,[17] an answer, perhaps, may be gleaned from a contemporary account of seeing the panorama performed, in which the viewing itself is articulated as a sort of moral journey:

> Beauteous meadows, gorgeous cities, and gliding streams follow in succession as we are alternately pleased or horrified by representations in figures of the various *temptations and ills that beset our daily life*, and of those blessings and rewards that counterbalance the evil.[18]

Though the story that Kyle and Dallas's canvas told — and still tells today — was first penned in seventeenth-century England, and though the tale itself is an allegory of human struggle that is meaningful outside of any particular time or place, still the panorama made the story of *The Pilgrim's Progress* immediate, palpable, and relevant for its nineteenth-century American audiences. It linked together a uniquely American penchant for technological innovation, entrepreneurship, and showmanship; a burgeoning interest in the arts and culture newly embraced by leaders of American religious life; and a desire to communicate that interest to a diverse populace. In these ways, the *Moving Panorama of Pilgrim's Progress* illustrates, in a way that few other works of art have done before or since, a moment when ideas about faith, art, and landscape all traveled along the same narrow highway in the course of American life.

The Pilgrim's Progress was first published in England in 1678 by John Bunyan, a reformist preacher who had been repeatedly imprisoned for delivering sermons that challenged the theology of the Church of England. The book, written while Bunyan was still incarcerated, was a runaway best seller from the moment it left the presses. In simple, often powerful, and affecting English, the book describes the trials, temptations, and triumphs of an Everyman named Christian journeying from his home in the City of Destruction to his final destination, the Celestial City, and eternal life. Part Two, published in 1684 (and also illustrated in the panorama), recounts the corresponding journey of Christiana, his wife. Allegorical conventions notwithstanding, *The Pilgrim's Progress* unambiguously stresses the importance of leading a Christian life and argues that each individual has the power and the obligation to seek and find salvation within his or her own life's journey.

Both parts of *The Pilgrim's Progress* had enduring significance for American audiences,[19] beginning with the early New England colonists who shared Bunyan's Protestant faith and similarly dissented from the Church of England. A century later, the book was a favorite among the founding fathers not only for its theological message but also for its topical theme of overcoming hardships to reach an ultimate goal. By the mid-1800s it was at a peak of popularity.[20] Nearly every American home with any books at all had a copy of *The Pilgrim's Progress*. Its characters, distinctive plot structure, and message had become so familiar to Americans that it became a useful trope for parodies that drove home their point by employing Bunyan's motif of a journey through a treacherous landscape.

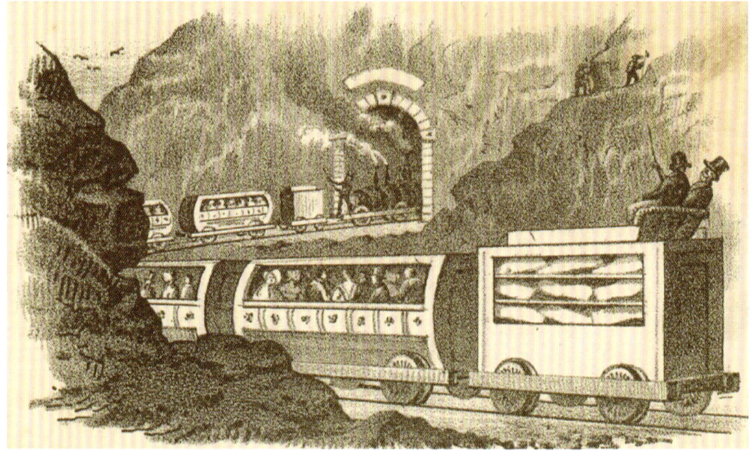

FIGURE 1.2. Illustration for Nathaniel Hawthorne, *A Visit to the Celestial City*. Printed by the American Sunday School Union, Philadelphia, 1844.

One such parody that predates the panorama is Nathaniel Hawthorne's 1843 short story *The Celestial Railroad*.[21] Hawthorne's modern-day pilgrims traverse Bunyan's landscape in the comfort and speed of steam travel. They stow their burdens of sin in the baggage car and evade pitfalls such as the Slough of Despond and Hill Difficulty by way of trestle bridges and tunnels, while the malevolent monster Apollyon serves as conductor (figure 1.2). Similarly satirical political cartoons (figures 1.3 and 1.4) printed between 1844 and 1848 lampooned candidate, and then president, James K. Polk, depicting him drawn helplessly to Bunyanesque landscape elements such as "The Salt River" and the "Mansion Despair."[22] The centrality of landscape to both of these parodies is obvious; in fact, one of the Polk cartoons takes the form of a map entitled "A Correct Chart of the Salt River," which winds through the Slough of Despond and has its terminus in the Lake of Oblivion.[23] The place names and the use of a moralized landscape, in these cartoons as well as in Hawthorne's story and its accompanying illustrations, clearly allude to *The Pilgrim's Progress* while maintaining an essential respect for its moral message. Even Hawthorne, who was famously critical of his own Puritan roots,

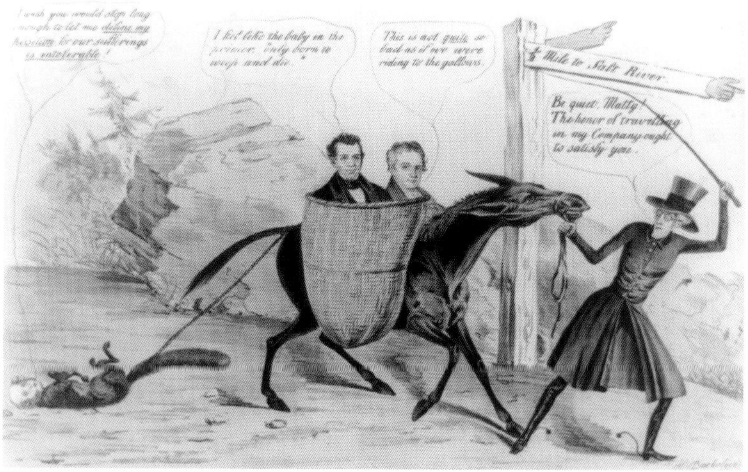

FIGURE 1.3. *Pilgrim's Progress*, 1844, lithograph. Published by James Baillie, New York, 1844. Photo courtesy Library of Congress.

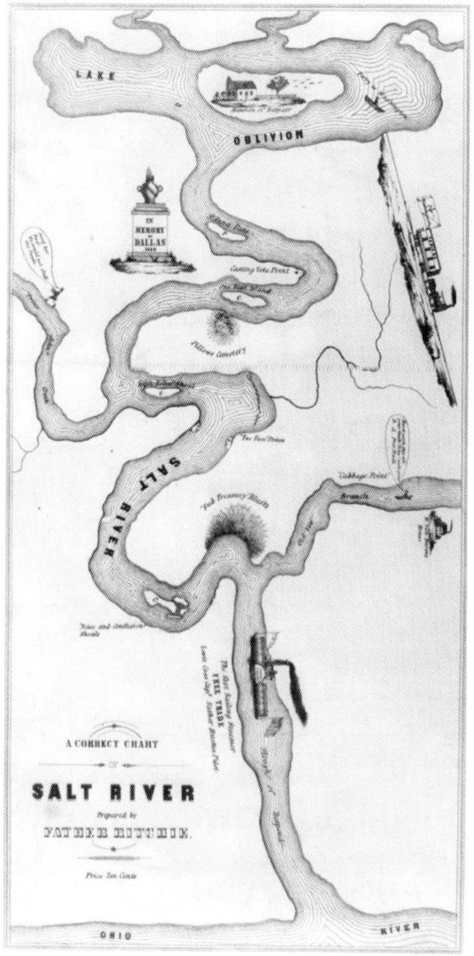

FIGURE 1.4. Artist unidentified, *A Correct Chart of Salt River*, lithograph. Published in Philadelphia, 1848. Photo courtesy Library of Congress.

pokes fun not so much at the moral hierarchy of Bunyan's allegorical landscape, but instead at the smug, modern-day pilgrims — seduced through Apollyon's wiles by the convenience of train travel — who seem to think there is a fast and easy way to get through it.

Joseph Kyle and Edward Harrison May knew that Bunyan's story and characters were woven intimately into the daily lives of their potential audience. So they assumed, correctly, that an eight-foot high, eight-hundred-foot long panorama of *The Pilgrim's Progress,* "Life-sized!" and "In Color!" as the promotional brochures boasted (see figure 2.1), would have mass popular appeal. To design their panorama, they had nearly two hundred years of pictorial precedents to guide them. Since the book's original publication in 1678, printed copies of *The Pilgrim's Progress* had featured lively black-and-white illustrations of many of the major events in the story, developing a standard iconography that would be repeated and varied over the centuries.[24] In the early nineteenth century, the allegory was a popular subject for handheld, rolled paper panoramas as well as "metamorphoses," a kind of paper-folding novelty;[25] it had even been the theme of at least one earlier moving panorama that seems not to have caught on like Kyle's and May's would.[26] Academically trained British artists such as John Martin and Henry Courtney Selous had begun to illustrate Bunyan's text with engravings for limited-edition printed volumes (figures 1.10, 2.3, and 1.22–1.24).[27] Additionally, the characters and major scenes in *The Pilgrim's Progress* had begun to draw the attention of some of the most admired American landscape painters of the day, including some of Kyle and May's talented colleagues at the National Academy of Design.

A connection between landscape painting, panoramas, and *The Pilgrim's Progress* at first may not be perfectly clear. But in fact, panoramas always had been closely connected to the travelogue tradition and, thus, to landscape painting. Earlier, stationary panoramas — which were installed in circular rooms designed to surround the viewer with a full 360-degree view — often depicted major cities or monuments,[28] offering a sort of virtual travel experience for their viewers. As Kevin Avery explains in his essay for this book, *moving* panoramas eventually became the preferred panoramic format for travelogues, since they better approximated the nature of traveling itself. As images passed through the viewing window of a moving panorama, each scene seamlessly blending into the next, spectators enjoyed the illusion that they themselves were journeying through the painted landscape. With the addition of often life-sized human figures, the landscape conceit was used to great effect in panoramas that took viewers down the length of the Mississippi, for instance, or followed a whaling ship around the world.[29] It was also an obvious fit for a panorama dedicated to *The Pilgrim's Progress*, where the theme of the protagonist's journey is central to the narrative itself.

The panoramic influence is strong in mid-nineteenth-century American landscape painting, with one scholar noting that both the panoramas and paintings of the time provided viewers with the breathtakingly powerful visual experience of simultaneously understanding a subject both in its "myriad details" and "extraordinary breadth."[30] Landscape painters sought to persuade patrons and audiences of the unique power of their art during this watershed period. Though landscape painting was on the rise, it previously had suffered from second-class status in two different ways. First, in the eighteenth and early nineteenth centuries, American landscape subjects were thought to be innately inferior to European views by artists such as Claude Lorrain and Salvator Rosa, whose Italianate subjects were imbued with "associations" bestowed by millennia of human history.[31] And second, while landscape painting would come to dominate salons and exhibitions in the Civil War period and later, prior to that time it was perceived as subordinate to figural art, especially history painting and even portraiture.[32] This woeful situation was bemoaned by critic John Neal in 1838 when he wrote, "It is a thankless calling, and at best a precarious one, that of a landscape-painter in our day."[33] The preternaturally gifted young landscape painter Thomas Cole sought to address and disarm these perceived disadvantages not only through the sheer virtuosity of his work, but also through his adoption of associations — stories, characters, messages — that had particular relevance for American art and audiences. Cole aspired to be not merely a painter of views, but also of historical and moral landscapes.

A glorious, early example of Cole's ambition is his pair of paintings *The Garden of Eden* (figure 1.5) and *Expulsion from the Garden of Eden* (Museum of Fine Arts, Boston), completed in 1828 and exhibited at the National Academy

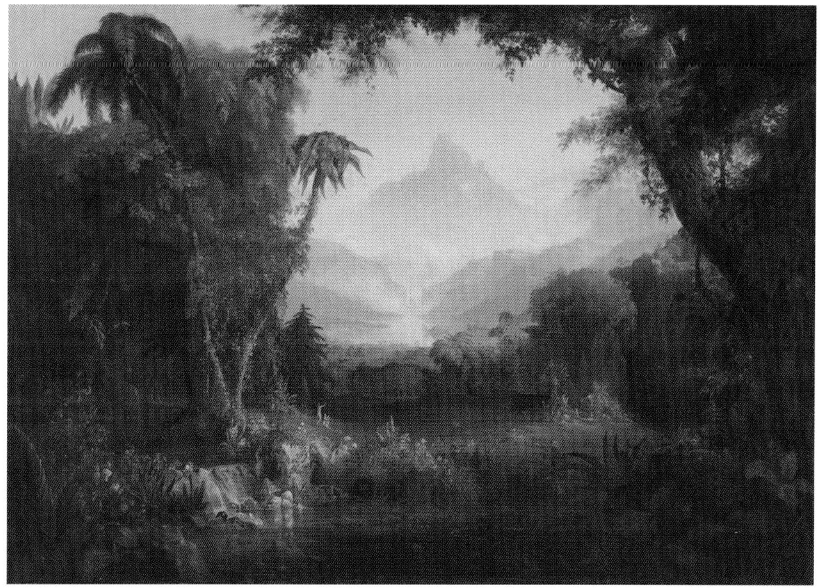

FIGURE 1.5. Thomas Cole (1801–1848), *The Garden of Eden*, 1828, oil on canvas, $38\frac{1}{2}$ x $52\frac{3}{4}$ inches. Amon Carter Museum of American Art, Fort Worth, Texas, 1990.10.

that same year. At first glance a fairly straightforward (albeit sublimely rendered) interpretation of the Bible, the paintings gain an additional layer of meaning when we recall that the American wilderness itself often was viewed as the "new Eden." Cole himself would use this metaphor eight years later in the conclusion of his influential "Essay on American Scenery,"[34] in which he simultaneously advocates for environmental conservation and appreciation for landscape painting. The Eden of Cole's paintings is not just a mythic view of the biblical past; it also contains real relevance to contemporary concerns in mid-nineteenth-century America. Religion, nature, and their stewardship by human beings are inextricably linked in Cole's art, not the least in the *Garden of Eden* paintings. They set a precedent for the moralized landscapes (of the type seen in the panorama) that would follow. They also set a pictorial precedent: motifs such as the crystalline waterfall seen in the background and the carpet of variegated flowers in the foreground would appear later in the *Land of Beulah* scenes in the *Moving Panorama of Pilgrim's Progress*, as well as in a study by Cole's student Jasper Cropsey.

The *Garden of Eden* paintings are also of interest because together they form a narrative of human experience. One picture comes first in the story, and then the next one; they proceed in turn like chapters in a book or scenes in a panorama. Throughout his career Cole would create several similar series of paintings, including his famed, five-part *The Course of Empire*, tracing the downfall of a pre-Christian society. More relevant to the panorama is his 1840 *Voyage of Life* series (figures 1.6–1.9), which was clearly informed by the popularity of Bunyan's *The Pilgrim's Progress*.[35] Like the Eden paintings, the *Voyage of Life* series was exhibited at the National Academy the same year that it was completed, making it at once part of the canon of American landscape painting. In this series of four paintings, titled *Childhood*, *Youth*, *Manhood*, and *Old Age*, a solitary figure like Bunyan's Christian journeys through a landscape that is alternately treacherous and inviting, growing older as he goes. Again, the paintings derive their meaning from being viewed together in sequence: they tell a story of a journey through life that advances only as the viewer moves from one absorbing scene to the next, just as in the panorama.

Both the Eden paintings and the *Voyage of Life* series were, in turn, heavily influenced by the work of British painter John Martin, who had established himself as the foremost painter of biblical, religious, and allegorical scenes of his time and whose work had once been reinterpreted in a stationary (as opposed to moving) panorama in London.[36]

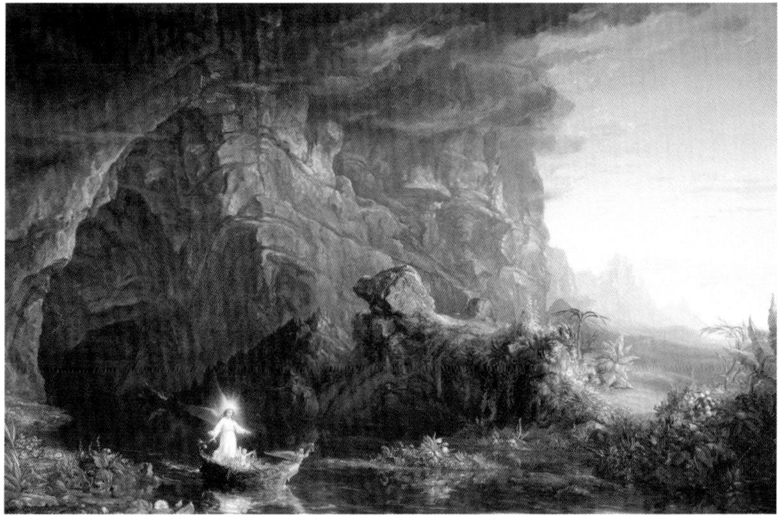

FIGURE 1.6. Thomas Cole (1801–1848), *The Voyage of Life: Childhood*, 1839–40, oil on canvas, 52 x 78 in. Munson-Williams-Proctor Arts Institute, Utica, New York, museum purchase, 55.105. Photo courtesy Munson-Williams-Proctor Arts Institute/Art Resource, New York.

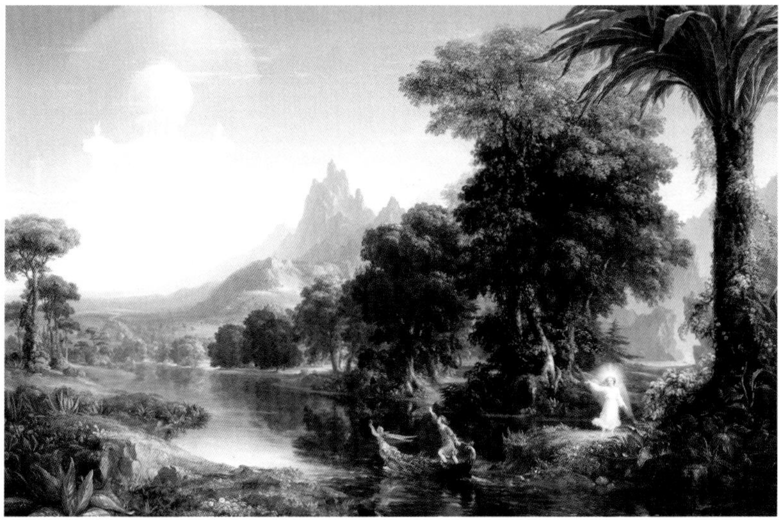

FIGURE 1.7. Thomas Cole (1801–1848), *The Voyage of Life: Youth*, 1840, oil on canvas, 52½ x 78½ in. Munson-Williams-Proctor Arts Institute, Utica, New York, museum purchase, 55.106. Photo courtesy Munson-Williams-Proctor Arts Institute/Art Resource, New York.

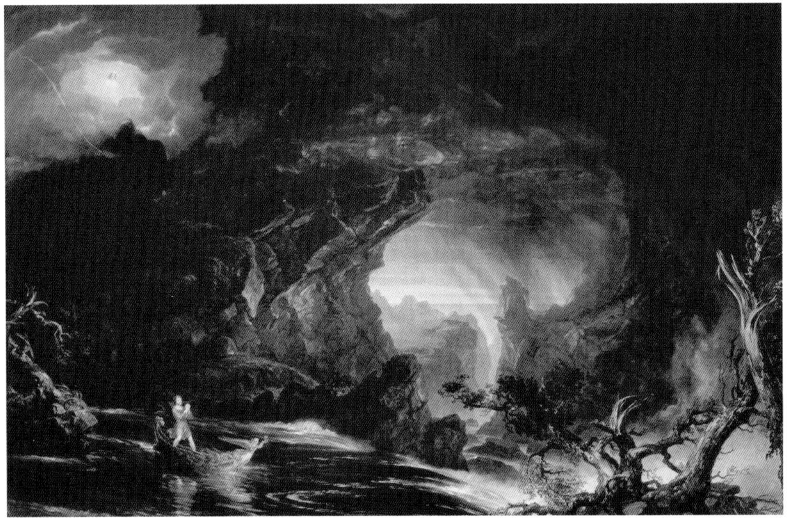

FIGURE 1.8. Thomas Cole (1801–1848), *The Voyage of Life: Manhood*, 1840, oil on canvas, 52 x 78 in. Munson-Williams-Proctor Arts Institute, Utica, New York, museum purchase, 55.107. Photo courtesy Munson-Williams-Proctor Arts Institute/Art Resource, New York.

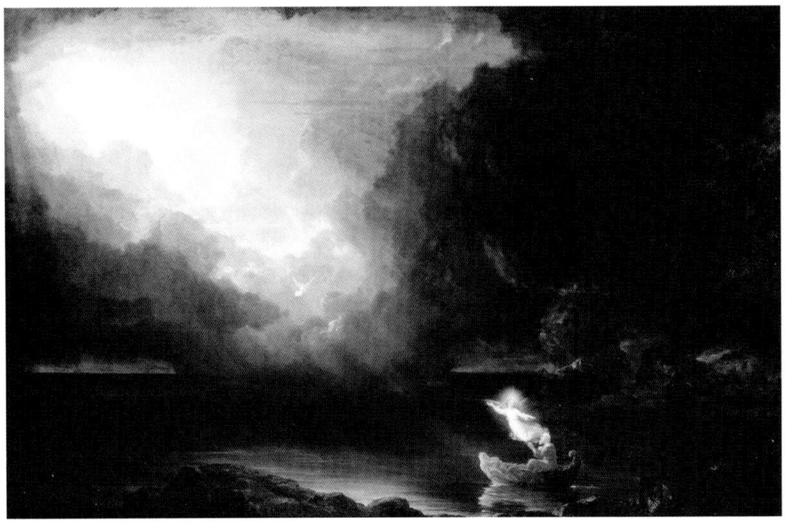

FIGURE 1.9. Thomas Cole (1801–1848), *The Voyage of Life: Old Age*, 1840, oil on canvas, $51\frac{3}{4}$ x $78\frac{1}{4}$ in. Munson-Williams-Proctor Arts Institute, Utica, New York, museum purchase, 55.108. Photo courtesy Munson-Williams-Proctor Arts Institute/Art Resource, New York.

Martin's work was widely known in America through engravings that he produced for printed editions of John Milton's *Paradise Lost* (1827) as well as *The Pilgrim's Progress* (1830).[37] Features of Cole's *Expulsion* were virtually quoted from Martin's engraving of the same subject for *Paradise Lost*. Similarly, the *Childhood* and *Manhood* scenes from the *Voyage of Life* — with the yawning, womblike cave and imposingly vaulted rock formations — were also influenced by Martin's engraving for *The Valley of the Shadow of Death* (figure 2.3), while *Youth*'s castles in the air seem informed by the glittering city in the sky in Martin's *The Celestial City* (figure 1.10), both scenes from the 1830 edition of *The Pilgrim's Progress*. Translated into slightly different and distinct thematic subjects for Cole's paintings, Martin's pictorial elements, through the lens of Cole's interpretation, once again reappear in their original context in the *Moving Panorama of Pilgrim's Progress*.

When the *Voyage of Life* paintings are set alongside images from the panorama, for instance, it seems unavoidable to conclude that they provided a direct and specific pictorial language for Kyle and May's panorama. The felicitous colors and luminescent castle-in-the-sky of *Youth* are a clear precedent for *The Land of Beulah* (plate 30); the glowering orange clouds of *Manhood* become the fire and smoke of the Valley of the Shadow of Death (plates 19, 20, and 37); and the dark quietude of *Old Age*, pierced by the gold and white of a celestial messenger, has more than a little in common with both Christian's and Christiana's passages through the River of Death (plates 31 and 39). There is a sense of motion

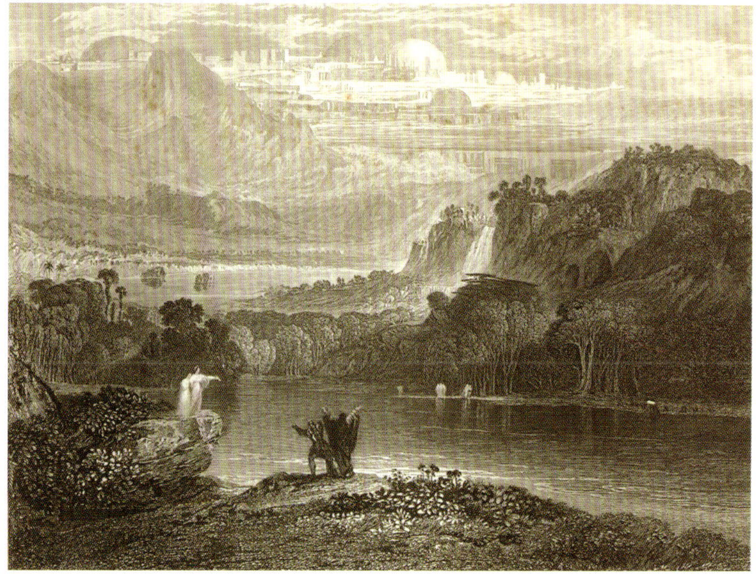

FIGURE 1.10. After John Martin, *The Celestial City*, engraved by W. R. Smith. Published in *The Pilgrim's Progress* (London: J. Murray and J. Major, 1830). Collections of the Dyer Library and Saco Museum, Saco, Maine, museum purchase.

and theatricality here that also prefigures the performance-based idiom of the moving panorama — the angel, arms outspread, introduces the child as he emerges from the cave, while the man, hands clasped in prayer, hurtles toward seemingly certain doom. The marriage of figure and landscape in this series — the dependence on one to give meaning to the other — imbues these works with dramatic power. Cole's *Voyage of Life* then, both thematically and pictorially, sets the stage for the panorama's dynamic blend of art and performance.

The *Youth* canvas of *The Voyage of Life* had particular visual currency. After Cole's death in 1848, it was the composition chosen by the American Art-Union for reproduction in an 1849 engraving "to take advantage of the interest attached by the public to the memory of Mr. Cole."[38] As such it was the first and most frequent *Voyage of Life* scene to be replicated. With its gardenlike setting and bright-eyed protagonist, it is certainly less disquieting than the others in the series; it also has one of the series' most alluring pictorial elements: the dazzling, incandescent castle in the sky that is the goal of the young man's journey, so similar to John Martin's and the panorama's interpretations of Bunyan's Celestial City. Cole himself would repeat that motif in his later series *The Cross and the World* (unlocated), left uncompleted when he died. Known only from photographs[39] and four somewhat murky studies, this series apparently was meant to catalogue the separate journeys of two pilgrims, one whose journey takes him to "the cross" and the other to "the world." The former is rewarded, at both the beginning and the end of his journey, with visions of a glowing cross in the sky, while the latter views a glimmering, ethereal palace in the distance of the scene entitled *The Pilgrim of the World on His Journey* (figure 1.11). Paradoxically, it is the misguided "pilgrim of the world" whose vision anticipates most closely the panorama's distant views of the Celestial City in the *Land of Beulah* scenes,[40] indicating the beginning of a shift away from the more traditional view of heaven (illustrated in the panorama) as a city paved with gold. It would not take long for Americans to view this kind of city-in-the-sky imagery with a degree of suspicion and irony; for instance, the motif is featured in the illuminated title page (figure 1.12) of Mark Twain's 1867 *The Innocents Abroad, or the New Pilgrims' Progress*, a travelogue in which the author pokes fun at Americans seeking the fulfillment of all their hopes and dreams in a European tour.[41]

Ideal as Cole's works were as the model for a "painters' panorama" of *The Pilgrim's Progress*, Cole himself was not available to contribute designs or advice; he had died

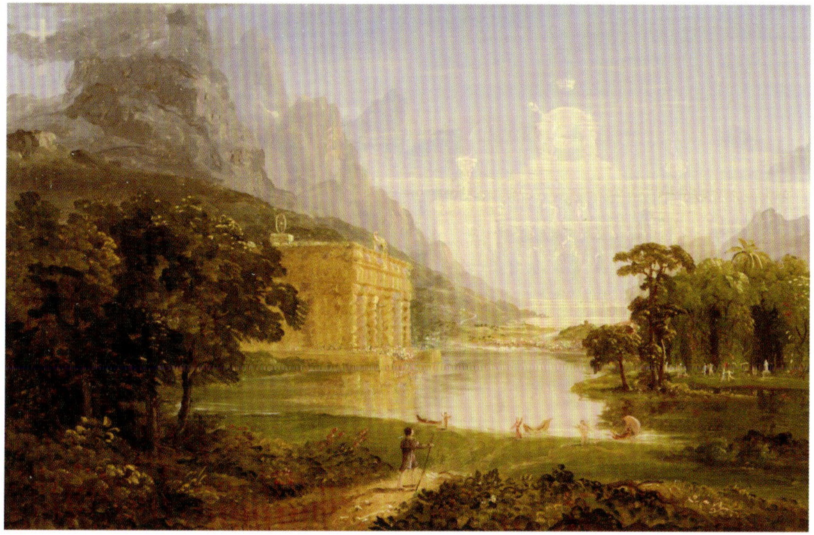

FIGURE I.11. Thomas Cole (1801–1848), sketch for *The Cross and the World: The Pilgrim of the World on His Journey*, circa 1846–47, oil on canvas, 12 x 18 in. Albany Institute of History and Art, Albany, New York, purchase, 1943.82.

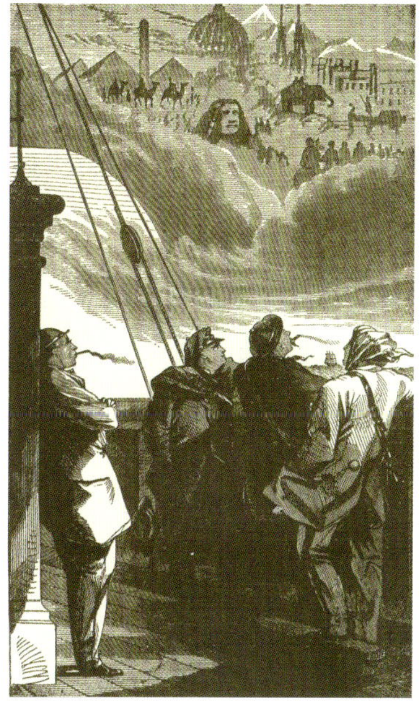

FIGURE I.12. Fay and Cox, "The Pilgrim's Vision." Illuminated title page for *The Innocents Abroad, or The New Pilgrims' Progress* by Mark Twain (Hartford, Conn.: American Publishing, 1867). Collections of the Dyer Library and Saco Museum, Saco, Maine.

early in 1848 at his Catskill home. His death caused widespread mourning, especially among those artists and men of letters who had most admired and emulated him, leaving many to fear that the future of American landscape painting would be uncertain in his absence. "It is as if the voyager on the Hudson were to look toward the great range of the Catskills," grieved William Cullen Bryant at Cole's funeral, "and were to see that the grandest of its summits had disappeared — had sunk into the plain from our sight."[42] Though there is no documentation to support such a theory, it seems entirely plausible that Cole's death — the journey's end of American landscape painting's most devoted pilgrim — may have inspired the creation of the panorama itself.[43] What is certain is that Kyle and May looked to Cole's students and heirs apparent to help them conceptualize and design their masterpiece.

Frederic Edwin Church was an obvious choice. A student and acolyte of Cole's, he had already established himself as a painter of note with views of familiar landscapes in New York and New England, showing a particular talent for dramatic effects of storms and sunsets. Atmospheric effects are also at play in his allegorical scenes, including *Christian on the Borders of the Valley of the Shadow of Death* (figure 1.13), a scene from *The Pilgrim's Progress* that was exhibited at the National Academy in 1847. This painting was only one of several large-scale religious paintings that Church would complete and exhibit at the Academy in the years preceding the panorama's completion. Unfortunately, *The River of the Water of Life* (1848), another scene from *The Pilgrim's Progress*, and *The Plague of Darkness* (1849), a scene from Exodus, are currently unlocated. No doubt the size and ambition of these works, noted in contemporary accounts, compelled Kyle and May to approach Church to contribute designs for the panorama. Church's religious paintings also seem to have favorably impressed the voting members of the academy, for Church became the youngest full-fledged member (a distinction that stands today) in 1849.

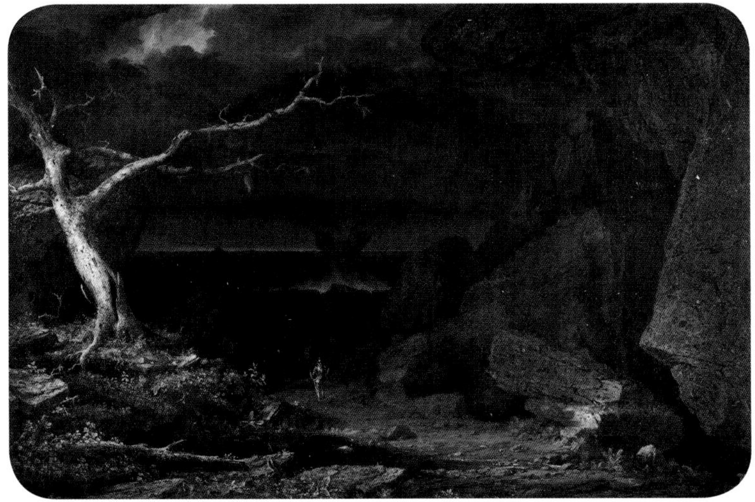

FIGURE 1.13. Frederic Edwin Church (1826–1900), *Christian on the Borders of the Valley of the Shadow of Death, Pilgrim's Progress*, 1847, oil on canvas, 40½ x 60½ in. Olana State Historic Site, Hudson, New York, New York State Office of Parks, Recreation, and Historic Preservation, OL.1981.50.

Church's contribution to the panorama, according to the 1851 catalogue,[44] is the scene entitled *Dawn of Day over the Valley of the Shadow of Death* (plate 20). It is loosely based on his 1847 oil *Christian on the Borders of the Valley of the Shadow of Death*. The black-and-orange palettes are similar, as are the rocky outcroppings on the right side of each composition and the flat, smoldering horizon, suggesting the limitless expanse of the dreaded valley. In both works, low-lying shadows lurk, recalling how Christian was warned that "Death also doth always spread his wings" over the valley. The most notable similarity between the two scenes is the sense of the painted landscape as a metaphor for the darkest and most dangerous chapters of life's journey, just as Bunyan uses the Twenty-third Psalm's Valley of the Shadow of Death as a literary metaphor for the same. Church's scenes are deliberately vague: the 1847 view is inscrutably dark, with a largely illegible middle ground, and the threatening landscape forms in the panorama scene are likewise unarticulated. Church's dark and shifting forms suggest a landscape of the mind and soul as much as an actual place.

Dawn of Day is the only panorama scene attributed to Church, yet his influence also seems evident in the scene entitled *Christian at the Cross* (plate 10), for which the design is attributed to Edward Harrison May. It is difficult not to see a precedent in Church's 1848 *To the Memory of Cole* (figure 1.14)[45] — the shape of the baroque cross with its capped ends, the flowers and vegetation winding around it from base to tip, and the hilltop setting are all marked similarities. This quotation from Church's elegy to his teacher is particularly meaningful given that the panorama as a whole seems to pay homage to Cole. In fact, *To the Memory of Cole*, which

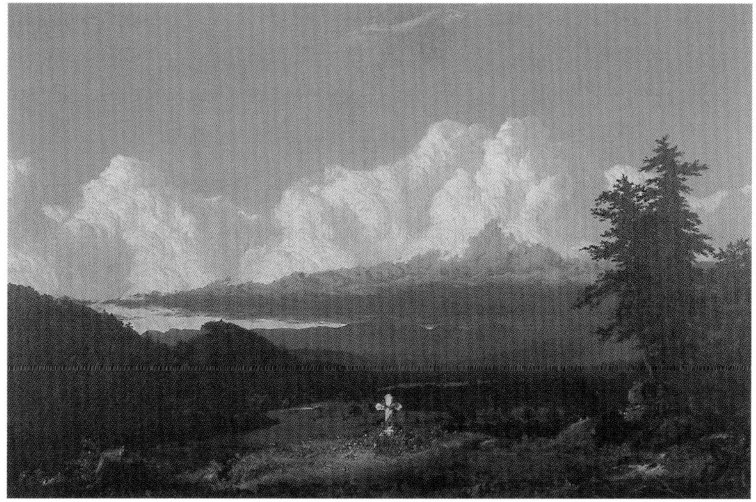

FIGURE 1.14. Frederic Edwin Church (1826–1900), *To the Memory of Cole*, 1848, oil on canvas, 32 x 49 in. Private collection. Photograph courtesy of Sotheby's, Inc. © (2014).

Church completed just two months after Cole's death, in April 1848, was shown in the memorial exhibition of Cole's work at the American Art-Union later that year, where it appeared alongside both *The Voyage of Life* and the uncompleted *Cross and the World*.[46] Those who saw the paintings together in this exhibition — and Edward Harrison May was almost certainly among them — were likely inspired to regard Church's composition as part of a piece with Cole's religion- and narrative-infused landscape series. Interestingly, *Christian at the Cross* was also the subject for a painting by Jesse Talbot exhibited at the National Academy in 1847 (figure 1.15).[47] Talbot's skillful and lush landscape, with its decided left-to-right narrative action, seems as though it easily might have been adapted for the panorama; the fact that it was not could further suggest that May's alternative composition was a calculated and very intentional nod to both Cole and Church.

Church was Cole's most acclaimed follower, but possibly not his most ardent one. The young Jasper Francis Cropsey was indelibly affected by Cole's death just as he had been affected by his work. As he wrote to his wife, "Though the man has departed, yet he has left a spell behind him that is not broken."[48] Cole's religious paintings were certainly on Cropsey's mind in 1850 when he painted *Ideal Landscape* (figure 1.16), presumed to be a study for the panorama's *Land of Beulah* (plate 30), which also has been labeled *Homage to Thomas Cole*.[49] Cropsey had never before grappled with *The Pilgrim's Progress*, or indeed any overtly religious or allegorical theme, as a subject; scholars hypothesize that he was asked to participate in the panorama purely because of his growing reputation as well as his connection to the National Academy and Cole.[50] Like most American landscape paint-

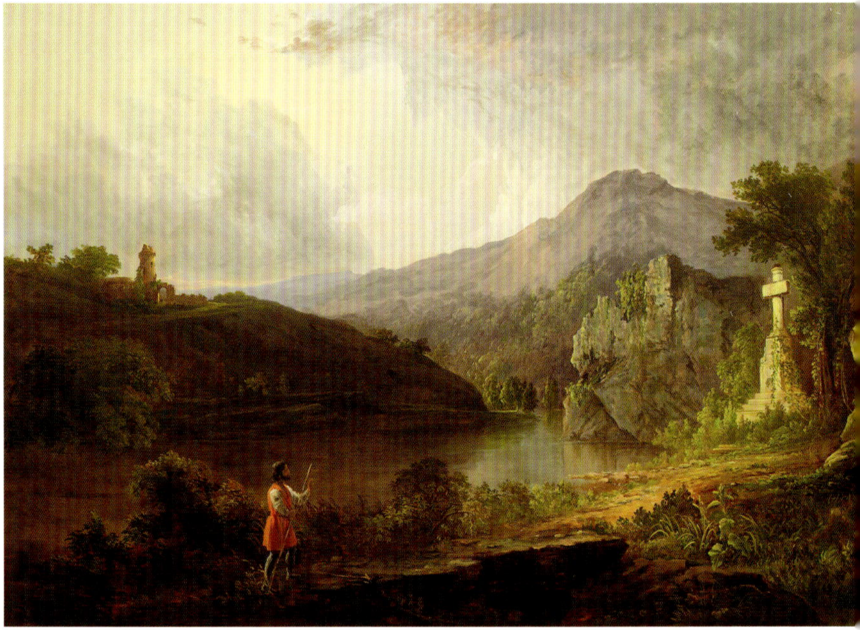

FIGURE 1.15. Jesse Talbot (1806–1879), *Christian at the Cross*, 1847, oil on canvas, 39 x 57 in. Private collection. Photo by Bif Hendrix.

opposite:
FIGURE 1.16. Jasper Francis Cropsey (1823–1900), *Ideal Landscape: Homage to Thomas Cole*, 1850, oil on canvas, $8\frac{1}{8}$ x $12\frac{1}{8}$ in. Thyssen-Bornemisza Collections, 1981.47.

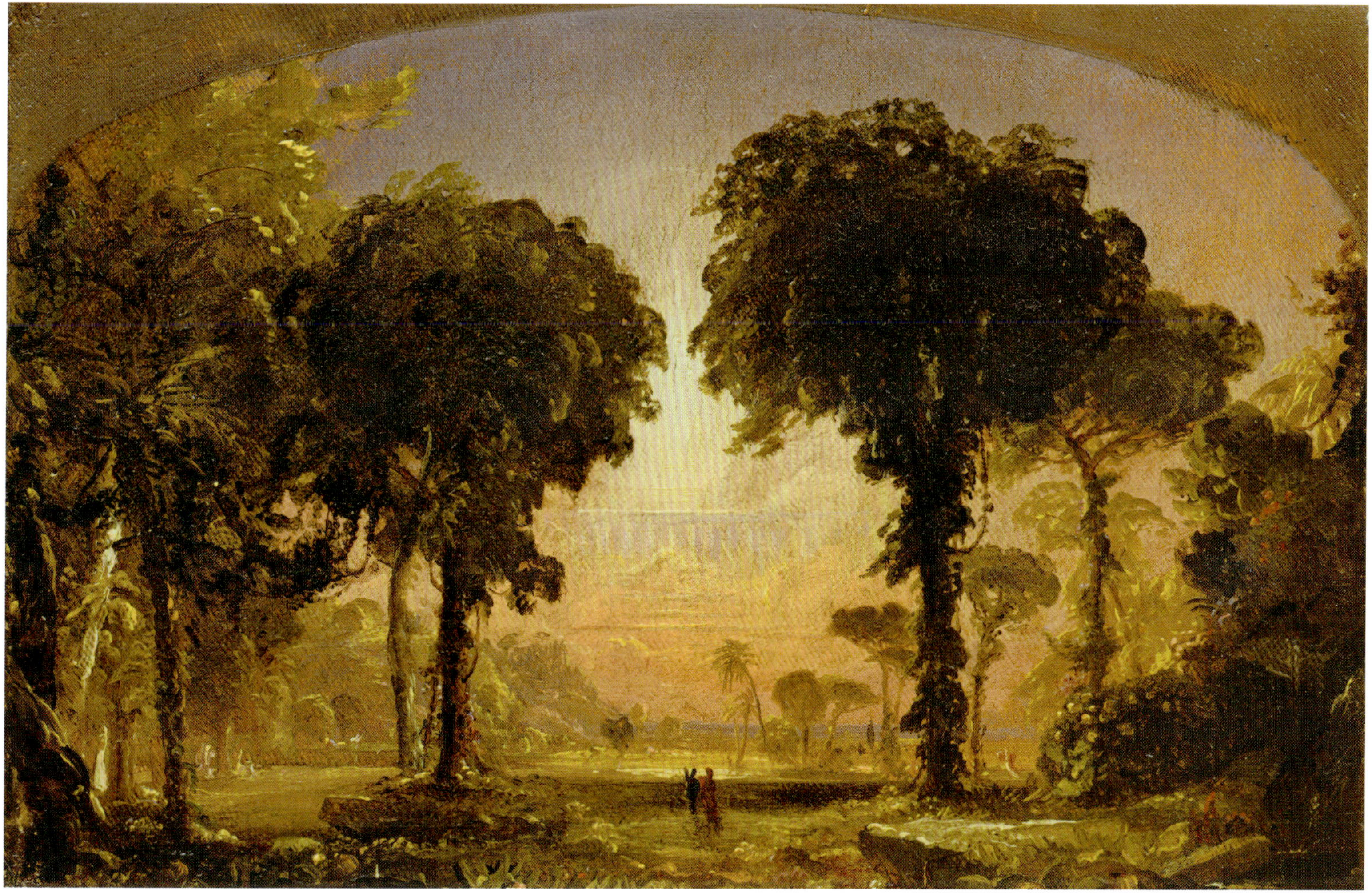

ers of his era, however, Cropsey held to the belief — variously informed by traditional Christianity and the influence of the rising Transcendentalist movement — that all landscape was sacred; that nature was God's "second book," a post-biblical revelation.[51] A painter who celebrated and shared this miracle of the natural world, then, did so in service of God and faith, as a kind of ministry: "Only he who has been under the influence of art, sees nature," proclaimed the Reverend Samuel Osgood at the opening of an 1851 exhibition at the American Art-Union. "Art, the interpreter of Nature, Nature, the interpreter of God."[52]

Cropsey looked not only to nature but also to the work of the artist he most admired in imagining this idealized heaven on earth: the last stop for Bunyan's heroes before reaching the Celestial City. The lush foreground vegetation, the tiny figure of a pilgrim in the center ground, and the distant, gleaming hint of architecture are all closely connected to Cole's *Garden of Eden* and the *Youth* canvas in the *Voyage of Life*. All of these elements, in an altered form, find their luminous manifestation in the panorama's *Land of Beulah* (plate 30), in which Cropsey faithfully and satisfyingly interprets Bunyan's description of a place "where the sun shines night and day" and the pilgrims "hear nothing, see nothing, feel nothing, smell nothing, taste nothing that is offensive" and depicts the Celestial City literally as a majestic city of gold in the sky. *The Land of Beulah* was one of the scenes most frequently lauded by critics of the panorama, with one reviewer saying that "nothing could go beyond the exquisite conception . . . of the lovely land of Beulah."[53] For at least one audience member, too, it seems to have served as a source of artistic inspiration. In 1854 the African American painter Robert S. Duncanson wrote to a friend about his plan to make a major easel painting on the subject and included a sketch (figure 1.17) that could only have been inspired by the panorama's interpretation.[54] Duncanson does not mention having seen the panorama — though he almost certainly did in 1853[55] — but his sketch bears so much in common with Cropsey's composition that its influence seems irrefutable.

Cropsey is also credited with designing the panorama's version of *The River of the Water of Life*, the same subject Frederic Edwin Church used for his unlocated easel painting of 1848.[56] Presumably this was the subject of the second painting, which, according to Cropsey's journal, he sold as "studies for the panorama of Pilgrim's Progress."[57] Just like Church's painting, the location of Cropsey's second study is unknown, and the related scene for the panorama also has been lost, for reasons that are unknown, along with thirteen other consecutive scenes. Fortunately, some sugges-

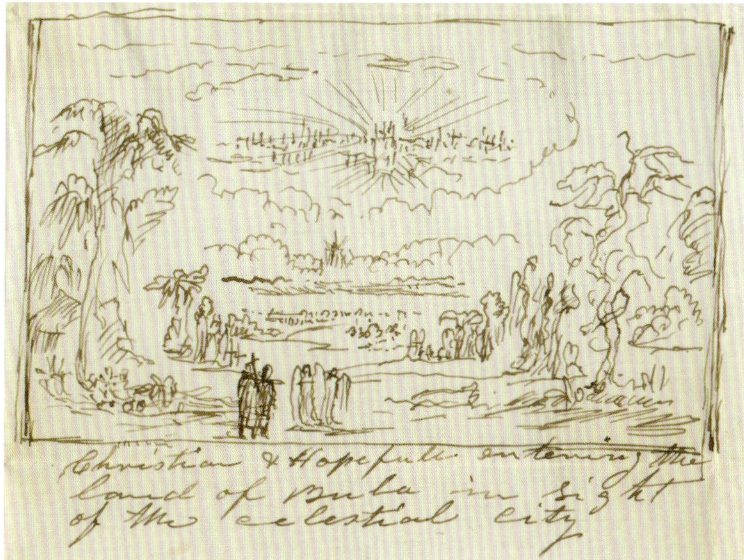

FIGURE 1.17. Robert S. Duncanson, *The Land of Beulah,* after Jasper Cropsey in the *Moving Panorama of Pilgrim's Progress.* From a letter from Duncanson to Junius R. Sloan, September 27, 1854. Robert Spencer papers, Newberry Library, Chicago.

tion of the panorama scene's appearance survives in an 1867 poem by Alfred B. Street. The poem, entitled "River of Life: Suggested by Cropsey's 'River of Life,' in the Bunyan Tableaux," begins with an evocative description of Cropsey's mise-en-scène:

> Thy winding wave, so lucent and so tender;
> Thy flowers so lovely in their glittering white;
> Thy stately palms, their changeless foliage gleaming
> Under a sky so radiant and so bland,
> Thy purple hill-tops, surging far, and seeming
> A stairway leading to some distant land."[58]

This first stanza confirms all we know of Cropsey's strengths and interests as a landscape painter. The archaic use of the word "bland" conveys well the painter's talent for atmospheric effects that are more pleasingly eternal than dazzlingly temporal. The poet also observes a motif in Cropsey's far distance that is carried throughout the panorama, and indeed throughout Bunyan's story: the idea that the distant goal of the journey, the Celestial City (or at least some further signpost on the way to it) is visible at key intersections of the landscape. Without the original work or its study to examine, there is no way to know whether the "stairway to some distant land" is a corporeal vision in the sky, as in the artist's *Land of Beulah* or his study for it, or instead the mere suggestion of stairs among the mountains' ridge.[59] Either way, and in both of his panorama scenes, Cropsey seems to have fully grasped the narrative and theological point that these landscapes, as lovely as they are, must be passed through and left behind in order for the traveler to reach the ultimate reward.

Cropsey's easel paintings were affected meaningfully by his participation in the panorama. In the years to follow, he first experimented with allegorical series of paintings in the mode of Thomas Cole, including *Spirit of War* (1851, National Gallery, Washington) and *Spirit of Peace* (1851, Woodmere Art Museum, Philadelphia). He also produced landscapes with openly religious themes, including *The Millennial Age* of 1854 and *The Good Shepherd* of 1855 (Newington-Cropsey Foundation). In fact, he considered grappling with *The Pilgrim's Progress* once again. In 1855 he wrote to a friend that he planned a five-part series entitled *Pilgrim of the Cross*, inspired by *The Pilgrim's Progress*, explaining that the subject would "afford as much purity of purpose and fullness of religious thought as any other I at present think of."[60] Cropsey's deep religious faith, and his desire to make that faith manifest in his work, is a frequent topic in his personal correspondence.[61] Although the better part of his *ouevre* — masterful but ostensibly secular landscapes — reflects his piety in less explicit ways, his work for the panorama and in the years following its creation unreservedly broadcasts his mutual promotion of art and Christian ideals.

These principles were shared, and more outwardly expressed, by Daniel Huntington, another National Academician and contributor to the panorama's design. Huntington contributed designs for the panorama scenes *They Lost Their Way in the Valley of the Shadow of Death* (plate 37) and *Mercy's Dream* (plate 36), granting permission for Kyle and May to use compositions he had already worked up in easel paintings of the same subjects.[62] Both scenes are from Part Two of *The Pilgrim's Progress*, which recounts the journey of Christian's wife, Christiana. By the 1840s Huntington had fully perfected a pictorial language that united art, religion, and the idealized female form, so the second part of Bunyan's narrative readily matched his interests.[63] Also, although all the panorama artists were observant Christians, Huntington was perhaps the most directly engaged in the religious discourse of the time, and therefore well equipped to deal with these depictions of spiritual crisis (*They Lost Their Way*) and enlightenment (*Mercy's Dream*). Just after the panorama's debut, Huntington would pointedly compare his role as a painter to that of John Bunyan as a preacher and writer,[64] praising "those Pilgrims in art, who have kept their eyes steadily fixed on the Heavenly city."[65] In concert with the thinking of the time, Huntington's words suggest a commitment to illustrating his religious ideals in art that was ministerial in approach.

Huntington was raised Congregationalist, but he converted to Episcopalianism as an adult along with his brothers Gurdon and Jedidiah, the latter of whom was ordained an Episcopal minister in 1841.[66] The Huntingtons were not alone in rediscovering the Episcopal Church in mid-nineteenth-century America; its popularity increased as a direct reaction against two centuries of dominance by New England Puritanism. As it translated into Daniel Huntington's artwork, Episcopalianism offered a middle ground between strict Calvinist theology, which was suspicious of all religious imagery, and the opulence of Roman Catholicism, whose artistic traditions were belittled by some as "old church": antiquated or out of touch. The appeal of that middle ground to artists is articulated in an early review of the panorama's revised version, which states, "The Catholic Church has long attempted to teach by means of pictures; but this is, perhaps, the first instance in which it has been practiced to any extent by Protestants."[67] In fact, Huntington's work — so often featuring women engaged in prayer or spiritual study — has much in common with the emerging American Evangelical movement which, according to scholar Wendy Greenhouse, "promoted the home and family as the nursery of religious feeling and championed the notion of women — with their supposed natural susceptibility to spiritual sentiment — as 'ministers' to their families."[68]

That ideal is readily apparent in Huntington's compositions of Christiana and her family, including an 1842–1844 easel painting entitled *Christiana and Her Family Passing through the Valley of the Shadow of Death* (figure 1.18), which supplied the model for the corresponding scene in the panorama (plate 37). Contemporary accounts suggest that Huntington "granted [Kyle and May] his permission to copy his well known picture,"[69] phrasing that helps to explain both the similarities and the differences between the painting and the panorama scene. Although there are variations between the two, in both Christiana is situated at the apex of a pyramid containing her family (in the panorama scene their guide, Great Heart, towers above the pyramid of Christiana and her children). Her pose, embracing and protecting those around her, is reminiscent of the traditional subject of the "Virgin of Mercy,"[70] reflecting Huntington's (and the panorama impresarios') interest in motifs from Renaissance art. In both compositions, Christiana looks heavenward while her youngest son, James, clings to her, and Mercy, their young traveling companion, kneels at her feet. In the panorama scene, Mercy is draped across Christiana's lap in an attitude of either despair or supplication. Her pose is al-

FIGURE 1.18.
Daniel Huntington (1816–1906), *Christiana and Her Family Passing through the Valley of the Shadow of Death*, 1842–44, oil on canvas, 92¼ x 74 in. Courtesy of the Pennsylvania Academy of the Fine Arts, Philadelphia. Bequest of Henry C. Carey (The Carey Collection), 1879.8.8.

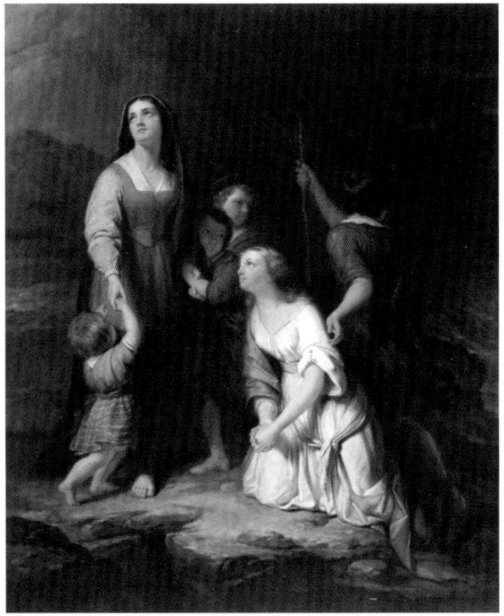

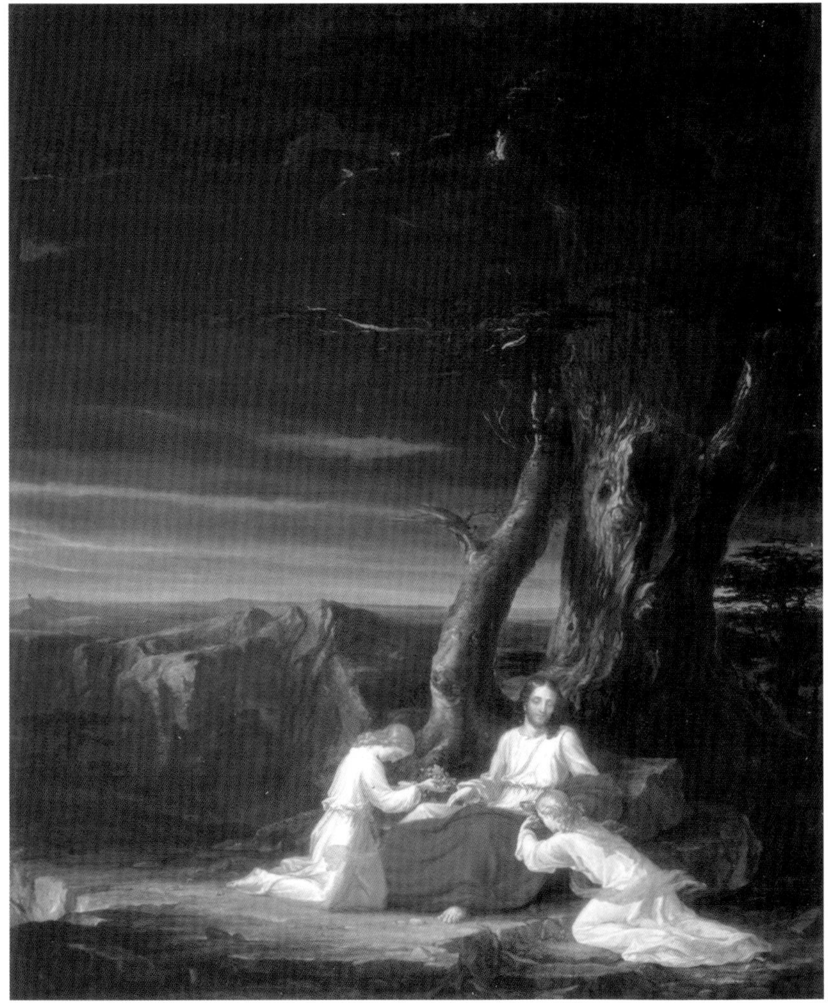

most an exact mirror image of the foremost figure in *Angels Ministering to Christ in the Wilderness* (figure 1.19), a rare figural scene by Thomas Cole that was well known to nineteenth-century audiences.[71] The poses of Christiana and her children in the panorama scene thus suggest her role as teacher, protector, and beloved shepherdess, protecting her flock and guiding them through life's journey even while she in turn receives their comfort.

If Christiana is the keeper of the faith in the Valley of

the Shadow of Death scenes, then Mercy is its recipient in *Mercy's Dream*. One of Huntington's most famous compositions, *Mercy's Dream* (figure 1.20, plate 36) was first realized in an easel painting completed and exhibited at the National Academy in 1841. Acclaimed as "transcendently beautiful,"[72] the canvas was soon reproduced and widely disseminated in an authorized engraving, which in turn inspired many amateur copies. Huntington himself produced two oil copies of *Mercy's Dream*,[73] in 1850 and 1858, ostensibly to aid in the production of additional prints. However, it seems possible that the 1850 copy (which never was delivered to the engraver)[74] may instead have been used as a model by the panorama painters. This hypothesis is supported by very minor compositional details: the blaze of light above the angel's arm is stronger in both the 1850 version and the panorama, and the vegetation behind Mercy is more articulated and recognizably a tree trunk, rather than generalized rock formations. Also supporting this theory is the fact that *Mercy's Dream* was a late addition to the panorama: it appeared only in the second version, which debuted in 1851 and thus would have been in production the year before. It also was demonstrably a late addition for that version itself, as it was painted on a discrete section of fabric that was spliced into the larger panorama, presumably sometime after most of the second version was completed.[75] Compellingly, *Christiana and Her Family* was also copied in 1850 (that version is now in the collection of the Ringling Museum in Sarasota, Flor-

opposite:
FIGURE 1.19. Thomas Cole (1801–1848), *Angels Ministering to Christ in the Wilderness*, 1843, oil on linen, $73\frac{3}{4}$ x $59\frac{1}{2}$. Worcester Art Museum, Worcester, Massachusetts, Charlotte E. W. Buffington Fund.

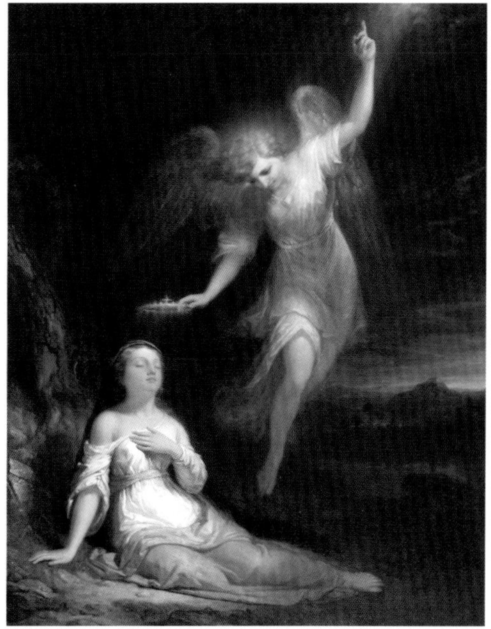

FIGURE 1.20. Daniel Huntington (1816–1906), *Mercy's Dream*, 1841, oil on canvas, $84\frac{5}{8}$ x $66\frac{1}{2}$ in. Courtesy of the Pennsylvania Academy of the Fine Arts, Philadelphia. Bequest of Henry C. Carey (The Carey Collection), 1879.8.10.

ida), suggesting that perhaps Huntington made both copies for the purposes of the panorama.

It is ironic that *Mercy's Dream* seems to have been something of an afterthought for the panorama, since its theme encapsulates the entire narrative structure of *The Pilgrim's Progress*: it is a dream within a dream, serving as a meta-allegory for Bunyan's own vision. Like Huntington's paintings of Christiana, *Mercy's Dream* is informed by Renaissance art. The subject and the composition have much in common with sixteenth- and seventeenth-century depictions of female saints in ecstasy,[76] experiencing a moment of direct contact with the divine. Indeed, the painting illustrates the revelation given to Mercy in a dream while spending the night in the Palace Beautiful. As she relates to Christiana the next morning:

> Methought I looked up, and saw one coming with Wings towards me. So he came directly to me, and said, Mercy, what aileth thee? Now when he had heard me make my complaint, he said, Peace be to thee. He also wiped mine eyes with his Handkerchief, and clad me in Silver and Gold: he put a Chain about my Neck, and Ear-rings in mine Ears, and a beautiful Crown upon my Head.

Mercy's story is replicated faithfully in the figures of Huntington's scene (minus the jewelry, which appears only in the 1858 copy), but he uses a degree of artistic license in the setting. Mercy describes her dreamscape only as "a solitary place" and makes no mention of being out-of-doors. But Huntington's setting, in both the easel paintings and the panorama scene, is a rocky, mountainous landscape, much like Frederic Edwin Church's interpretation of the Valley of the Shadow of Death (and indeed Huntington's own treatment of that subject, previously discussed).[77] In the panorama scene, particularly, the landscape behind the angel is fully developed, featuring a mountain, watery inlets looking out to sea, dark cloud formations, and a fiery sunrise.[78] The choice of setting was no doubt purposeful on Huntington's part. Though best known — now and in the mid-nineteenth century — for portraits and allegorical scenes, Huntington was a strong advocate for the power of landscape painting to embody higher ideals, proclaiming its ability to do just that in a speech on Christian art presented at the National Academy in 1851.[79] As it did for the other artists of the time, including those associated with the panorama, landscape anchored Huntington's religious scenes to the observable here and now, connecting abstract Christian ideals to the tangible world of God's creation.

This, of course, was the modus operandi for the panorama as a whole. Joseph Kyle and Edward Harrison May, its creators, were active participants in the artistic culture of the time, and thus they understood fully the power of landscape to partner sympathetically with religious themes. Landscape, both literally and figuratively, became the underpinning for their *Moving Panorama of Pilgrim's Progress*: John Bunyan's allegorical landscape of the King's Highway (the road to the Celestial City) gave their panorama its narrative structure, while the painted landscape under their characters' feet and extending limitlessly both beyond and behind them provided its visual structure. The unique confluence of art, religion, and landscape in the panorama, and its possibilities for reaching and enlightening a broad and diverse audience, did not go unnoticed by the critics. One even adopted the landscape metaphor in recommending specifically to the unschooled this "*new and easy road* by which this sweet book may get to the brain — and get there with music and pleasure and without leaf-turning and study."[80] Another praised the artists' skill in creating scenery that could elevate the senses "and work upon the imagination with such power and force as to lead the mind *from nature up to nature's God*."[81]

The same critic also noted the artists' abilities to pervert nature with their fantastic interpretations of Bunyan's words: "Entering into the dreamer's spirit, the artist has called into being . . . demons of horrifying deformity."[82] In imagining the gruesome scene entitled *The Pilgrims' Escape* (plate 24), Irish-born artist Peter Paul Duggan found his inspiration not in an ideal view of nature but in a despoiled one. A painter of religious and historical works who had been affiliated with the National Academy since 1844, Duggan was visiting the West Indies in 1848–49 while plans for the panorama were taking shape.[83] His 1849 *Lazar House in the Tropics* (figure 1.21), derived from that trip, depicts the denizens of a leper colony and may have been informed by the artist's own struggles with the wasting disease of tuberculosis. It appeared in the catalogue of the Academy's 1849 exhibition along with related lines from Milton's *Paradise Lost*: "A lazar house it seem'd; wherein were laid / Numbers of all diseased."[84] Embedded within the composition itself, inscribed on the paving stones, are cautionary words from William Shakespeare's *King Lear*: "Take physic, pomp." Though the subjects of *Lazar House* and *The Pilgrims' Escape* are entirely different, they share several features: sources in seventeenth-century literature, remarkable and fearsome things seen on a journey, and landscape infused with a moral message, all hallmarks of the panorama itself.

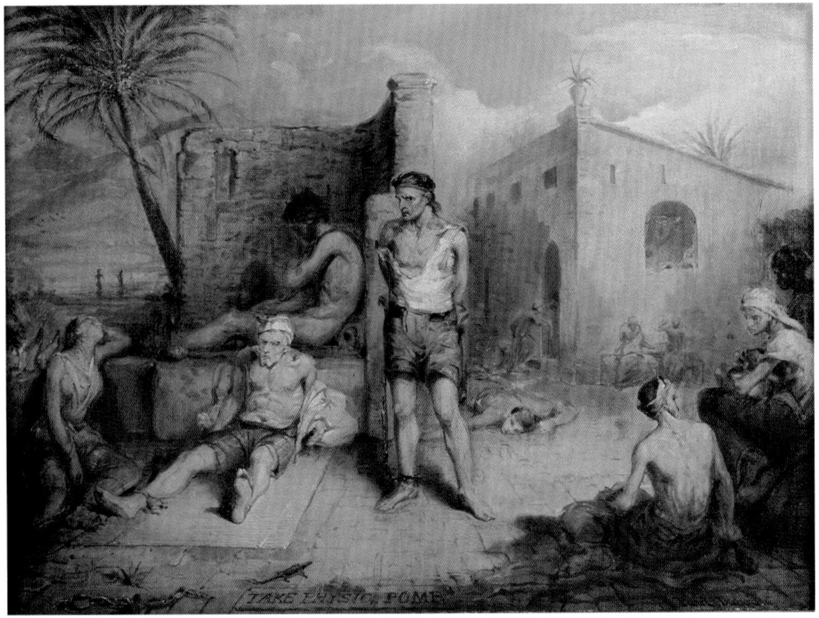

FIGURE 1.21. Peter Paul Duggan (?–1861), *Lazar House in the Tropics*, 1848–49, oil on canvas, $18\frac{1}{2}$ x $23\frac{7}{8}$. National Academy Museum, New York.

The two scenes are also compositionally similar. Both have a looming central figure (a leprosy victim in *Lazar House* and Giant Despair in *The Pilgrims' Escape*)[85] standing in front of a large fortresslike structure with plunging perspective lines. Given these similarities, and the fact that *Lazar House* was exhibited just one year before the panorama debuted, the painting may well have been the basic template for Duggan's panorama scene.

There can be no ambiguity, however, about the source for the panorama scenes attributed to British artist Henry Courtney Selous.[86] Following the lead of his teacher John Martin, who as previously noted illustrated an 1830 edition of *The Pilgrim's Progress* with influential landscape etchings, Selous produced a popular and highly acclaimed illustrated edition of *The Pilgrim's Progress* in 1844.[87] Kyle and May were no doubt moved to approach Selous to contribute to the panorama based on both the strength of that volume and his involvement in the creation of panoramas in England.[88] Since Selous lived in Britain, it is likely that Kyle and May merely secured permission from him to use his illustrations for some of their designs; he is not known to have been involved otherwise in the panorama's production. Indeed, the panorama scenes attributed to Selous (*Christian Passing through the Valley of the Shadow of Death*, *They Behold the Fate of Those Who Have Fallen from the Hill of Error*, and *They Behold the Fate of the Apostate*) (plates 19, 26, and 28) correspond closely with his 1844 illustrations (figures 1.22–24), all spirited line drawings in the mode of neoclassical artist John Flaxman.

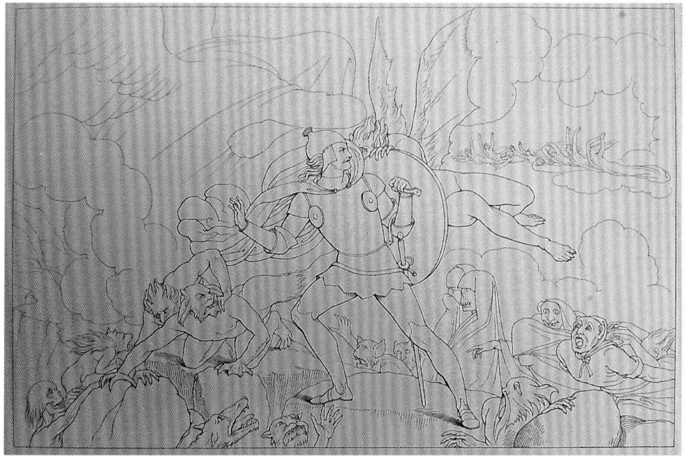

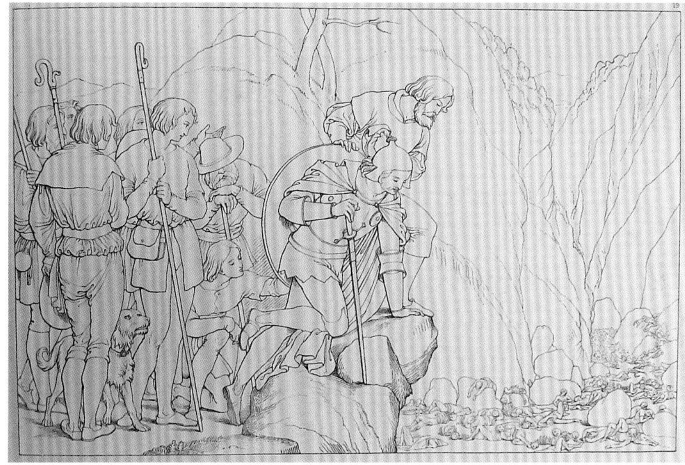

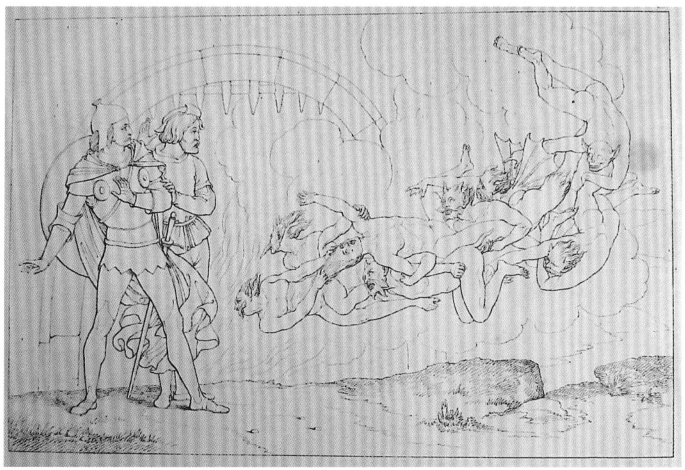

FIGURE 1.22. (top, left) Henry Courtney Selous (1803–1890), *Christian Passes the Valley of the Shadow of Death.* From John Bunyan, *Pilgrim's Progress Illustrated* (London: M. M. Holloway, 1844). Collections of the Dyer Library and Saco Museum, Saco, Maine. Gift of Peter Morelli.

FIGURE 1.23. (top, right) Henry Courtney Selous (1803–1890), *Christian and Hopeful Are Shewn the Pilgrims Who Have Fallen from the Hill of Error.* From John Bunyan, *Pilgrim's Progress Illustrated* (London: M. M. Holloway, 1844). Collections of the Dyer Library and Saco Museum, Saco, Maine. Gift of Peter Morelli.

FIGURE 1.24. (bottom, left) Henry Courtney Selous (1803–1890), *Christian and Hopeful Behold the Fate of the Apostate.* From John Bunyan, *Pilgrim's Progress Illustrated* (London: M. M. Holloway, 1844). Collections of the Dyer Library and Saco Museum, Saco, Maine. Gift of Peter Morelli.

Compared to many other paintings and illustrations based on *The Pilgrim's Progress*, landscape is a less overt presence in Selous's drawings and the panorama scenes they inspired. Still, landscape elements anchor his compositions. His figures have their feet firmly planted on a ledge of earth or rock in the foreground that appears, stagelike, at the same depth and latitude in the picture plane of each illustration (interspersed among the "frowning cliffs and yawning chasms," as the reviewer from the *Hamilton Banner* noted in 1857).[89] The repetition of this effect, something like that of actors on a proscenium, provides a sense of narrative continuity among all of Selous's *Pilgrim's Progress* illustrations: the viewer can imagine the figures stepping easily from one scene to the next. A similar conceit is fully employed throughout the *Moving Panorama of Pilgrim's Progress*, where the figures really do move from scene to scene, and one passage really does blend pictorially into another. Through their use of landscape, both Selous's engravings and the panorama's scenes focus on the relentless forward motion of the narrative, as Christian and his companions steadily erase the distance between themselves and the Celestial City.

Like Selous, Felix Octavius Carr Darley (who designed the single panorama scene *Entrance to Temple Beautiful, and Death of Giant Grim*) was an experienced book illustrator well before he became involved with the panorama.[90] The son of professional actors, Darley (1822–1888) established his reputation with illustrations for Philadelphia-based pictorial journals and then went on to contribute individual illustrations and frontispieces for largely forgotten books such as *The Quaker City* and *The John Donkey* in the 1840s. His career took off in 1848 with his move to New York and the publication there, through the American Art-Union, of illustrations for Washington Irving's *Rip Van Winkle* and *The Legend of Sleepy Hollow*. Darley's fluid and detailed line drawings for the American Art-Union have much in common with Selous's illustrations for *The Pilgrim's Progress*, published just four years earlier.

Darley's theatrical lineage, his work for the Art-Union, and his 1850 election to the Century Club,[91] another bastion of New York artists, all gave him the credentials to contribute to the panorama. Yet Kyle and May's interest in his participation may have been prompted by work he did well before 1850. An intriguing example has its source in Darley's series of fourteen illustrations for the book *Scenes in Indian Life*, published in Philadelphia in 1843, when the artist was only twenty-one years old and when both Kyle and Dallas were still living in that city. Darley's gripping illustration "Red-eyed and foaming, prone the monster falls" (published the following year as an engraving entitled *Hunting Buffaloe* [*sic*] in *Graham's Magazine*; figure 1.25) prefigures the combination of warrior, beast, and landscape that Kyle and May would represent so frequently in the *Moving Panorama of Pilgrim's Progress*.

There are notable compositional similarities between *Hunting Buffaloe* and Darley's design for *Death of Giant Grim*. In *Hunting Buffaloe*, inspired by the Western art of George Catlin,[92] a mounted Great Plains brave draws his bow on a colossal buffalo, already foundering in the grasses on the right side of the composition. The angle of the bow echoes that of Great-Heart's sword in the panorama scene, with its tip pointed at the same intimate juncture of the monster's body. The two warriors also share the same downward glance, and the crest on Great-Heart's helmet echoes the flying hair and buffalo cloak of the hunter. The leaden bearing of the vanquished opponent is also shared by both compositions: The buffalo and Giant Grim both collapse on their left sides, the foremost right extremities extended, the massive heads tilted warily but impotently at the instrument of their defeat.

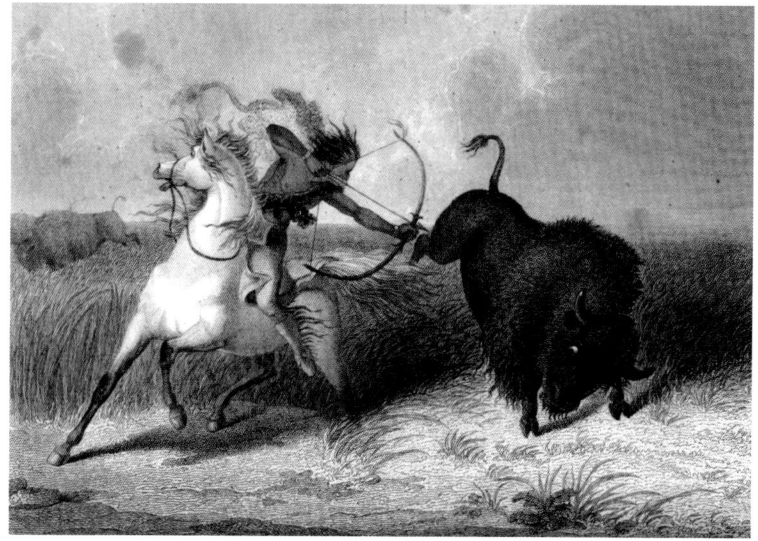

FIGURE 1.25. Felix Octavious Carr Darley (1822–1888), *Hunting Buffaloe* [*sic*], 1844, engraving. Engraved by "Cushman" for *Graham's Magazine* 26, no. 3 (September 1844).

The encounter between these two ill-fated American titans, depicted by Darley and others,[93] was a popular theme throughout the nineteenth century. Darley himself would revisit it frequently throughout his career, using it as the design for a bank note in 1860[94] as well as another engraving in 1870. As the century drew to a close, scenes like this were a poignant reminder of the passage of time and the relentlessness of progress; these concerns that had once gripped the American psyche were, by then, part of history. There is a parallel here to the matrix of the *Moving Panorama of*

Pilgrim's Progress itself. Dogged and defeated by magic lantern shows and other new visual entertainments, moving panoramas were all but extinct by the turn of the twentieth century. The panorama's largely unnoticed disappearance from public life for nearly a century further suggests how the new technologies and increasing secularity of the dawning twentieth century quickly made this grand achievement of popular art seem irrelevant.

Still unchanged even today, however, is America's appetite for spectacle, for epic battles and awe-inspiring views presented in visually dazzling ways designed to transport the viewer across space and time. Today's IMAX and 3-D movie screens are both theatrical conventions that owe a significant debt to the monumental scale and all-encompassing performance mode of nineteenth-century panoramas.[95] Sweeping landscape shots, capturing in a single "take" far more terrain than the human eye can absorb at one time, are also a standard motif of today's cinematography, again a panoramic paradigm. These powerful conventions, just like panoramas, can uniquely capture both the "myriad details" and "extraordinary breadth" of emotionally and culturally powerful subjects: faith, land, struggle, diaspora. Moving panoramas, then, rather than being a failed or short-lived experiment, were a bold innovation and a permanent game changer, setting the standard for the kinds of entertainments audiences would crave and demand from that time forward. The *Moving Panorama of Pilgrim's Progress* — with its evocative subject, artistic pedigree, and documented history of engaging and enthralling hundreds of thousands — endures today as a lasting example of the zenith reached by this revolutionary art form.

KEVIN J. AVERY

MOVIES FOR MANIFEST DESTINY

The Moving Panorama Phenomenon in America

We live in an overheated age, fueled by entertainment media and headed by what critics often generously term "film" or "the cinema." Assailed (or regaled) by special-effects blockbusters, multiple sequels, and then video versions that include "director's cuts" of the big-screen originals, we can scarcely imagine the pre-celluloid, pre-electronic forebears of today's movies that delighted American and British audiences a century and a half ago.

The *Moving Panorama of Pilgrim's Progress* (1850–51) is, in fact, a kind of director's cut — a slightly altered replica — of an original "motion picture" painted on cloth. Both versions of the panorama were but two among the hundreds, perhaps more than a thousand, of such productions that toured the English-speaking world from about 1845 until nearly the end of the century. "Moving panoramas," or "moving dioramas" as these entertainments were also called, flourished in England's Age of Empire and America's frontier era of Manifest Destiny.[1] Panoramas perfectly accommodated that age. Most of them were portraits of vast territories, represented in linear sequence and giving the viewer the impression of traveling over the landscape, often by boat or train. Today the nearest equivalent of the moving panorama is the travel or historical documentary. In length, moving panoramas typically reached a thousand or more feet and stood eight to twelve feet high.[2] They were generally presented (as Jessica Skwire Routhier has described of the *Moving Panorama of Pilgrim's Progress* in her preceding essay) in successive sections framed by a proscenium, which concealed the rollers around which the panorama was wound. Usually, a lecturer stood by the picture as a tour guide, describing the peculiar features and the history of the scenery as it passed by.

The *Moving Panorama of Pilgrim's Progress* was, like most of its contemporaries, painted in distemper, the transient, water-based medium of the theatrical scene painter. Very few of its kind have survived. Though they were never intended to be seen stationary or at close hand, moving pan-

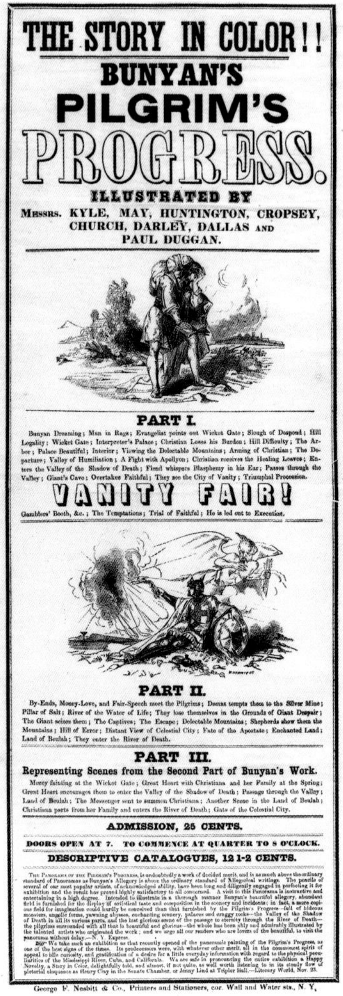

FIGURE 2.1.
The Story in Color!! Bunyan's Pilgrim's Progress, broadside, circa 1851–54, $21\frac{3}{4}$ x $7\frac{7}{8}$ inches. Printed by George F. Nesbitt, New York. Olana State Historic Site, Hudson, New York, New York State Office of Parks, Recreation, and Historic Preservation, OL.1981.1205.

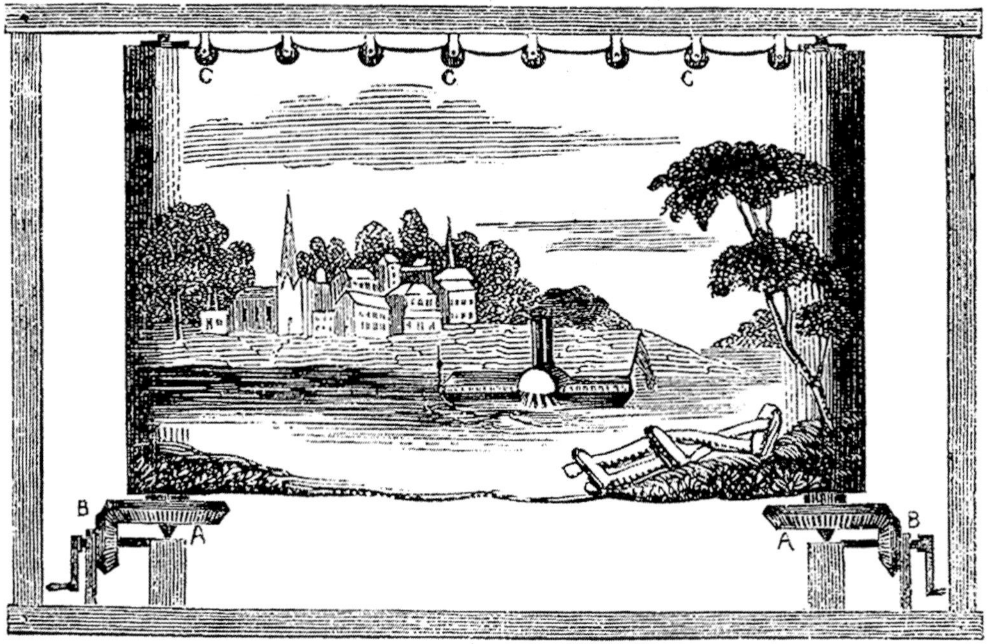

FIGURE 2.2.
Illustration of a moving panorama from *Scientific American* 4, no. 13 (December 16, 1848): 100.

oramas are virtually impossible today to exhibit as they originally were — in motion. With the notable exception of the Dyer Library and Saco Museum's recently created full-scale replica of the *Moving Panorama of Pilgrim's Progress*, as well as various digitized animations of panoramas that have appeared in recent years, we have perceived moving panoramas primarily as static historical artifacts. Understanding their former appeal begs some description of the panorama's history and its audience.

The word *panorama* (Greek for "all-sight" or "all-embracing view") was coined in the late eighteenth century to refer to the circular panorama invented by an Irish artist, Robert Barker, who resided at the time in Edinburgh, Scotland.[3] Barker was a portraitist who also created landscapes in the period just preceding the great age of landscape painting in Britain, which was dominated by J. M. W. Turner and John Constable. Around 1785, Barker had a novel idea: he ventured to draw, on four pieces of paper, everything he could see from the top of Edinburgh's famed Calton Hill. He now had a complete 360-degree view, which he transferred (with the help of Italian treatises on perspective) to a large canvas suspended within a wooden shed twenty-five feet in diameter. Barker cut a hole in the roof to admit light on the canvas and soon was charging a nominal admission to see his circular view of Edinburgh. The Scots showed sufficient interest that, in 1787, Barker moved his operation to London and obtained a patent for his invention. He sought the endorsement of Sir Joshua Reynolds, the president of the Royal Academy, who held that Barker's paintings in the round "represented nature in a manner far superior to the limited scale of pictures in general" and encouraged his colleagues and patrons to see them.[4] By 1794 Barker had erected a brick building ninety feet in diameter in Leicester Place, in which he could show two panoramas — one upstairs from the other. Fabric screens concealed skylights in the roof, and wood paling hid the bottom edge of the pictures. Thus displayed, the painted view seemed borderless as well as the sole source of available light. From the viewer's platform, the illusion of standing on a hill or a building overlooking an actual landscape was complete. Panoramas of London and of the British Fleet at Spithead were the first two of over one hundred subjects shown by Barker and his successors at the Leicester Square Panorama until its closing in 1863. Thanks to them, Leicester Square grew into the popular entertainment center of London that it remains today, and the world welcomed what some historians consider the first mass medium, the first true ancestor of the movies.[5]

By the early 1800s, the panorama had spread to countries all over Europe, but it came to America even earlier. In 1795 a copy of Barker's London panorama was exhibited in New York City. The medium's most renowned American projector — and author of the second-oldest surviving panorama — was the Paris-trained, neoclassical painter John Vanderlyn (1775–1852).[6] Foreseeing the American public's wariness and ignorance of the historical art he had been taught to paint, Vanderlyn looked to the new popular art of the panorama as a way of introducing European culture to New Yorkers. In Paris he had known the inventor Robert Fulton, who had taken the panorama idea to France in 1798. In 1814 Vanderlyn made drawings of the Palace and Gardens of Versailles, which he took to his hometown of Kingston, New York. In a barn there he transferred the drawings to a canvas measuring eighteen feet high by one hundred sixty feet in circumference. Vanderlyn completed the panorama in 1819 and installed it in a handsome, domed rotunda of brick he built with municipal blessing on the northeast corner of City Hall Park. On the second floor of the Rotunda, nearest the light source in the roof, Vanderlyn arranged the panorama, and in galleries on the first floor exhibited his portraits and historical subjects. All of it — high art and low — was available for twenty-five cents admission. It was an idealistic enterprise, really New York's first art museum. During the ten years of Vanderlyn's stewardship, panoramas from London also were shown in the Rotunda and even toured in other cities of America and in Canada. Vanderlyn died in 1852, and the Rotunda was torn down in 1870, but the *Panoramic View of the Palace and Gardens of Versailles* may still be seen at The Metropolitan Museum of Art.

By the 1830s, New York and other American cities were hosting newer forms of mass entertainment originating in both London and Paris, all capitalizing on the illusionistic novelty of the panorama's form and the cachet of its name. Just before the panorama painter Louis-Jacques Mandé Daguerre invented the daguerreotype (one of the earliest photographic processes), he developed the diorama in Paris, in 1822, and his brother-in-law soon established it in London.[7] The "di" (a variant of *dia,* from the Greek for "passing through") in diorama indicated the changing effect that Daguerre was able to produce in a large-scale view. His canvas was of conventional, rectangular format framed by a plain, dark proscenium like the movie screens of today. By rendering the scene in a combination of opaque and transparent pigments on both sides of the canvas, then lighting the image first from in front, then from behind, Daguerre conjured illusions of sunsets and oncoming storms, augmenting them, where appropriate, with sound effects. The "di" prefix also suggested the novel manner Daguerre devised to exhibit his customary double bill. As one dioramic image concluded its performance, the entire dais supporting the audience pivoted before a second feature.

Smaller and probably cheaper variations on Daguerre's invention by British artists introduced America to the diorama. The paintings and prints of John "Pandemonium" Martin, with their fiery imagery of biblical catastrophes, were translated into dioramas and prefigured "The Ten Commandments" and "Armageddons" of movie renown.[8] Martin's *Belshazzar's Feast* (1820; private collection), dramatizing the prophet Daniel's warning to the king of Babylon of the fall of his empire, became a diorama featured at Niblo's Garden on Broadway in March 1835.[9] It was pre-

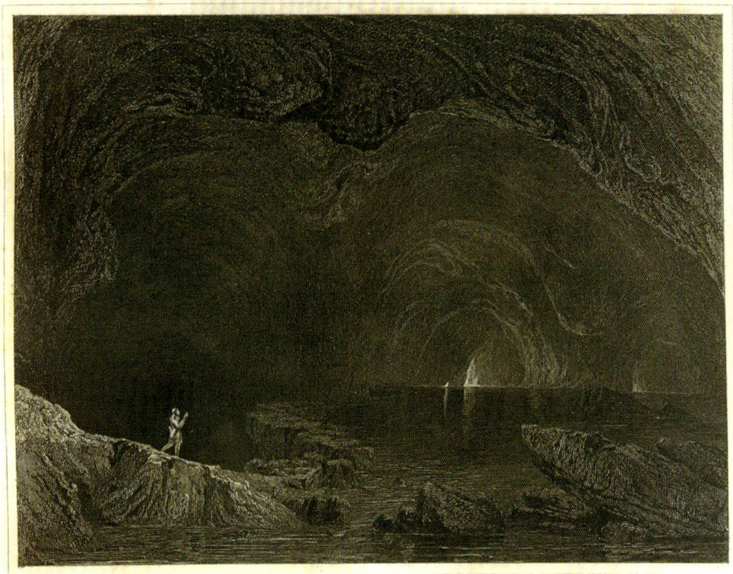

FIGURE 2.3. After John Martin, *The Valley of the Shadow of Death*, engraved by W. R. Smith. Published in John Bunyan, *The Pilgrim's Progress* (London: J. Murray and J. Major, 1830). Collections of the Dyer Library and Saco Museum, Saco, Maine, museum purchase.

ceded there by *The Departure of the Israelites from Egypt* (based on David Roberts's 1829 painting in the Birmingham City Museums and Art Gallery). Such subjects exploited the fears and buttressed the faith of Britons and Americans tested by the financial swings and the Protestant controversies of the early nineteenth century. The taste, by turn, reflected back on the moral and religious serial landscapes of the American painter Thomas Cole, respectively, *The Course of Empire* (1836; New-York Historical Society), *The Voyage of Life* (figures 1.6–1.9), and the unfinished *The Cross and the World* (figure 1.11). The first two series were shown, like panoramas and dioramas, as pay-admission spectacles.[10] As Jessica Skwire Routhier discusses in her essay, the *Moving Panorama of Pilgrim's Progress* was very much a natural successor to the latter two series by Cole, not merely in its theme but by virtue of the design contributions to the panorama by Cole's followers, the landscape painters Frederic Church and Jasper Cropsey.

For all the quantity and variety of panoramic fare in America, real public fever for it did not arise until 1846. That was the year an itinerant scene painter named John Banvard brought his "three-mile picture" of the Mississippi River from the frontier town of Louisville, Kentucky, where he had painted it, to genteel Boston.[11] By the time the painting had completed its tour in New York, London, the British provinces, and even Paris, an estimated two million people had seen one or the other of two versions of the subject that Banvard eventually produced. The folksy — and eventually wealthy — artist and raconteur became a fixture of Broadway show life through the Civil War; he had sired the most conspicuous mass entertainment phenomenon of the nineteenth century.

Banvard and his moving panorama seemed so fresh that many Britons erroneously thought he had invented the form.[12] Having learned from P. T. Barnum that what the public believed was money in the bank, Banvard never contradicted anyone who so credited him. In fact, the moving panorama, like most of the other "-oramas" except the diorama, had originated in Britain around 1820 almost simultaneously as a feature of dramatic stage presentations and as an independent showpiece.[13] It arrived in the former guise at the Park Theater on Broadway in 1828 as a scenic interlude to a play about a trip to London and Paris; the moving picture created the illusion of the actors' voyage across the English Channel, with the watery scenery passing behind their stationary ferry. New York impresarios lost no time producing a Yankee response in the same house later that year: a play entitled *A Trip to Niagara; or, Travellers in America,* featuring a two-hundred-foot moving canvas of the Hudson River from New York to Catskill Landing, as seen from the deck of a steamboat. Dioramic effects — transitions from day to night and oncoming storms, painted on the canvas and enhanced by modifying the theater lights — were integral to

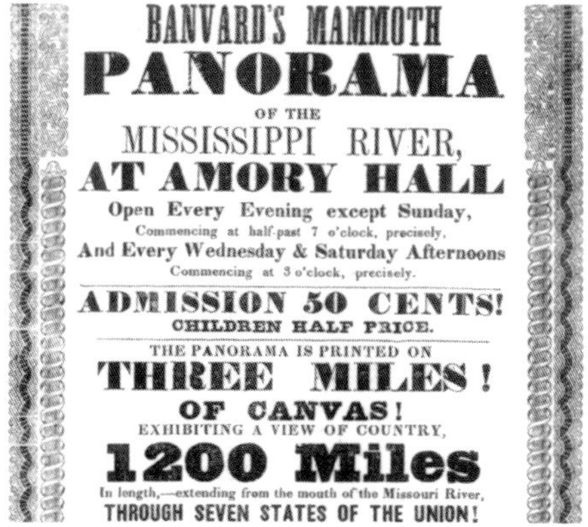

FIGURE 2.4. *Banvard's Mammoth Panorama of the Mississippi River*, broadside advertising a performance at Boston's Amory Hall, 1847.

the moving panorama from its inception and augmented such scenes in the Hudson River panorama as the cliffs of the Palisades and the Highlands at West Point.[14]

In a memoir, Banvard recalled visiting Vanderlyn's Rotunda as a boy growing up in New York City. Being artistically inclined, he had experimented with a few miniature dioramic subjects. But it was the vicarious steamboat journey represented in *A Trip to Niagara* and a few successors that prefigured his Mississippi River picture. By then, he had moved west to seek his fortune. At one point he converted a flatboat into a floating theater — which he parked at piers up and down the Wabash and Mississippi Rivers to invite the public in to see his dioramas — and often accepted farm produce for admission fees.[15] He also managed a museum in St. Louis, where in 1840 a few lucky financial investments permitted him to embark on what he claimed to be his abiding dream: to paint a moving picture of the Mississippi's major shoreline sites from its juncture with the Missouri south to the Gulf of Mexico. That same year in Boston, a scene painter named John Rowson Smith had painted a short moving panorama of the Mississippi, like the one of the Hudson River, for a Boston stage production.[16] Another later contender in the Mississippi panorama market, Henry Lewis, claimed that he had confided his idea to Banvard for such a picture before the latter had launched his project.[17] Banvard may well have dreamed of his Mississippi panorama since his earliest days on the river, but his dream was evidently in the air. He simply had the quickest reflexes.

For over a year, Banvard descended the Mississippi in a little skiff, sleeping on the banks in its meager shelter, penciling broad stretches of the shore in numerous sketchbooks. After finishing the preparatory work in New Orleans, he built a large studio in Louisville and ordered tremendous skeins of cotton muslin from the mills at Lowell, Massachusetts. It took him over four years to translate his sketches into a series of thirty-eight scenes covering the eastern bank of the Mississippi from the mouth of the Ohio River to New Orleans, on a twelve-foot-high bolt of cloth, said to have stretched thirteen hundred feet in length. Eventually, the picture was expanded to include the western bank of the Mississippi, as well as the scenery on the Ohio and Missouri Rivers, resulting in its being divided into two independent shows.[18] For sheer labor at least, Banvard might have claimed to be the Michelangelo of landscape painting.

In fact, Banvard had never benefited from any artistic training. The few easel paintings he left behind show that he was little more than a talented amateur, his chief métier being that of the theatrical scene painter, who produced merely broad, generalizing effects. His pretense to genius, which some critics cheerfully awarded him, lay chiefly in his proletarian charm and Yankee instinct for "modest" self-promotion, honed during his years on the river as an itinerant showman. When rain discouraged opening night attendance in Louisville, he gave away tickets to steamboat captains who, artistically innocent and flattered by their own familiarity with the scenes in the panorama, praised it ebulliently. Banvard promptly published their plaudits in newspapers and panorama programs, as he later did with those elicited from politicians, statesmen, clergymen, literary lions such as Charles Dickens, and even Queen Victoria, who reportedly bestowed upon him "a distinguished mark of her Royal Approbation."[19]

In London, the former New Yorker Banvard only exaggerated the frontier persona he had cultivated through his lectures with the panorama in Boston and New York, seasoning his remarks with original music played by his wife on the pianoforte. Hat in hand, he hastened to alert the audiences in Picadilly that he was not presenting his panorama "as a work of art, but as a correct representation of the country it portrays."[20] British reviewers, to be sure, criticized the picture's artistic qualities, especially measured against the circular panoramas at Leicester Square, but conceded patronizingly that the innocent qualities of Banvard's technique were one with the down-homeyness of the artist's stage presence, which was irresistible: "Upon a platform [next to his picture] is Mr. Banvard, who explains the localities as the picture moves, and relieves his narrative with Jonathanisms and jokes, poetry and patter, which delight his audience mightily."[21] Banvard's narrative, moreover, included his personal experience on the Mississippi, his picture illuminating the settings of the frontier adventures he unquestionably lived — and undoubtedly embroidered.

Almost as soon as Banvard reached England, he was hotly pursued by competitors envious of his fame and success. Understandably, John Rowson Smith, the creator of the early Mississippi panorama in Boston, was one of them. Smith rushed to Britain in 1849 with a "four-mile painting" of the river. Back in the States, at least four more panoramas of the subject circulated well into the 1850s, the decade of moving panorama fever.[22] Banvard had stimulated a transatlantic yen for moving travelogues that was only piqued by current events: the western explorations of the 1840s and 1850s, the wresting of Texas and California from Mexico in 1848, and the discovery of gold near Sacramento, all of which loosed a flood of emigrants from the eastern United States and Europe and supplied a host of new subjects to would-be panoramists. Pictorial voyages around South America to San Francisco and the Gold Regions became familiar fare in the northeastern cities, as did a few panoramas of the overland route to the West Coast through the South Pass of the Rocky Mountains.[23] One such picture traced the 1842–44 expedition route of the famed Colonel John C. Fremont. However, none of the painters of the panorama, including one John Skirving and the academic artist Joseph Kyle (who shortly afterward collaborated in the creation of both versions of the *Moving Panorama of Pilgrim's Progress*), had actually visited the west. They relied on the engravings of other artists' drawings that were published in Fremont's *Report of the Exploring Expedition to the Rocky Mountains . . . Oregon and North California* (1845) and in other recent western travel narratives.[24] This lack of direct experience must have been detectable in both the panorama itself as well as in the accompanying lecture. Critics in London bore down much harder on *Colonel Fremont's Overland Route* than they had on Banvard's *Mississippi*, charging that "the trees are without distinct character of foliage, and the men and beasts are one and all badly drawn."[25] So much for the critics. By 1851 more than 350,000 Britons had paid a shilling each to see it.

By the Civil War decade, frontier panoramas — as well as the huge landscape paintings of western subjects by Albert Bierstadt that traded on their popularity — had become subjects of ridicule. Both were lampooned by the humorist Artemus Ward (an inspiration to Mark Twain), who lectured with a caricature panorama of the West in New York and London after the War.[26]

Despite a gradual dwindling of interest in moving panoramas since the 1850s, novel subjects usually served to prompt brief popular resurgences. Such a variety of subjects continued thanks to the tireless exploratory impulse of the times. The decades' long search for the expeditionary party of England's Sir John Franklin, lost in the ice of coastal Labrador in 1845, inspired several moving panoramas. Perhaps the most popular was the first of several pictures based on the thrilling narrative of the naval surgeon Elisha Kent Kane, *Arctic Explorations* (1855).[27] Kane purported to have discovered the chimerical Open Polar Sea, then commanded the escape and rescue of his crew from their icebound ship down the coast of Greenland to civilization. The tropics of Costa Rica, including a trek into a volcanic crater, were illuminated in a panorama explained by the Irish orator and journalist Thomas Francis Meagher in New York and Washington in 1858.[28] The British were treated to panoramas of their empire, including Australia and the overland mail route to India.[29] Akin to the exploration panoramas were those representing whaling voyages; one in particular, Benjamin Russell and Caleb Purrington's *Whaling Voyage Round the World*, successfully toured throughout the East and Midwest from 1848 through 1851. Like the *Moving Panorama of Pilgrim's Progress*, *Whaling Voyage* escaped the destruction of most moving panoramas; its broad and hasty execution, measured against its evident popular appeal, is testimony both to the uncritical aesthetic standards of its audiences and to the lively appetite for travel and adventure among Americans at midcentury. Such taste was accommodated similarly by the early South Sea novels of Herman Melville, who based *Moby*

Dick (1851) on true-life accounts of an 1820 whaling incident that is also portrayed in the panorama.[30]

The development of fast and cheap steam transportation on both land and water combined with the increasing size of the middle class to usher in the phenomenon of mass tourism by the 1850s. Panoramists rushed to cater to it, producing scores of pictorial excursions. Probably the most famous was Godfrey N. Frankenstein's *Moving Panorama of Niagara Falls*, whose opening at Broadway's Hope Chapel in July 1853 coincided exactly with the introduction of a railroad line to Niagara, which produced a huge increase in visitors to that perennially wondrous landmark. Frankenstein was a painter of considerable accomplishment: he had founded and originally led the Cincinnati Academy of Fine Arts, and since 1844 he had visited the Falls almost annually to make paintings of the site from all angles and in every season.

The moving panorama phenomenon (and probably awareness of the railroad project) stimulated Frankenstein to turn his Niagara pictures into a grand enterprise. By necessity, the design of the panorama proved a departure from the vehicular, linear conceit of typical moving panoramas. The sequence of scenes most closely approximated a walking tour around the Falls, encompassing the various points of view Frankenstein had sketched, including a tour in the Cave of the Winds, the damp, deafening passage behind the American Falls, and a ride on the Maid of the Mist, the tour boat that still plies the Niagara River below the Falls. At occasional intervals, however, the scenery segued suddenly from a daytime to a moonlight setting and from a summer to a winter portrait of the cataract. As performances went on, the artist inserted topical scenes: the collapse of Table Rock at the Canadian Falls and a hapless boatman's fatal plunge over the American Falls. By staying current, Frankenstein kept his show thriving in New York for six months and showed it elsewhere in America until at least 1865.[31] The panorama was perhaps the most conspicuous example of a glut of Niagara imagery in the 1850s, culminating in the panorama-like presentation of Frederic Church's wide-angle painting, *Niagara* (Corcoran Gallery of Art), in 1857. Both *Niagara* and Church's ten-foot-wide painting of South America, *The Heart of the Andes* (1859, Metropolitan Museum of Art; see figure 2.5) were displayed in darkened rooms with overhead lighting focused exclusively on each painting to dramatize its effect.[32]

Many other North American landmarks became panorama fodder — the Great Lakes and St. Lawrence River, the Mammoth Cave in Kentucky, even the western prairies[33] — but a host of moving panoramas of the Old World

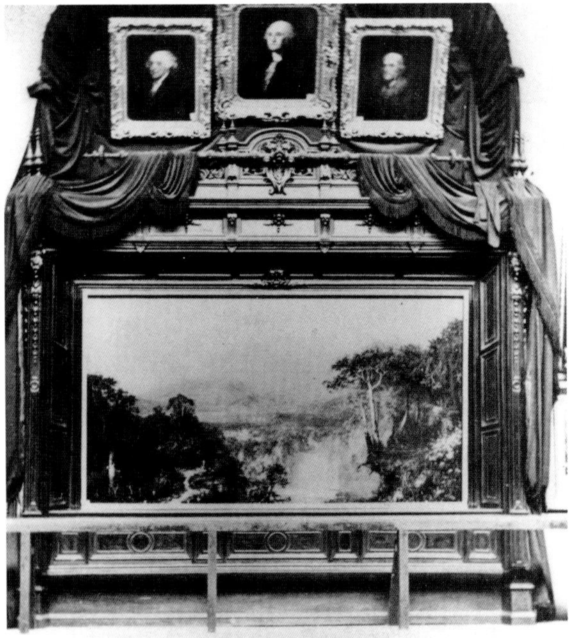

FIGURE 2.5. Frederic Edwin Church's *Heart of the Andes* on display in 1864.

testify to the rising interest in travel to Europe and beyond among the many Americans who had either acquired or expected to acquire the means to go there. Then again, part of the audience for such pictures were the hordes of immigrants — from Ireland, Italy, Germany, Scandinavia, and elsewhere — who yearned for reminders of the homelands many of them had reluctantly forsaken. Indeed, a mob of neo-Americans are portrayed in the only surviving scene of the Philadelphia artist Samuel B. Waugh's *Mirror of Italy*, or *Italia*, which opened in Philadelphia in 1849. Waugh's panorama toured the country on and off for at least eighteen years and enjoyed lengthy New York runs in 1850 and 1859. The extant fragment, now in the Museum of the City of New York, constitutes the very first scene of the panorama. It shows the pier at Manhattan's Battery crowded with newly arrived Irish immigrants; a queue of them files into the processing station of Castle Garden, decades before Ellis Island was even contemplated. It may be that the ragtag regiment in this opening view was intended as an inducement to Yankee audiences to embark in the opposite direction across the Atlantic. That is surely where the panorama took them — on an old-fashioned grand tour of Italy, from the northern Lake District and Milan through Venice, Florence, and Rome, culminating in Naples and Pompeii with a grand "Eruption of Vesuvius."[34]

Our survey might well conclude, if not chronologically then thematically, with the *Panorama of the Holy Land*, a product of the prodigiously popular European tour of the redoubtable Banvard and his "three-mile" Mississippi panorama. Humbled by his success, and responding to a sermon on good works he had heard in London, Banvard justified his piety and his purse in touring Palestine and then created what was probably the largest moving picture ever — variously described as measuring twenty-five or forty-eight (!) feet high. Back in America, on Broadway, he acquired his own theater, the "Georama," and ran performances there, as well as in Boston and Philadelphia, from 1854 to 1859. The passing imagery — with, of course, Banvard on hand to describe the scenes — transported the viewer by Mount Lebanon and the ruins of Baalbeck, on to Tyre, Sidon, Nazareth, the River Jordan, the Plains of Jericho, Bethlehem, and finally Jerusalem, the Holy City of the Old and New Testaments.[35] With the healthy profits of his Mississippi and Holy Land panoramas, Banvard built a palatial house for his family at Cold Spring Harbor, Long Island, and remained a Broadway entertainment fixture for decades.

The taste for subjects like the Holy Land illuminate not merely Americans' territorial curiosity but also the reflexively moralistic and religious mind-set of a citizenry still predominantly Protestant in the mid-nineteenth century. Banvard's *Holy Land* was surely a geographic tour, but its geography, as his professed inspiration for the panorama demonstrates, is also the landscape of Christian faith — indeed, the goal of the Christian pilgrimage since the Middle Ages. The distinction between it and Kyle and Dallas's *Moving Panorama of Pilgrim's Progress* is only one of literal versus figurative landscape: John Bunyan's Christian, the embodiment of the Protestant Everyman, makes a pilgrimage to his eternal reward (the Celestial City, or Heaven) through a landscape of trial and occasional consolation. The seventeenth-century allegory seems customized not only for Bunyan's fellow Puritans, some of whom — the Pilgrims of Massachusetts — had already gone to the New World to assume their predestined salvation, but also for the Pilgrims' descendants two hundred years later, who righteously fulfilled their Manifest Destiny to occupy the vast continent west of Plymouth Rock. If the tale's durability owes much to the Protestant revival in the early nineteenth century, it also seems, from our perspective, to have been tailor-made for a nation of God-fearing emigrants whose remaking of the New World required an ongoing redevotion of themselves. Thus, the story's appeal in panoramic form must have been irresistible to its makers and to its contributors, including, in this almost unique instance, some of America's foremost artists.

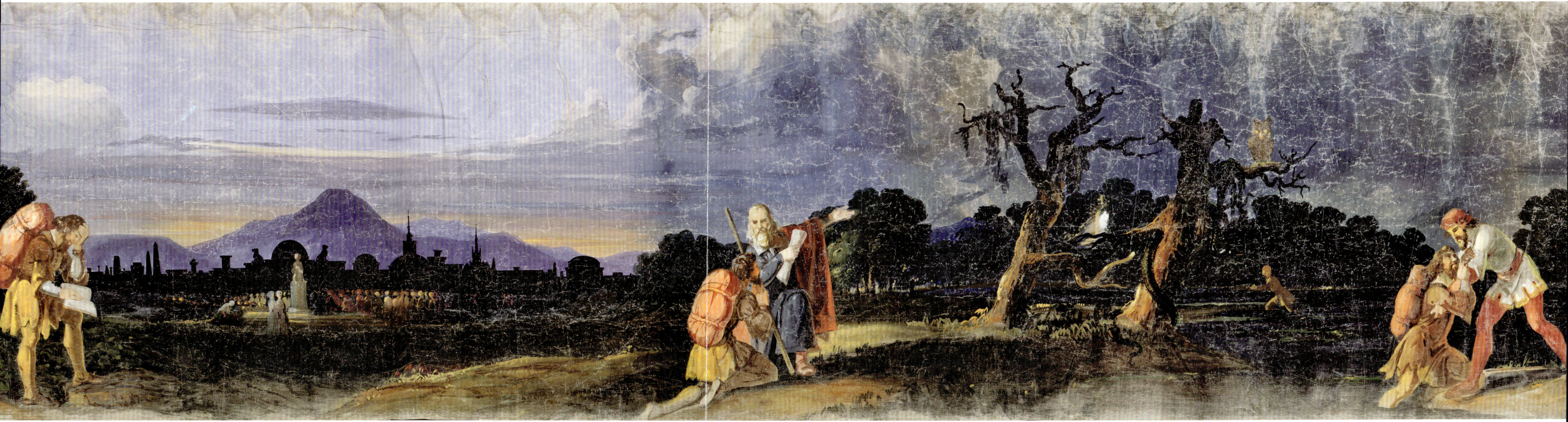

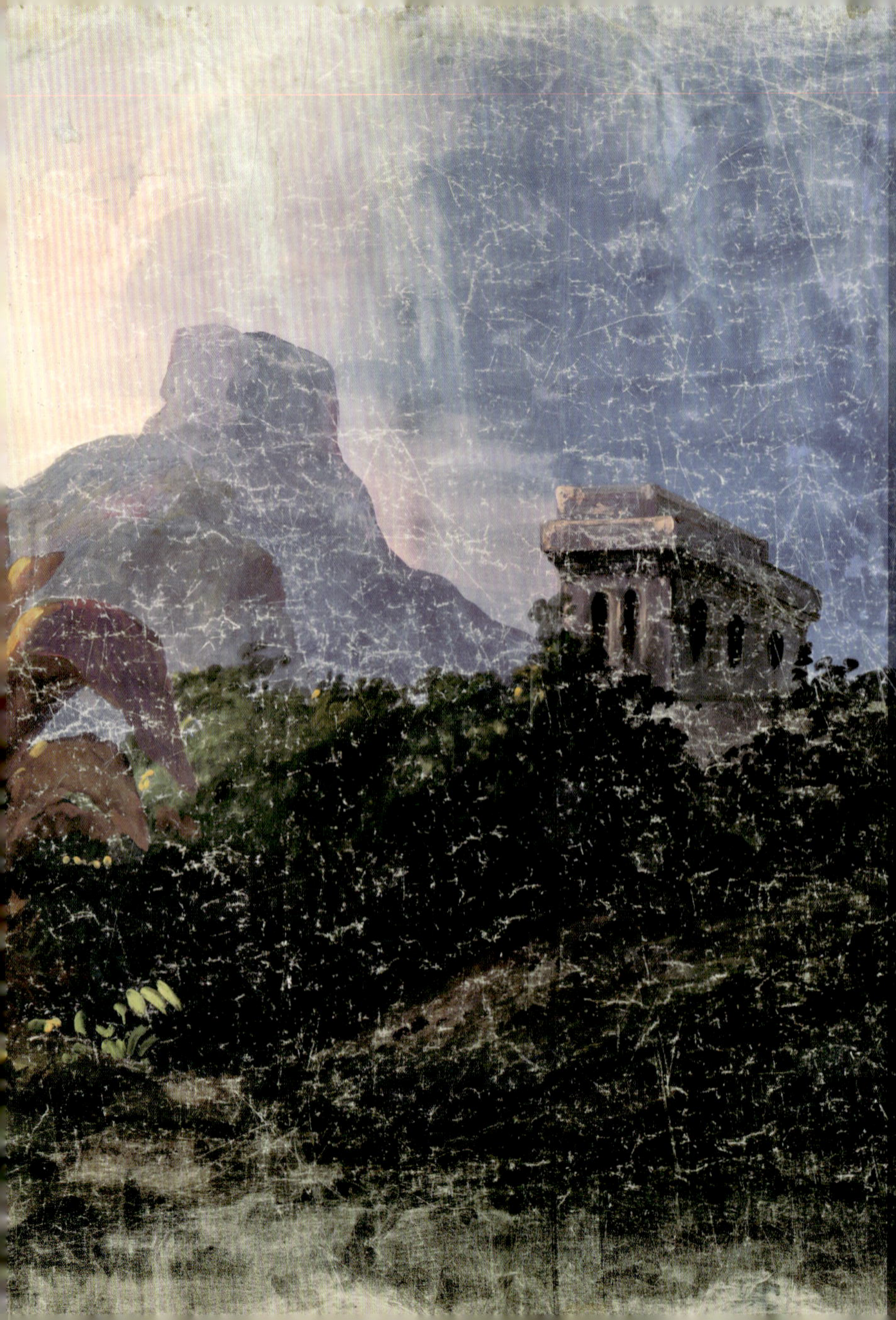

The *Moving Panorama of Pilgrim's Progress* is a continuous painting on eight hundred feet of muslin, encompassing in sequence most of the major scenes from John Bunyan's *The Pilgrim's Progress*, a book-length religious allegory first published in 1678. Historically, the panorama was presented in motion to a seated audience, rolled continuously from one gigantic roller to another so that only one scene was visible at a time, creating the illusion that the events were unfolding in real time. Pictured here are some of the panorama's most striking and recognizable scenes: *Palace Beautiful* (this page), *Mercy Faints at the Wicket Gate* (verso), and on the interior, a continuous succession of opening scenes, including *Christian Meditating in the Field*, *Evangelist Pointing out the Wicket Gate*, *Slough of Despond*, *Legality Hill*, and *Christian at the Wicket Gate*.

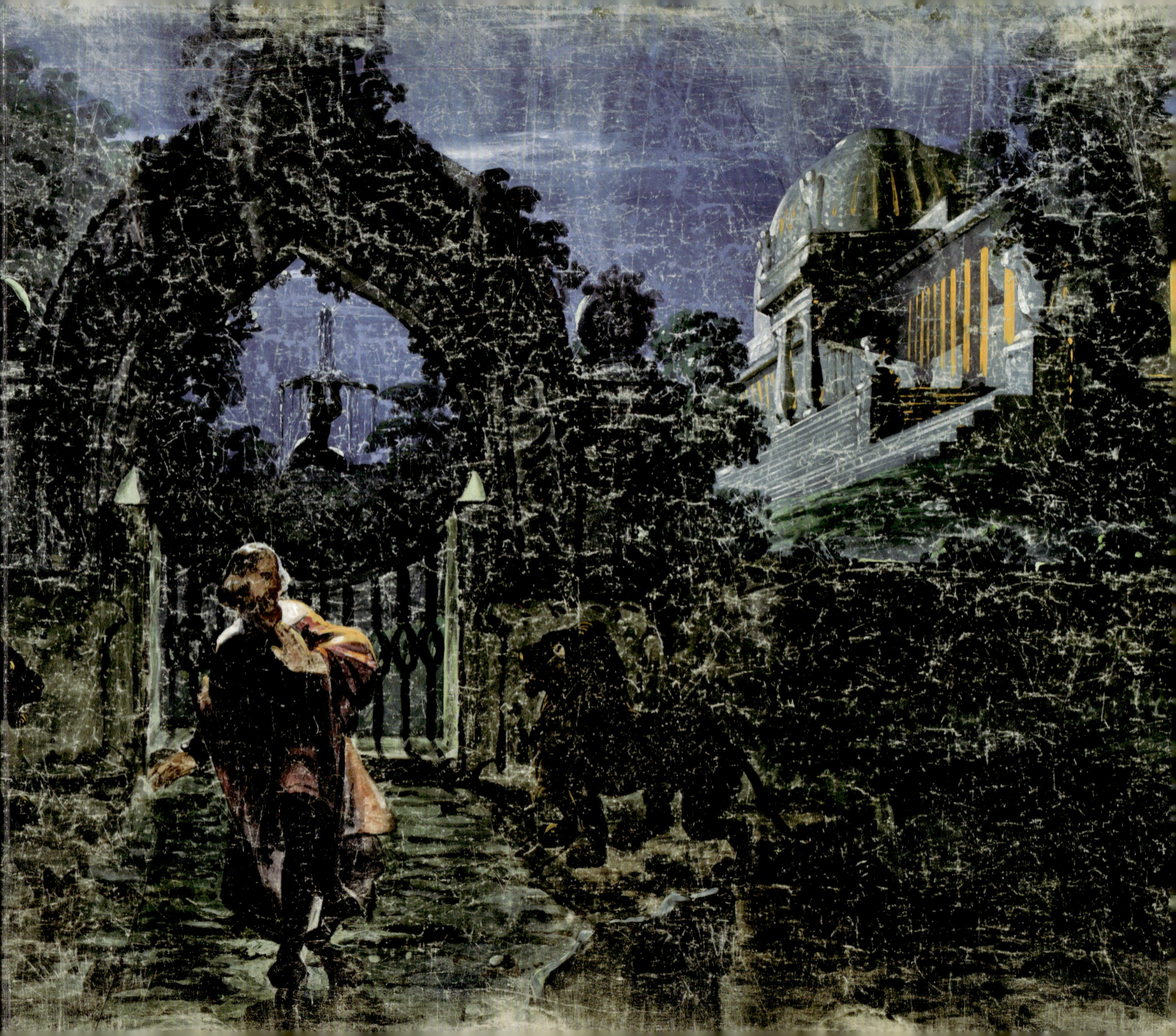

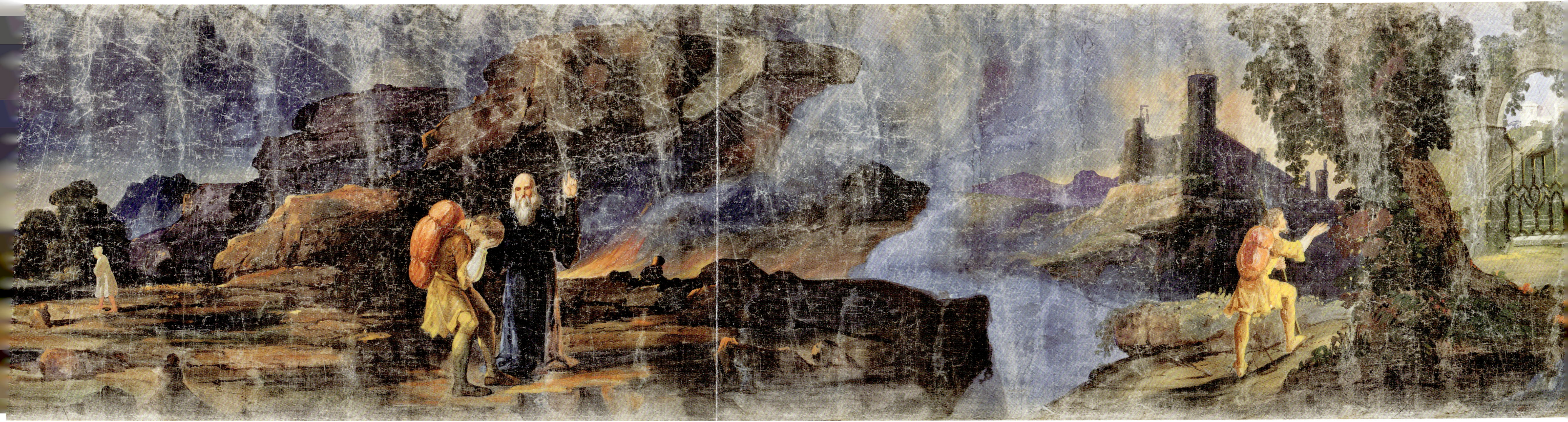

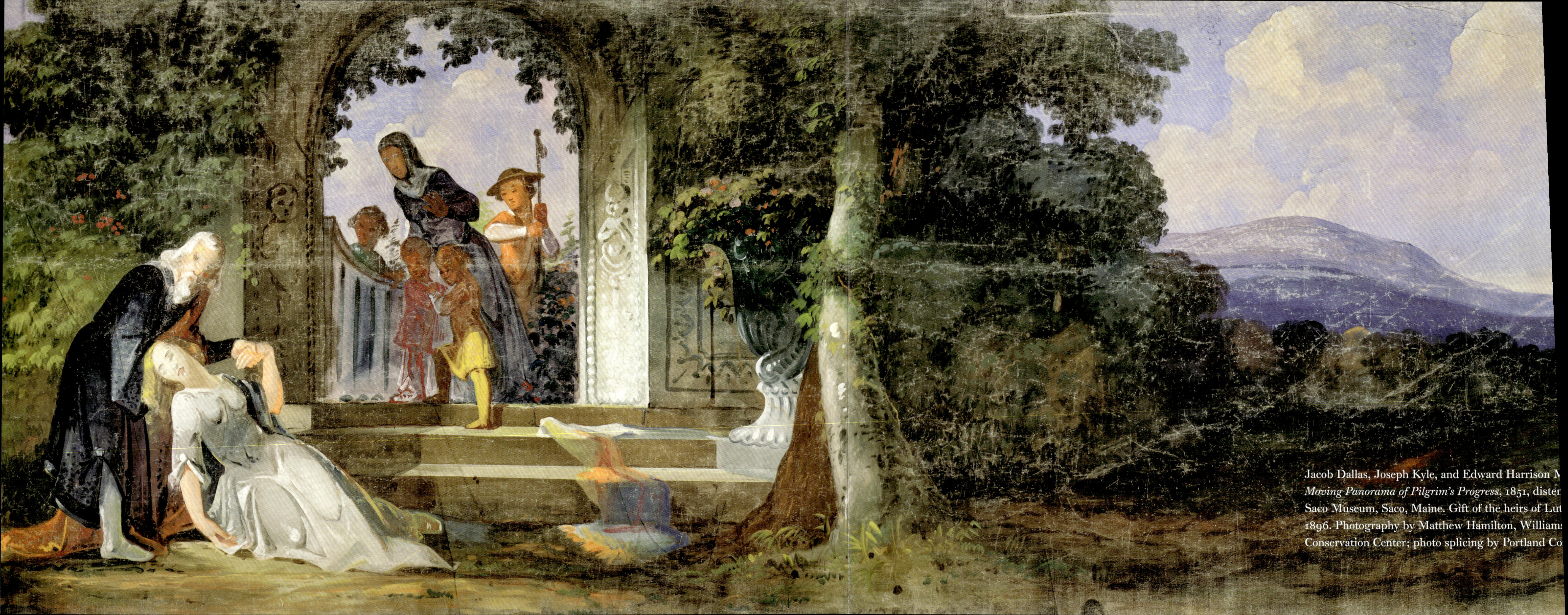

Jacob Dallas, Joseph Kyle, and Edward Harrison M
Moving Panorama of Pilgrim's Progress, 1851, dister
Saco Museum, Saco, Maine. Gift of the heirs of Lut
1896. Photography by Matthew Hamilton, Williams
Conservation Center; photo splicing by Portland Co

PLATES

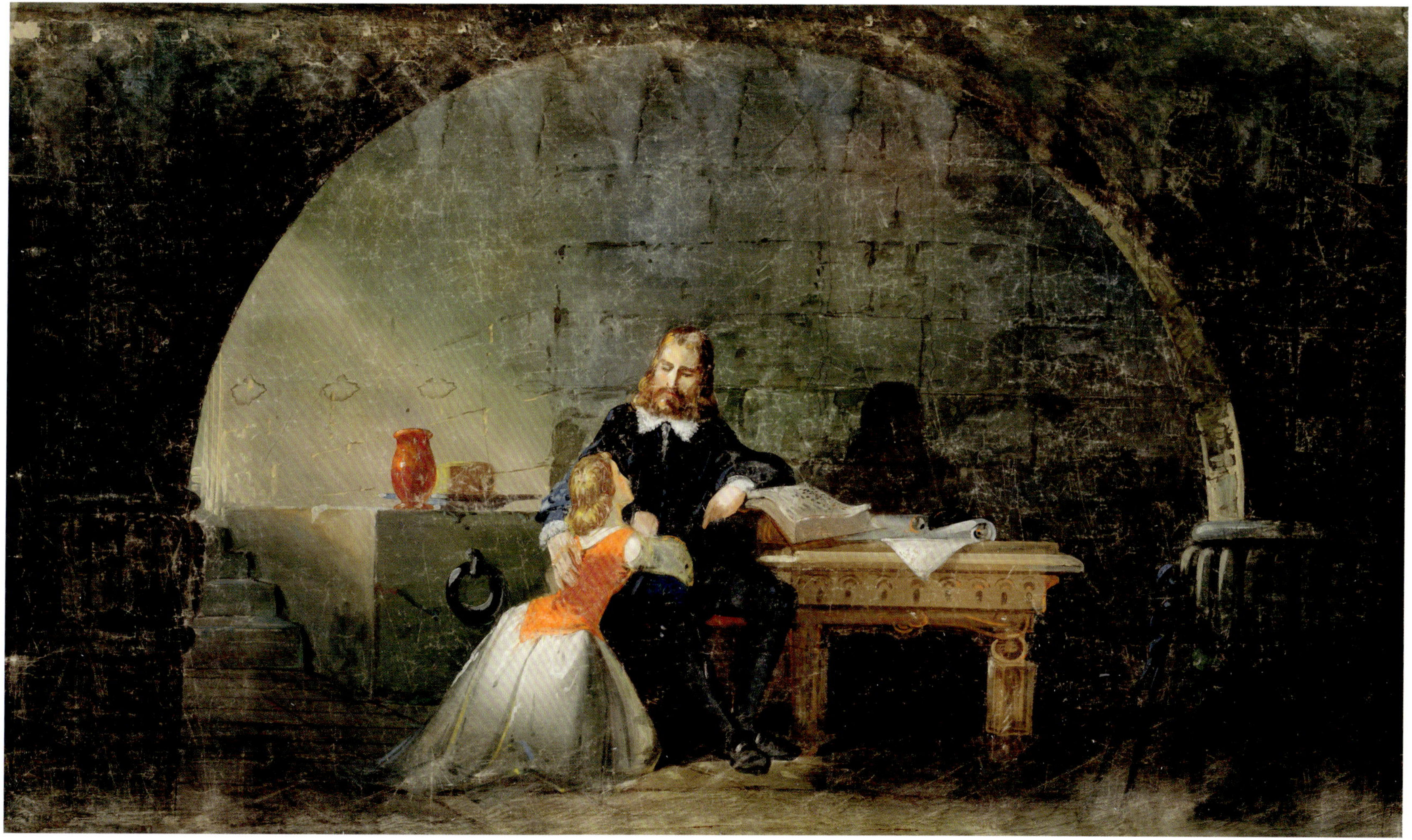

PLATE 1. *Bunyan Parting with His Blind Daughter*, design attributed to Edward Harrison May.

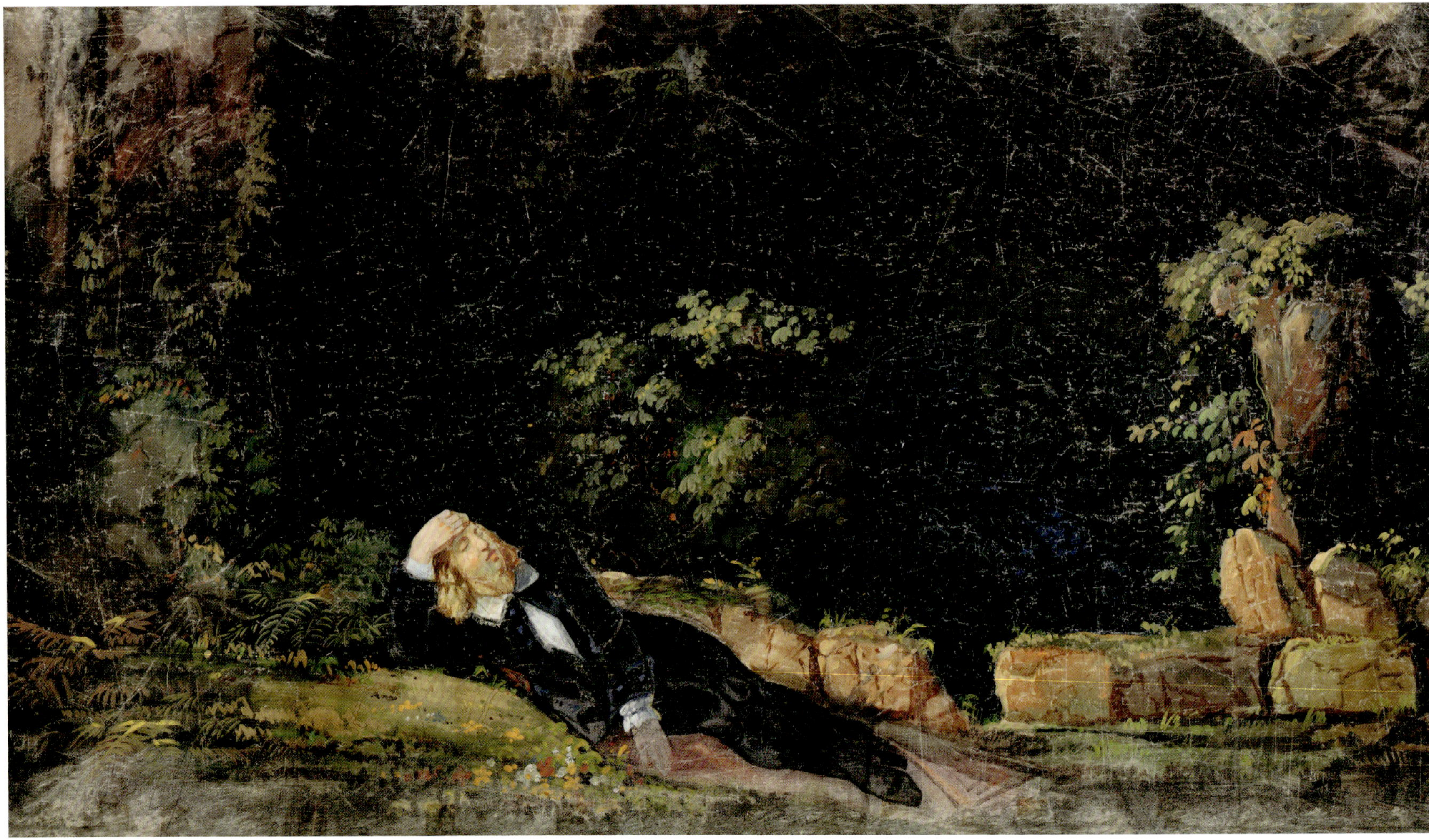

PLATE 2. *Bunyan Dreaming*, design attributed to Edward Harrison May.

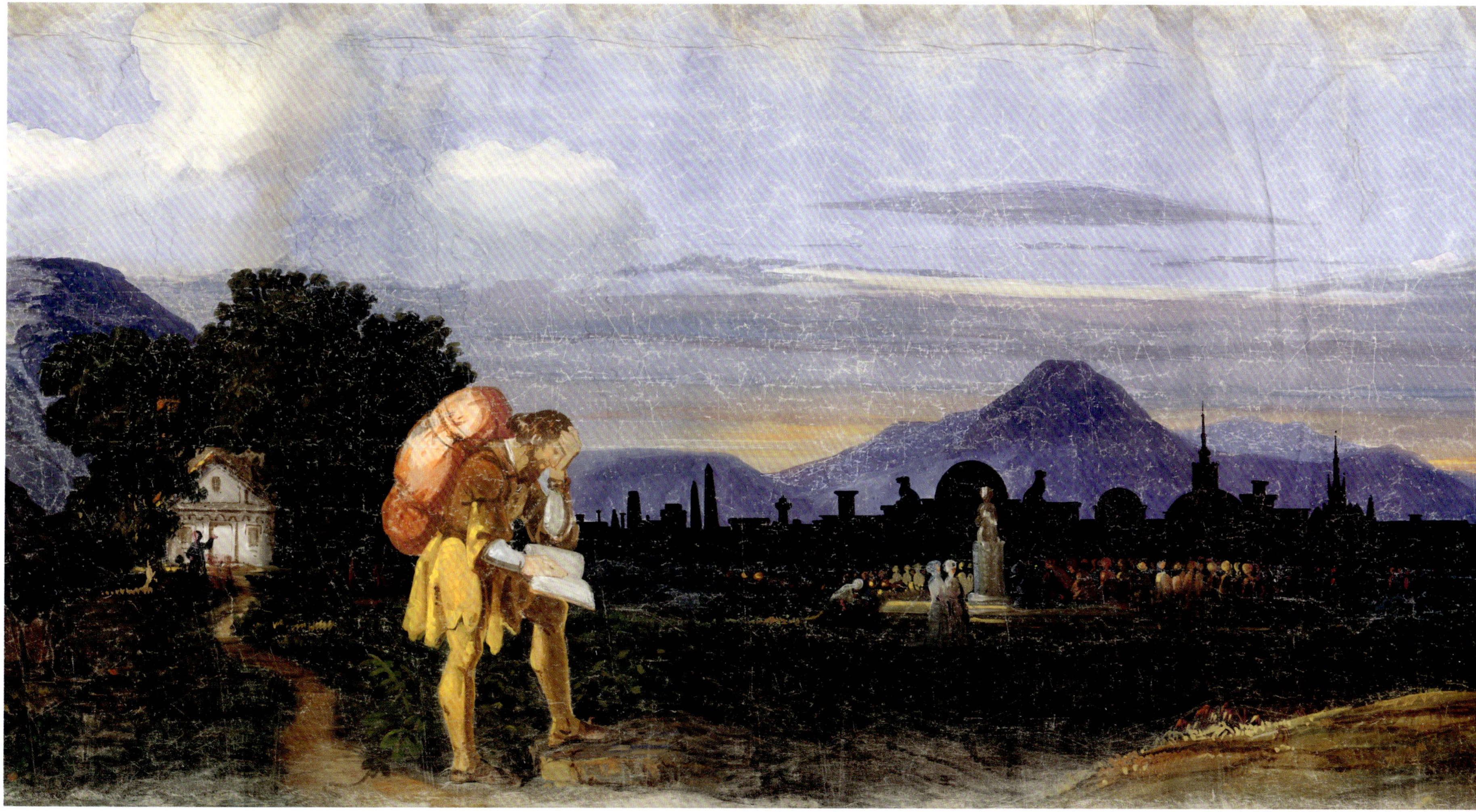

PLATE 3. *Christian Meditating in the Field*, design attributed to Edward Harrison May.

PLATE 4.
Evangelist Pointing Out the Wicket Gate,
design attributed to Joseph Kyle and
Edward Harrison May.

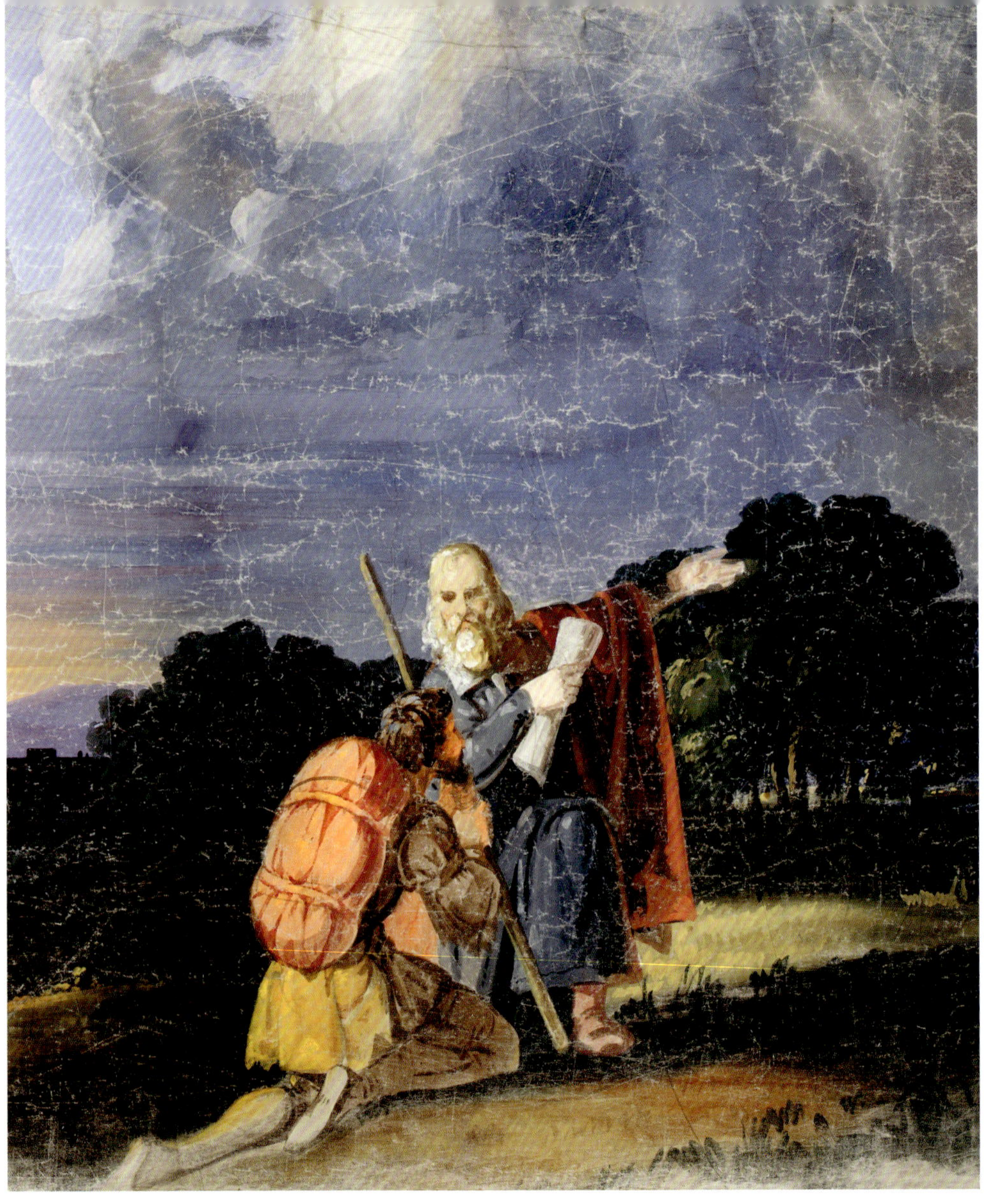

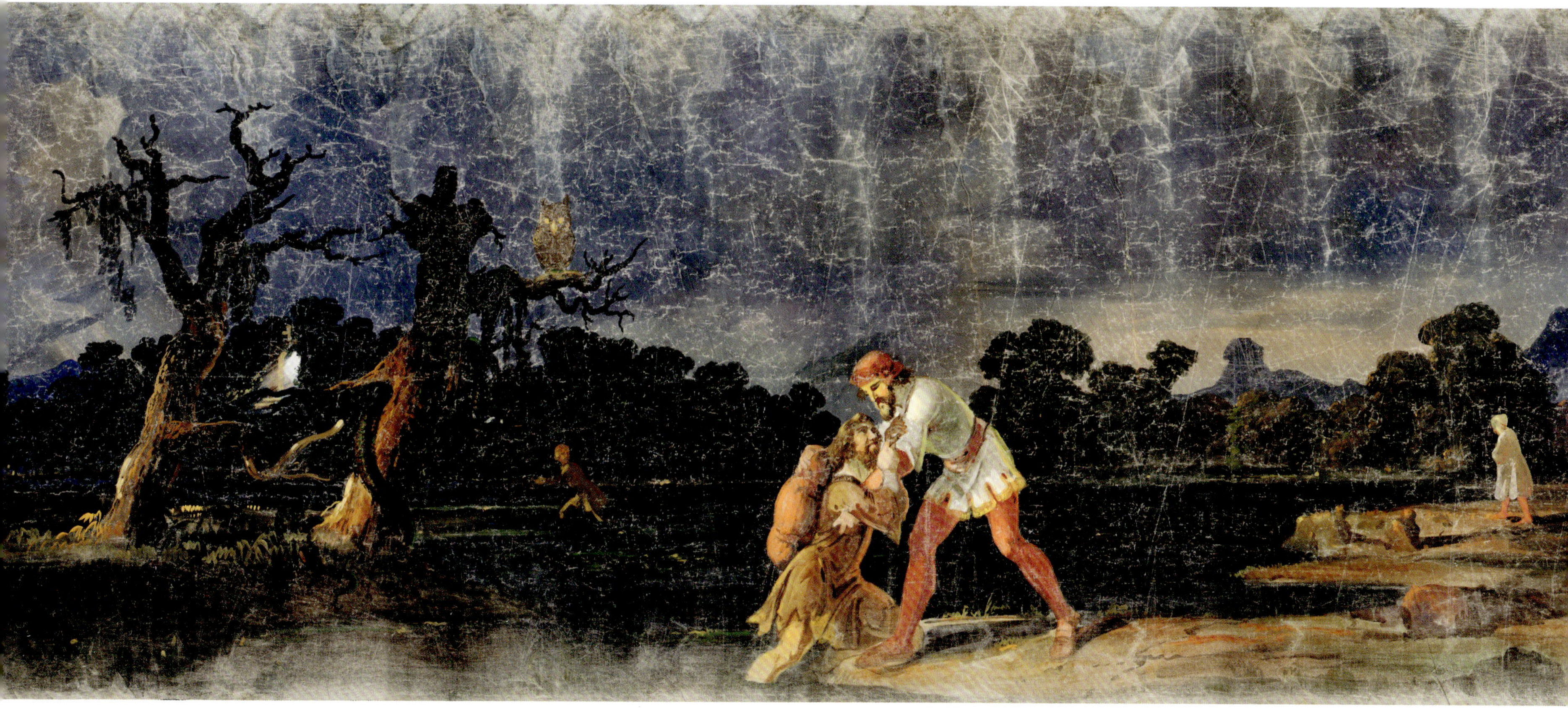

PLATE 5. *Slough of Despond*, design attributed to Joseph Kyle and Edward Harrison May.

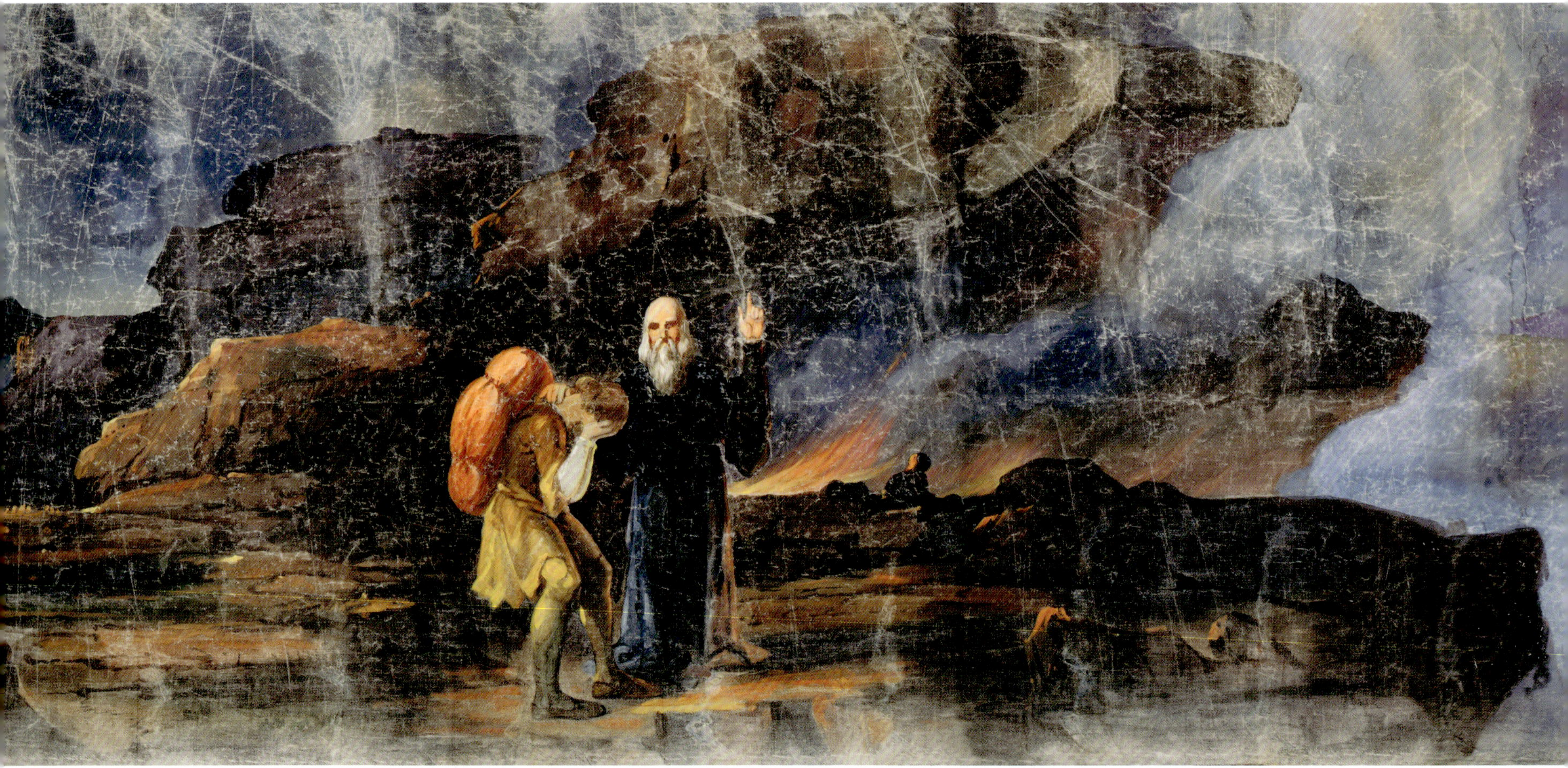

PLATE 6. *Legality Hill*, design attributed to Joseph Kyle and Edward Harrison May.

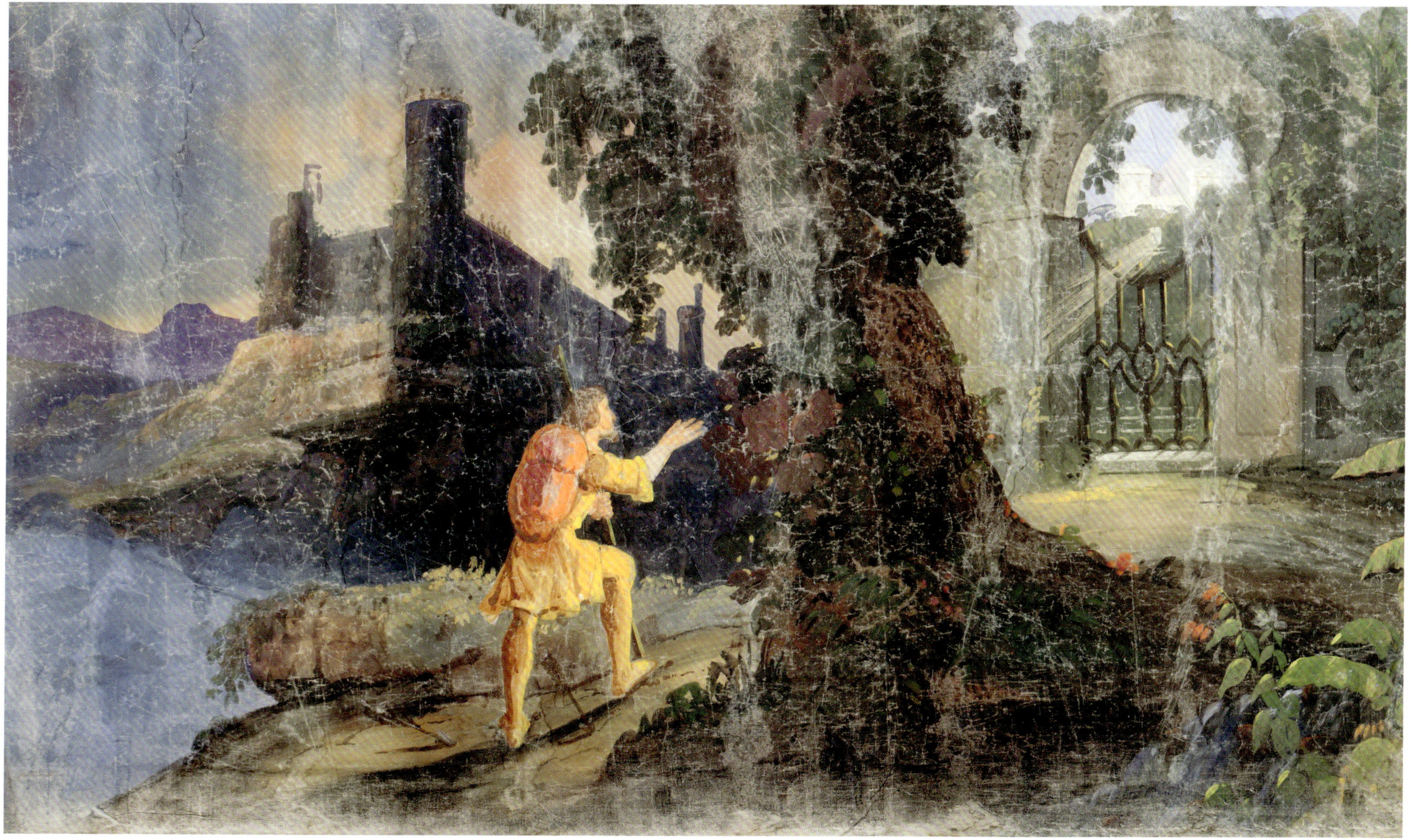

PLATE 7. *Christian at the Wicket Gate*, design attributed to Edward Harrison May.

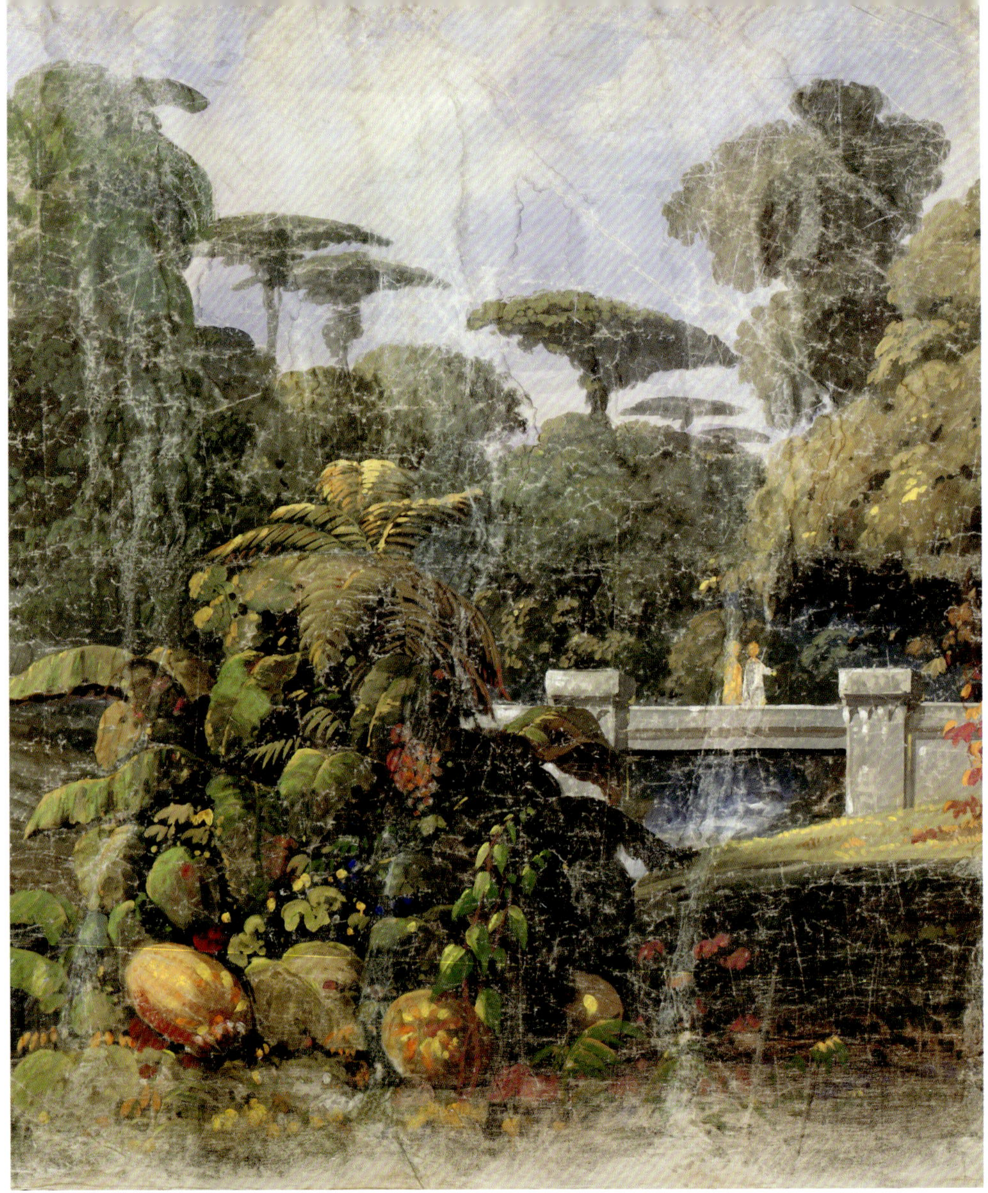

PLATE 8.
The Interpreter's House,
design attributed to
Joseph Kyle.

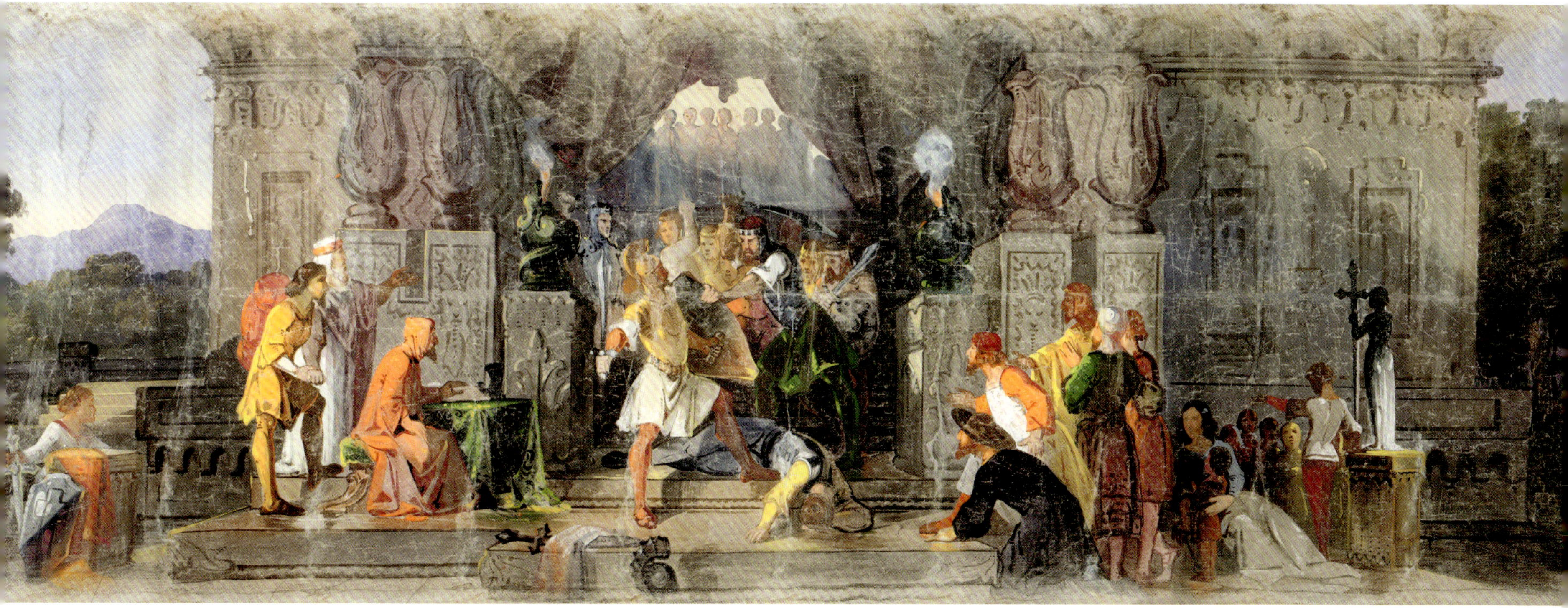

PLATE 9. *Interpreter Showing Christian the Wonders of His House*, design attributed to Edward Harrison May.

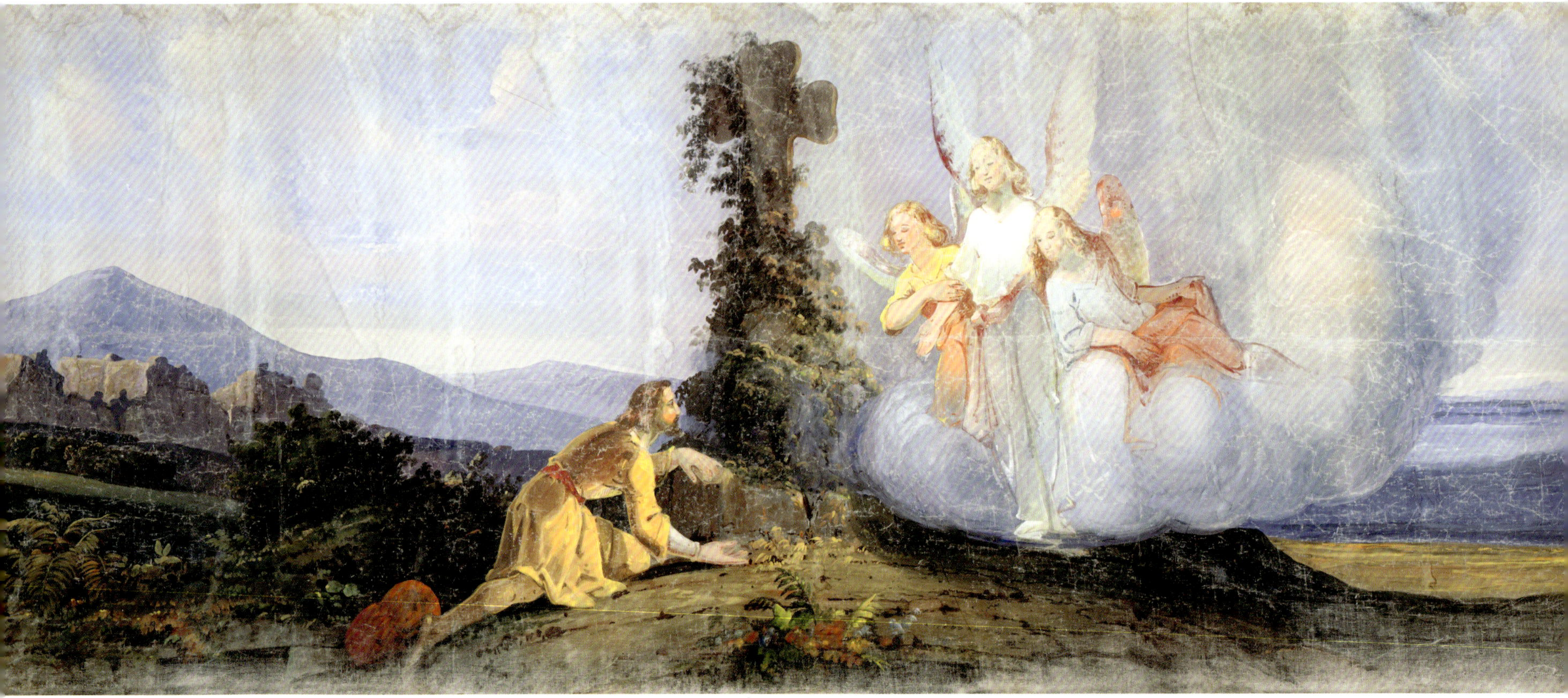

PLATE 10. *Christian at the Cross*, design attributed to Edward Harrison May.

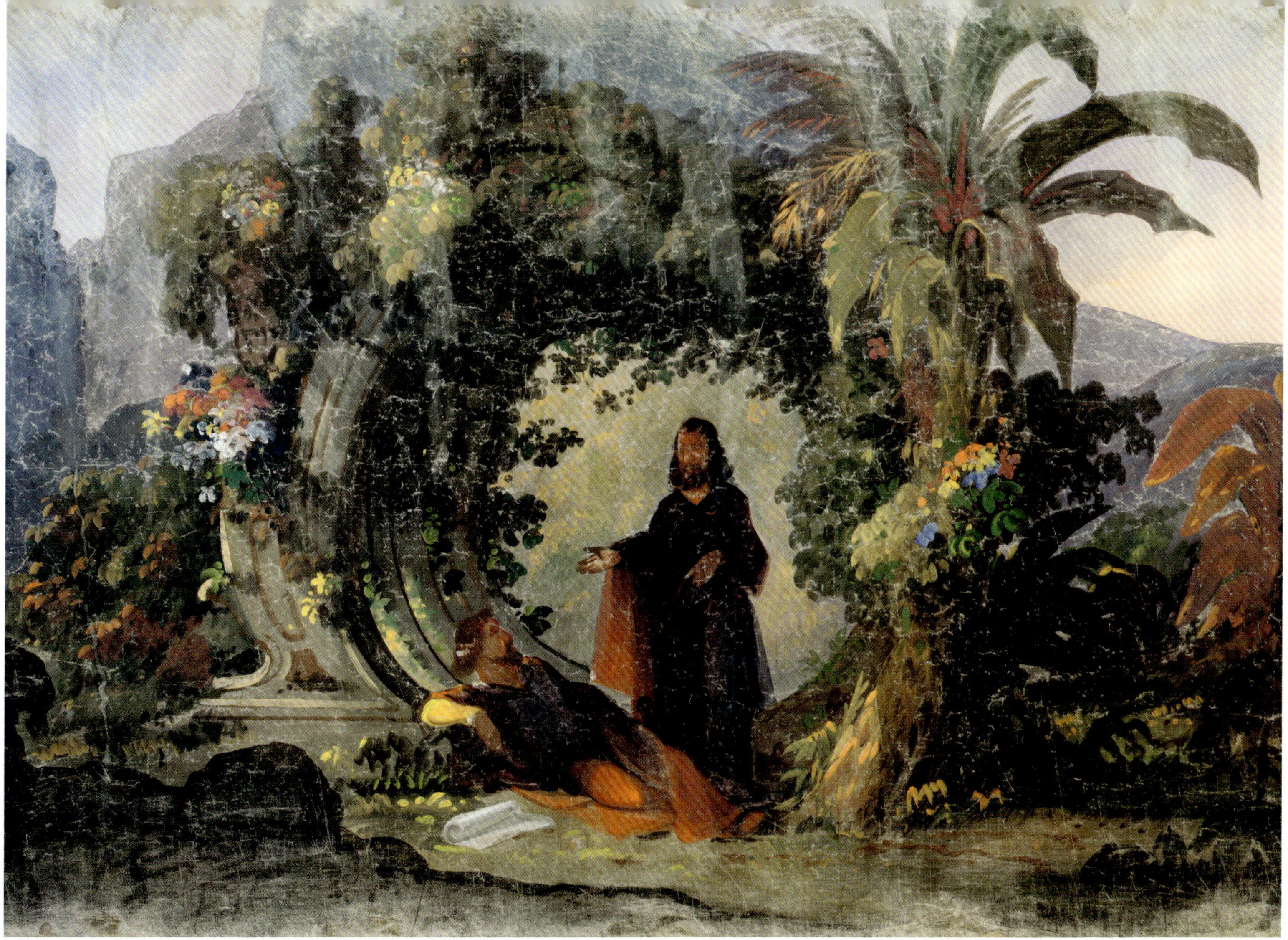

PLATE II. *The Arbor*, design attributed to Edward Harrison May.

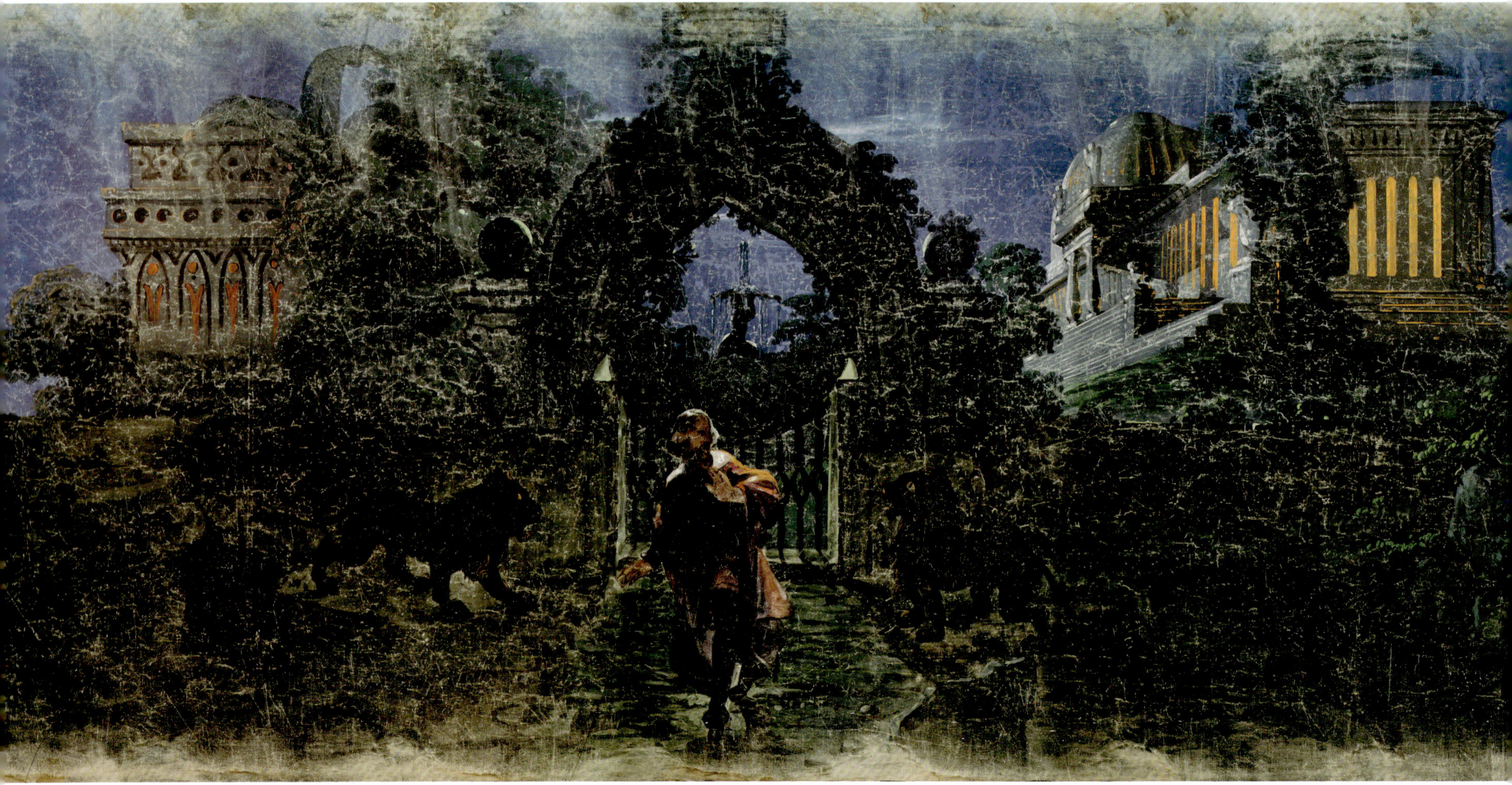

PLATE 12. *Palace Beautiful*, design attributed to Edward Harrison May.

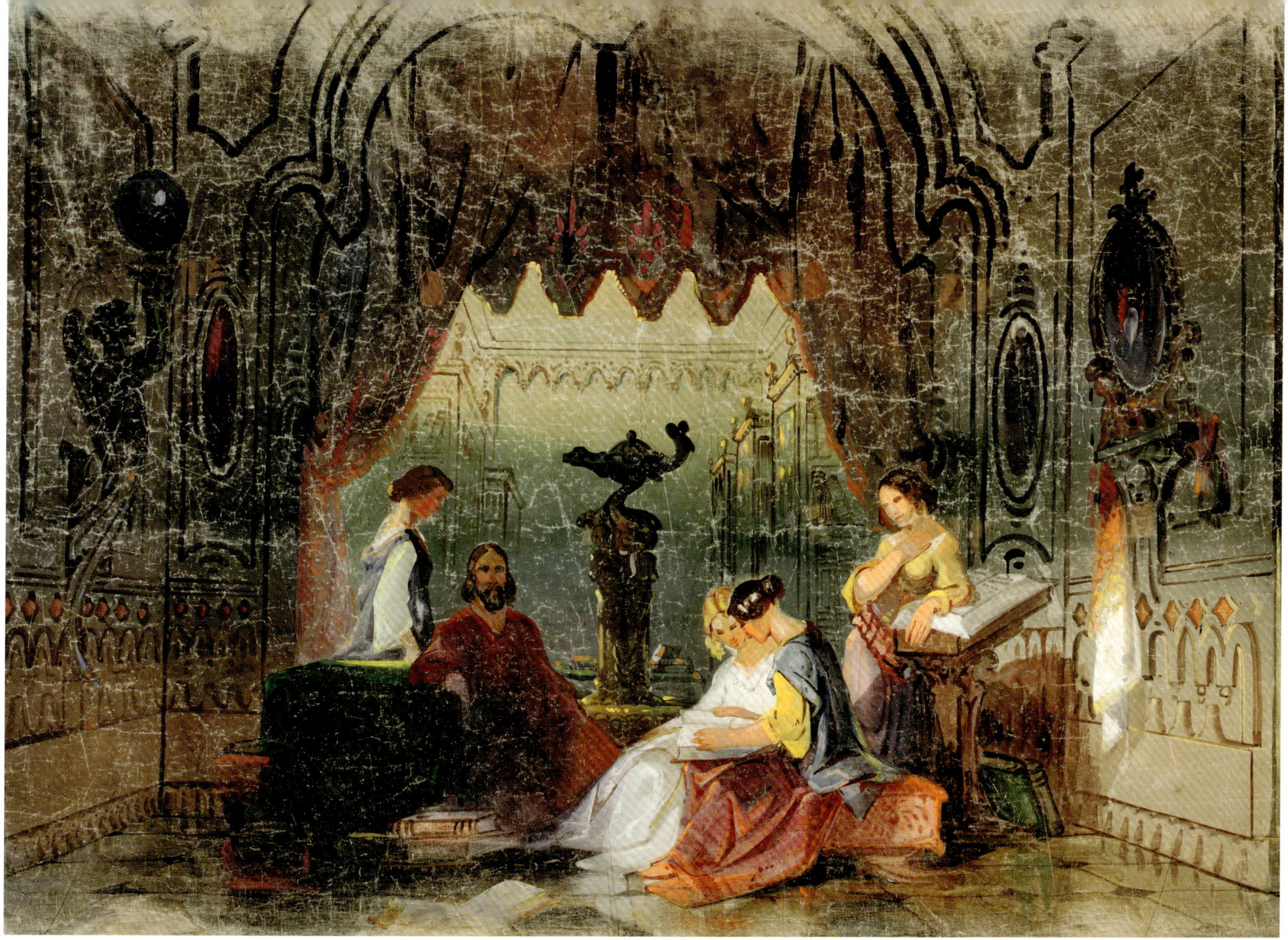

PLATE 13. *Interior of the Palace Beautiful*, design attributed to Edward Harrison May.

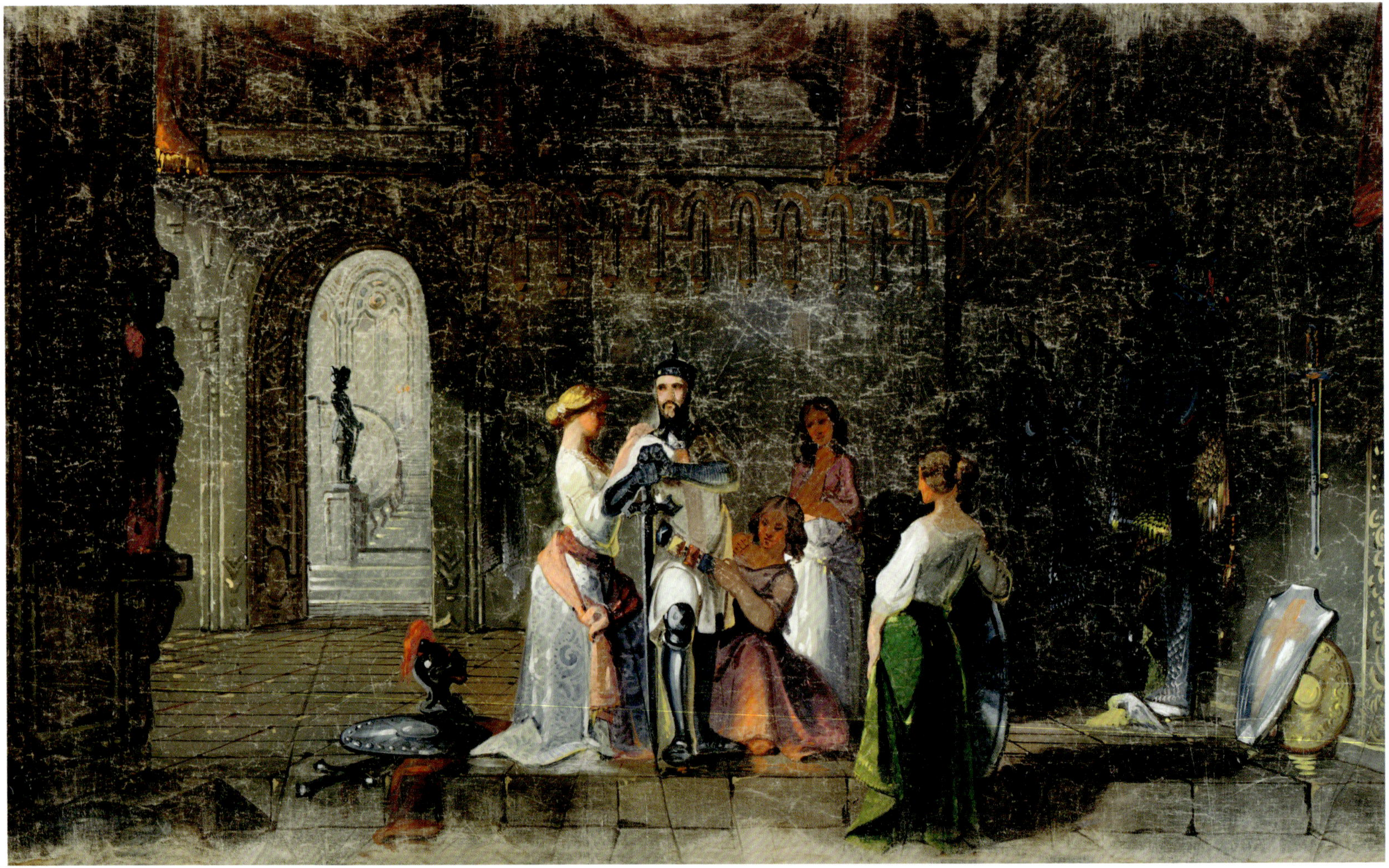

PLATE 14. *Arming of Christian*, design attributed to Jacob Dallas.

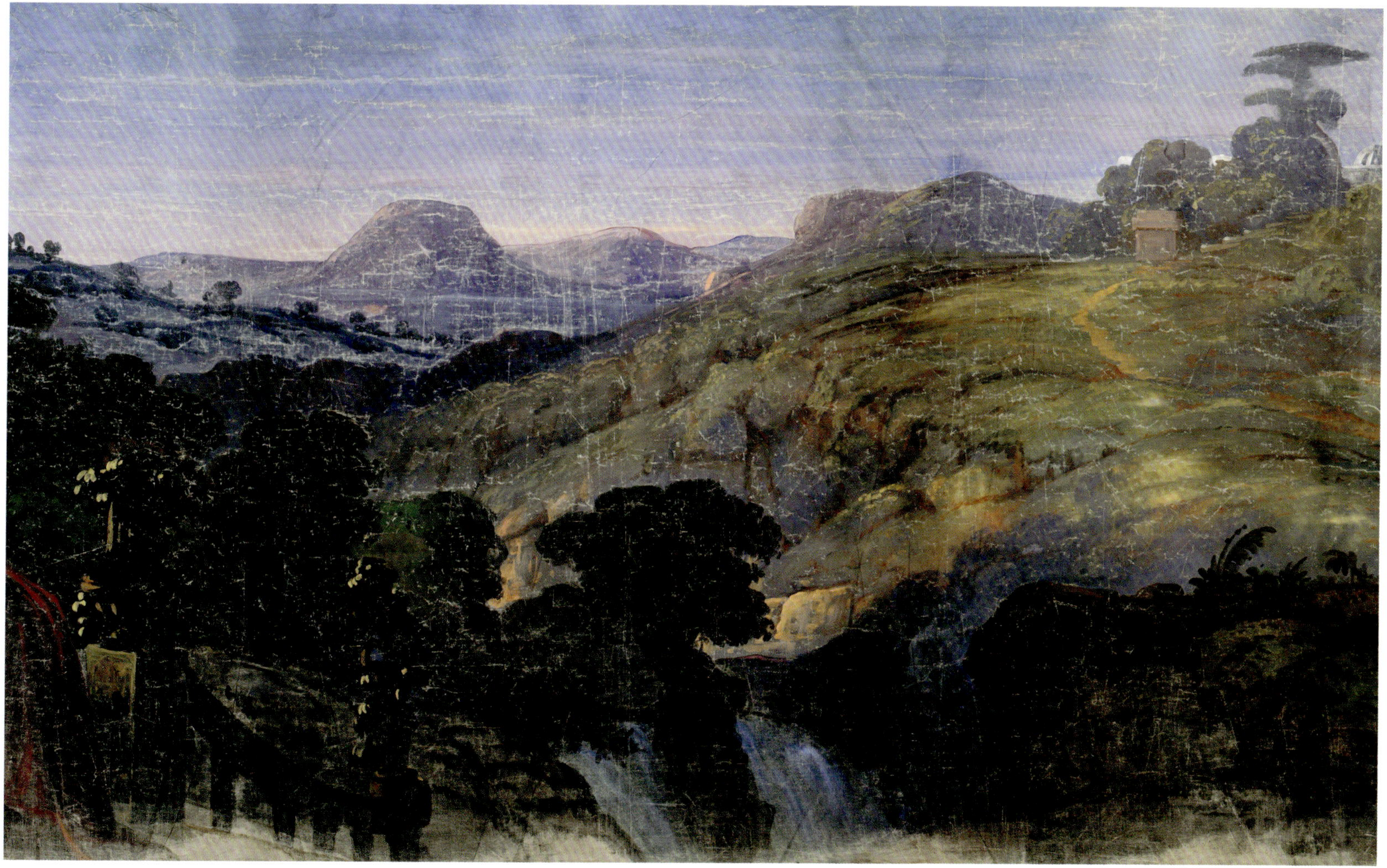

PLATE 15. *Virgins Pointing Out the Delectable Mountains*, design attributed to Edward Harrison May.

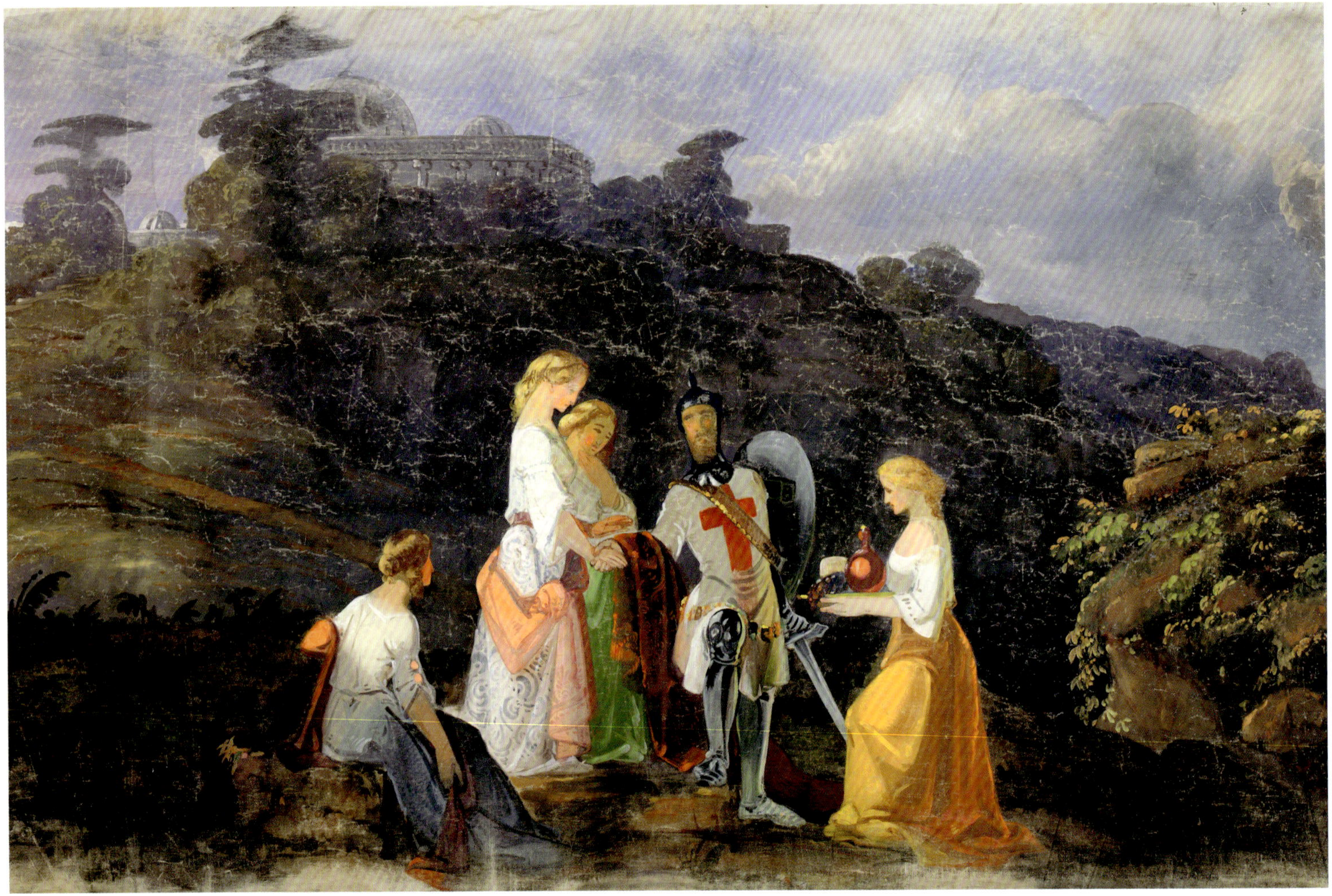

PLATE 16. *The Sisters Accompany Him to the Valley of Humiliation*, design attributed to Jacob Dallas and Joseph Kyle.

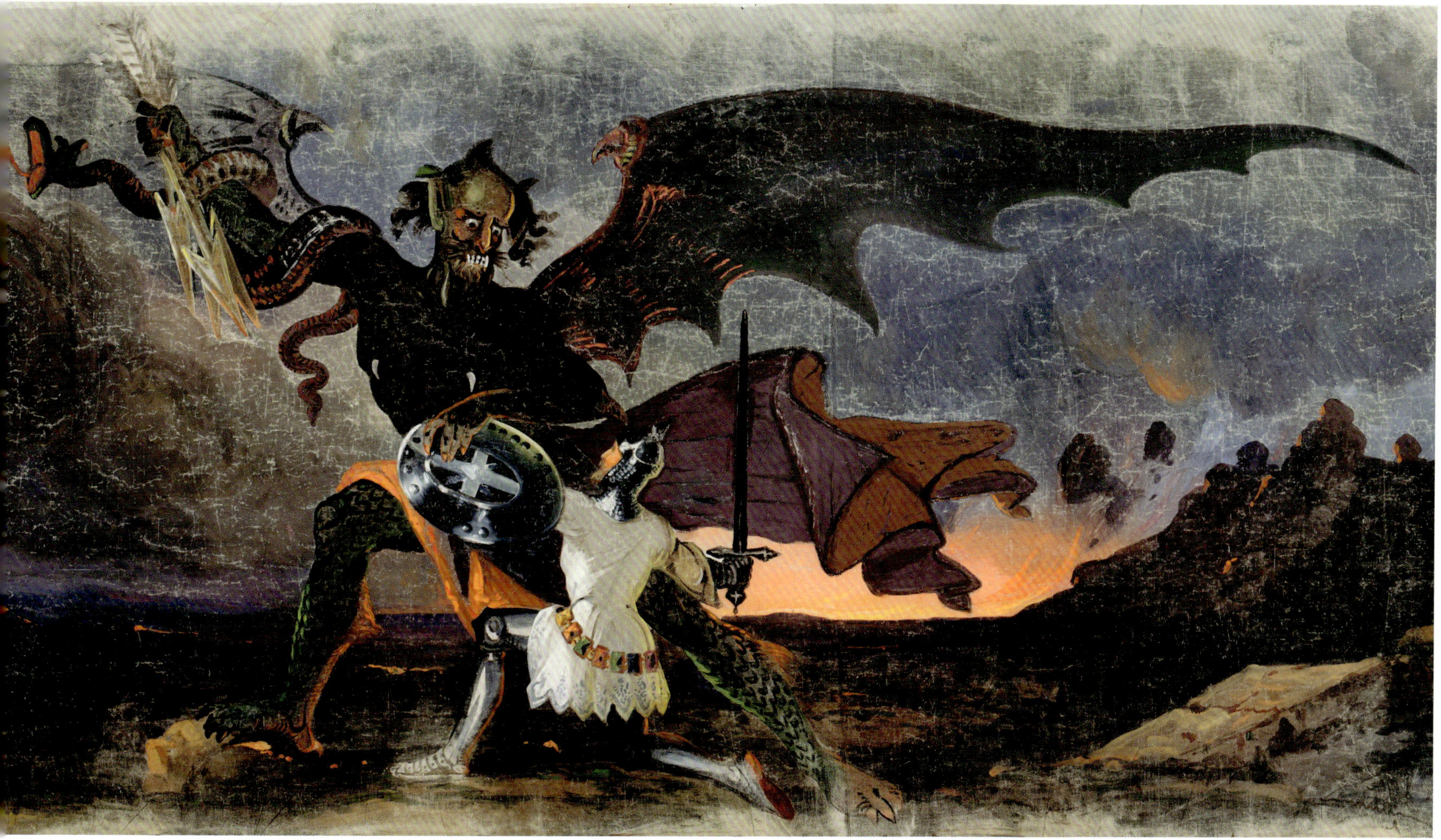

PLATE 17. *Fight with Apollyon*, design attributed to Edward Harrison May.

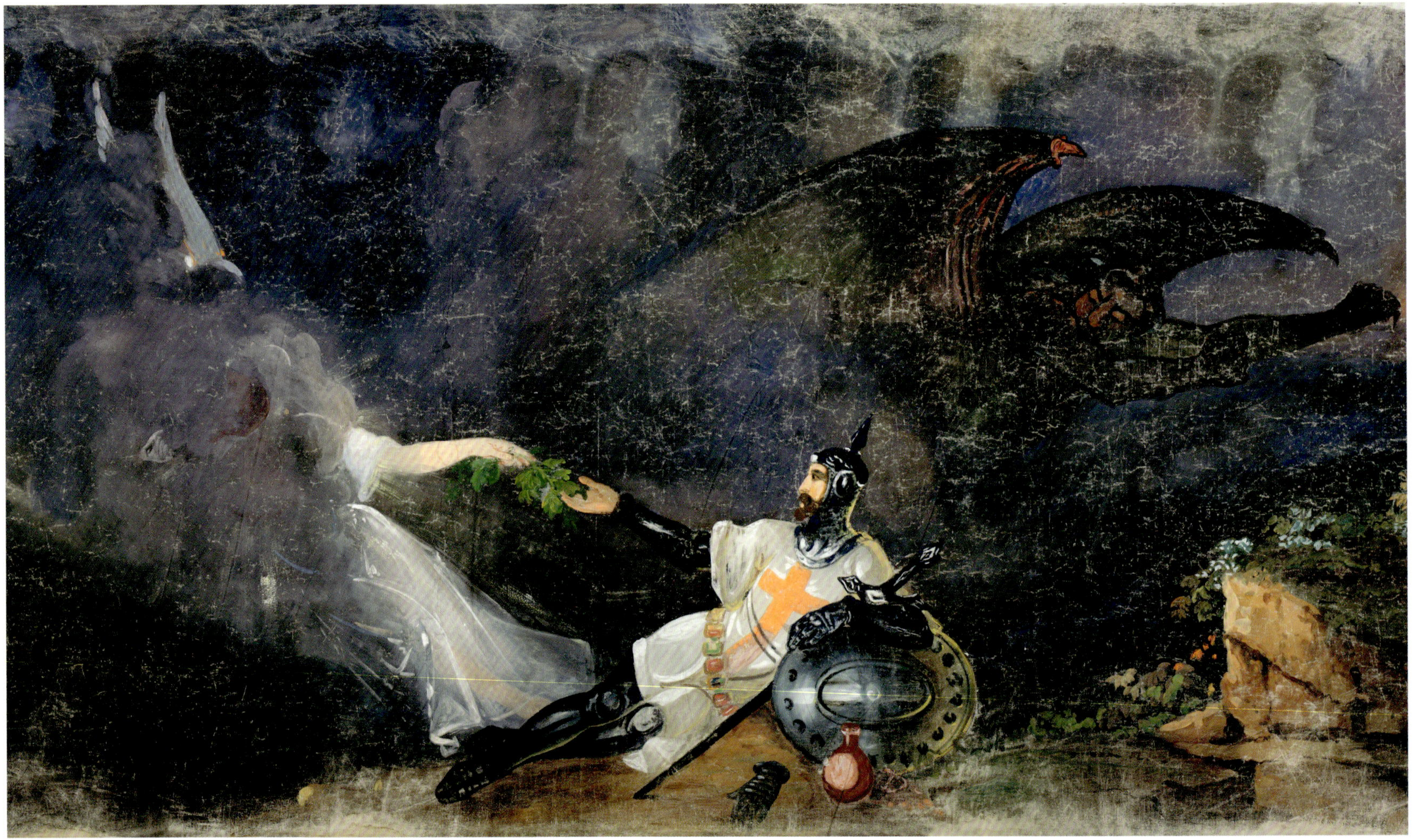

PLATE 18. *Christian Reposing after the Combat*, design attributed to Joseph Kyle.

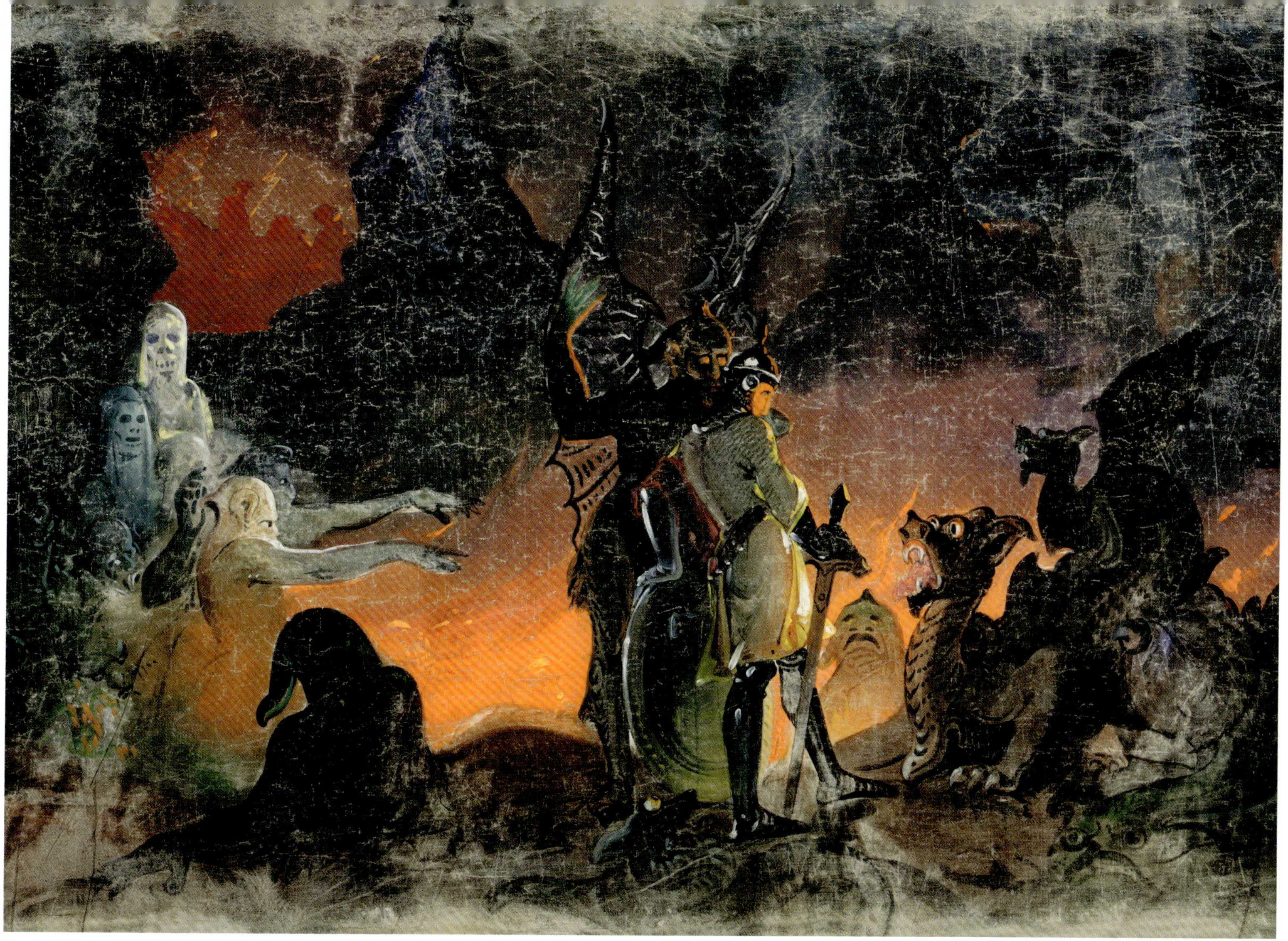

PLATE 19. *Christian Passing through the Valley of the Shadow of Death*, design attributed to Joseph Kyle and Henry Courtney Selous.

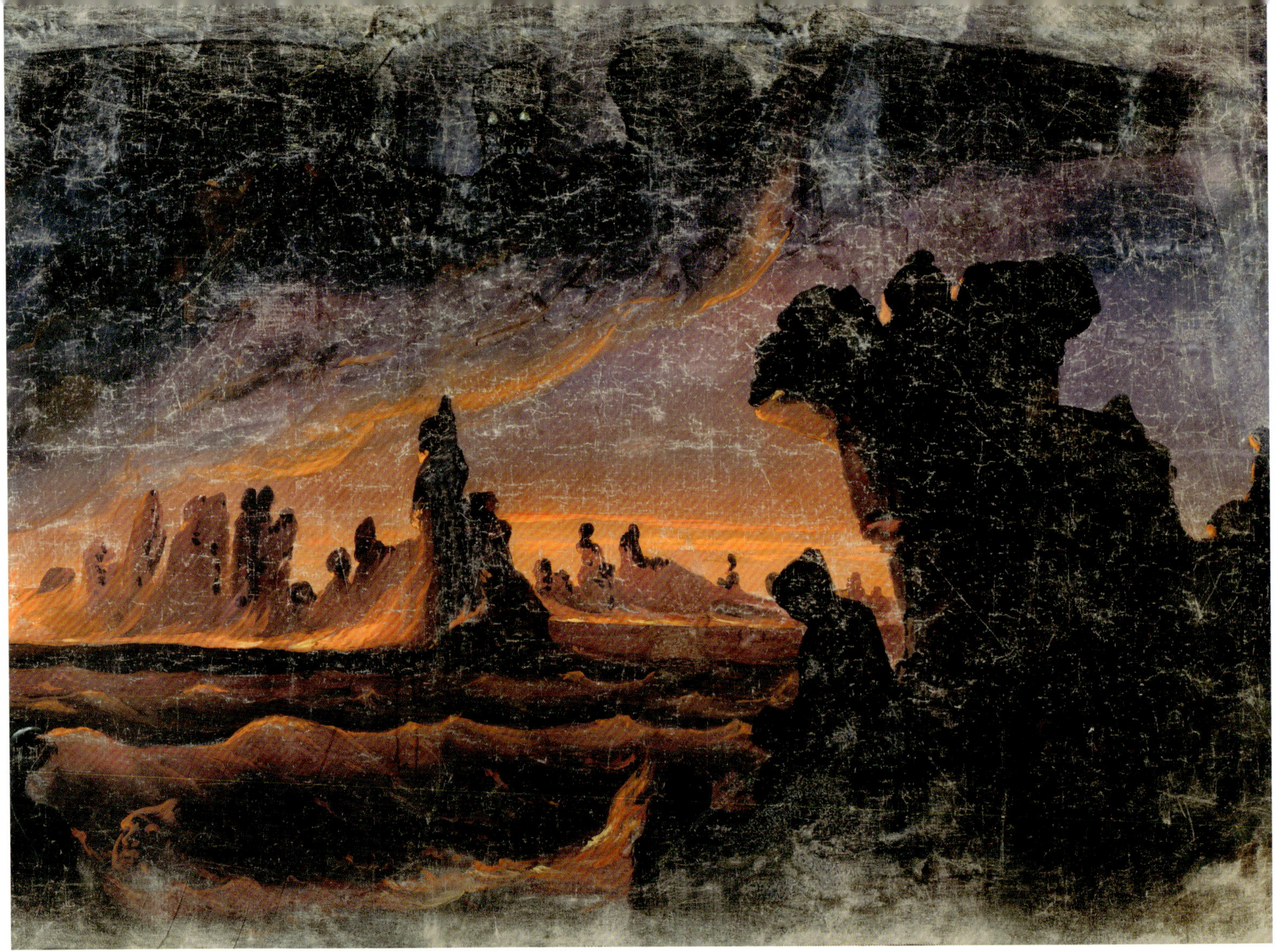

PLATE 20. *Dawn of Day over the Valley of the Shadow of Death*, design attributed to Frederic Edwin Church.

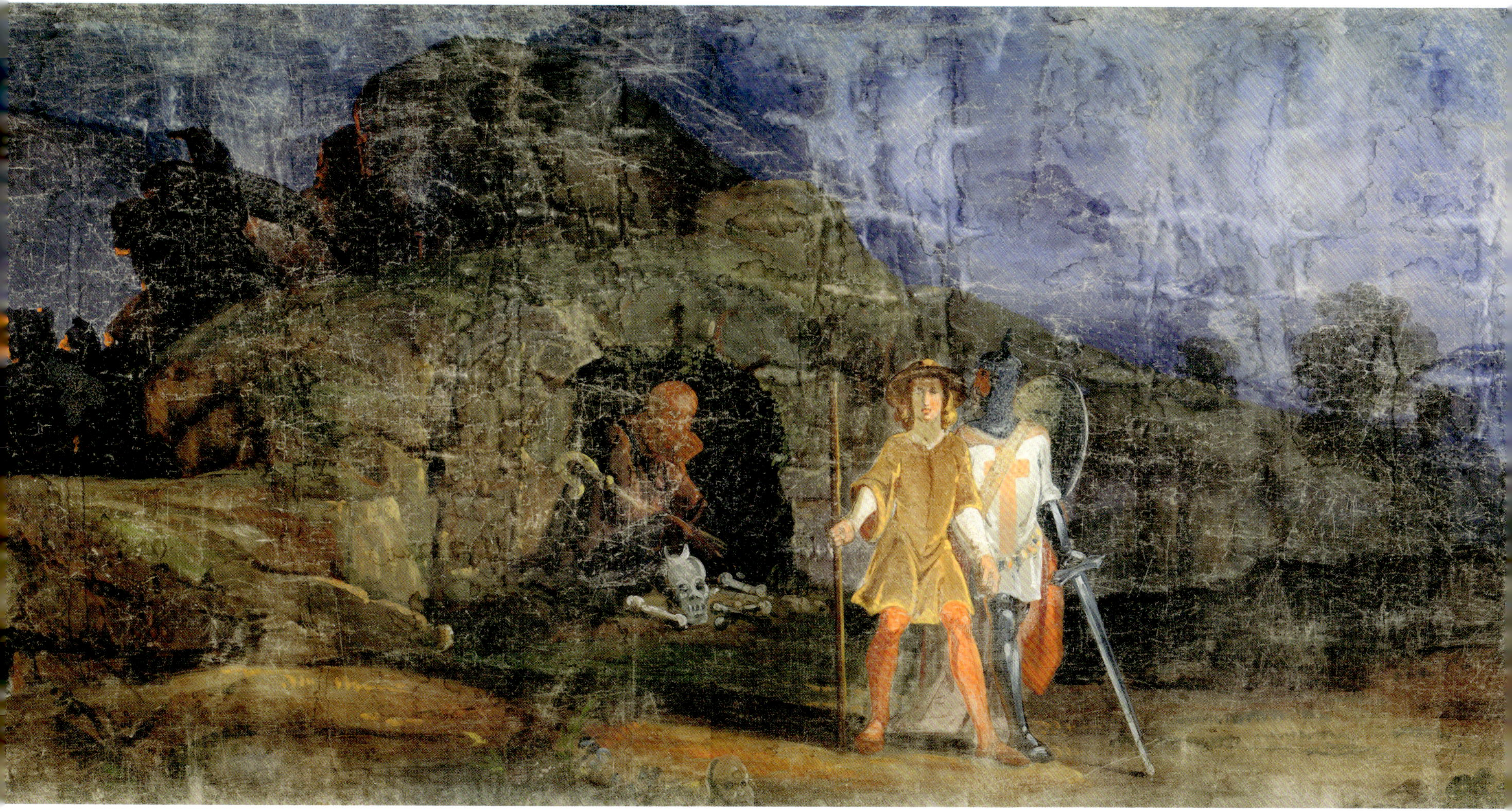

PLATE 21. *Giants Pope and Pagan*, design attributed to Joseph Kyle and Edward Harrison May.

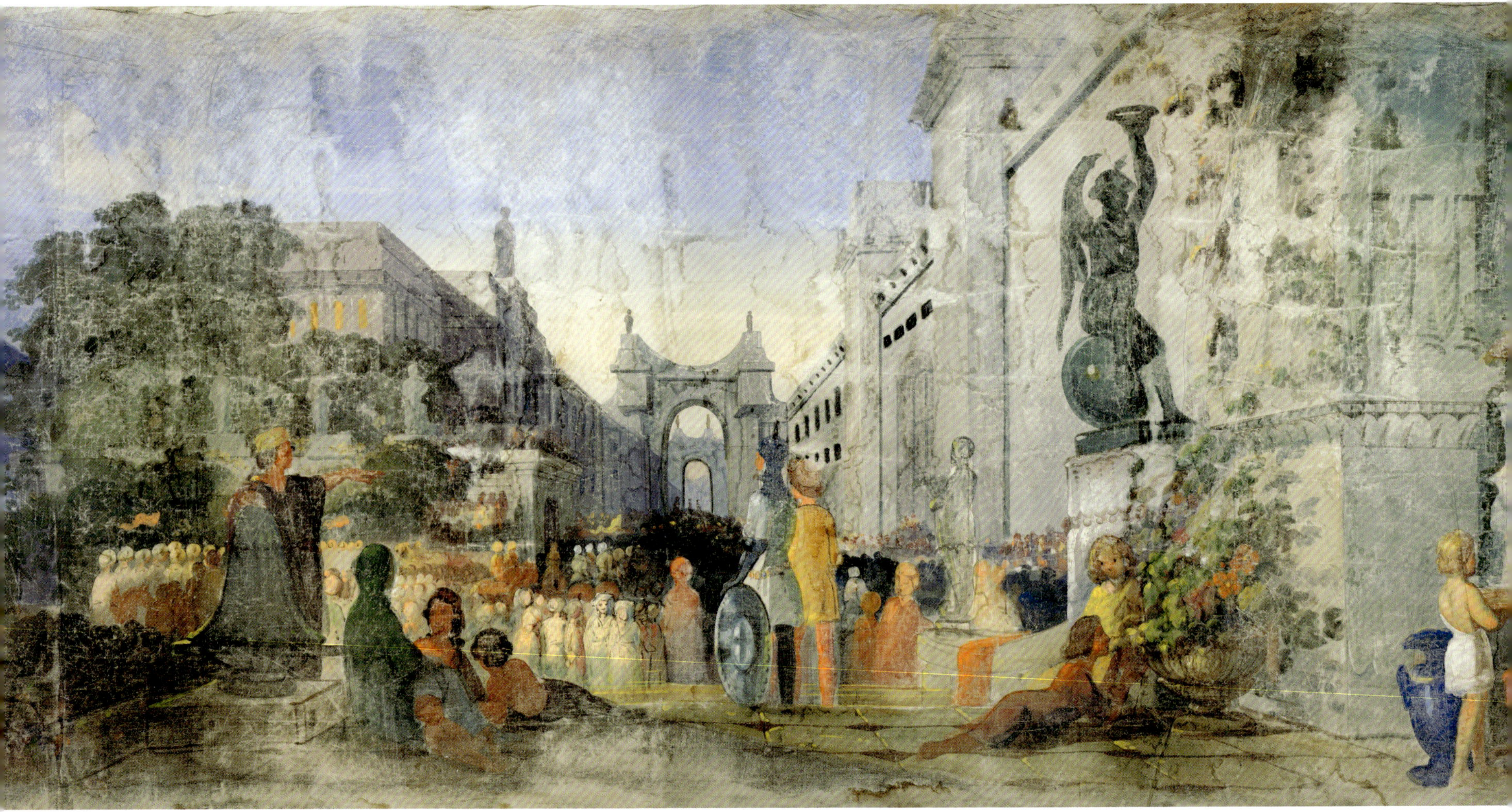

PLATE 22. *Evangelist Pointing Out Vanity Fair*, design attributed to Joseph Kyle.

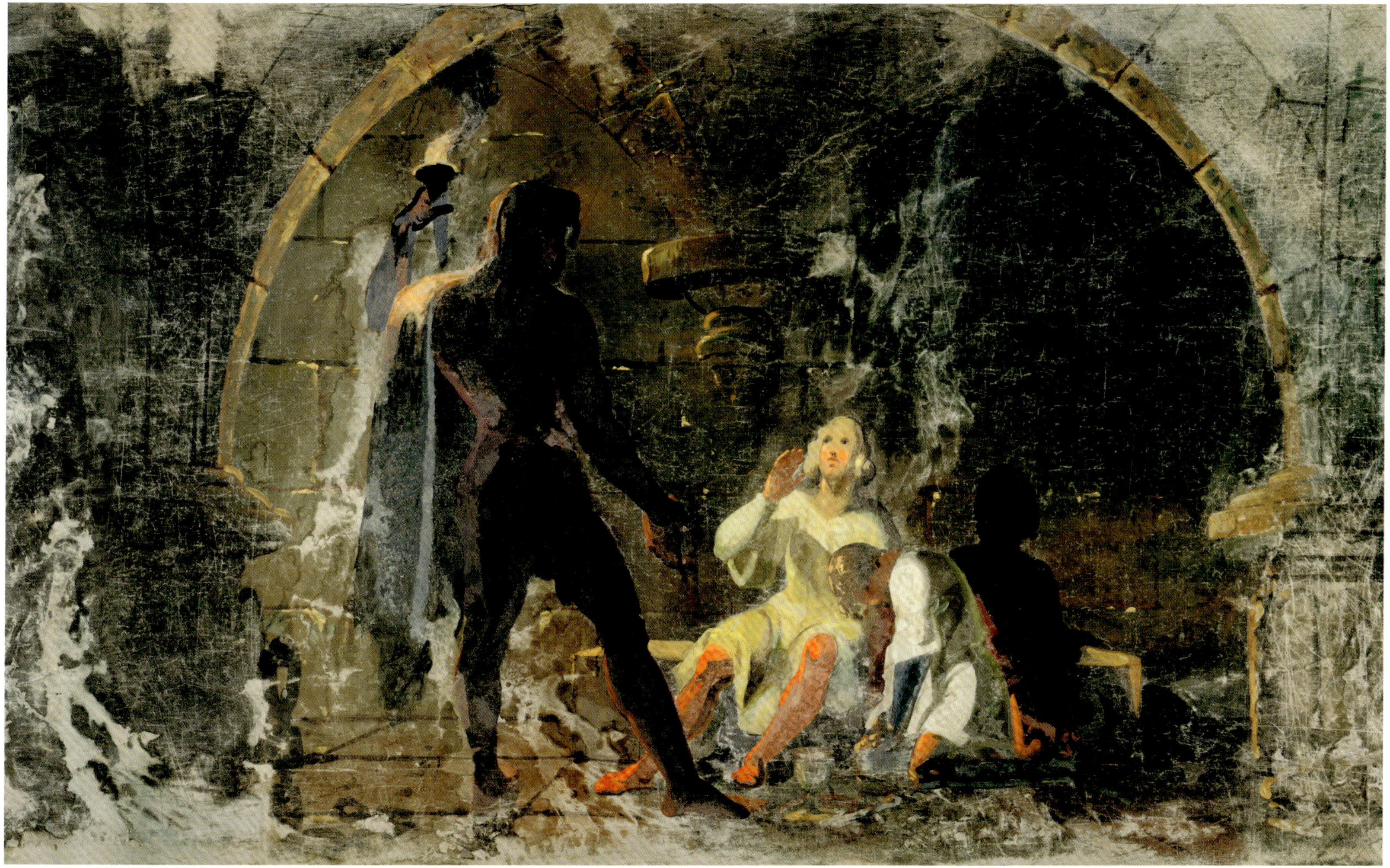

PLATE 23. *Giant Despair Visits the Pilgrims in Their Dungeon, and Advises Them to Commit Suicide*, design attributed to Edward Harrison May.

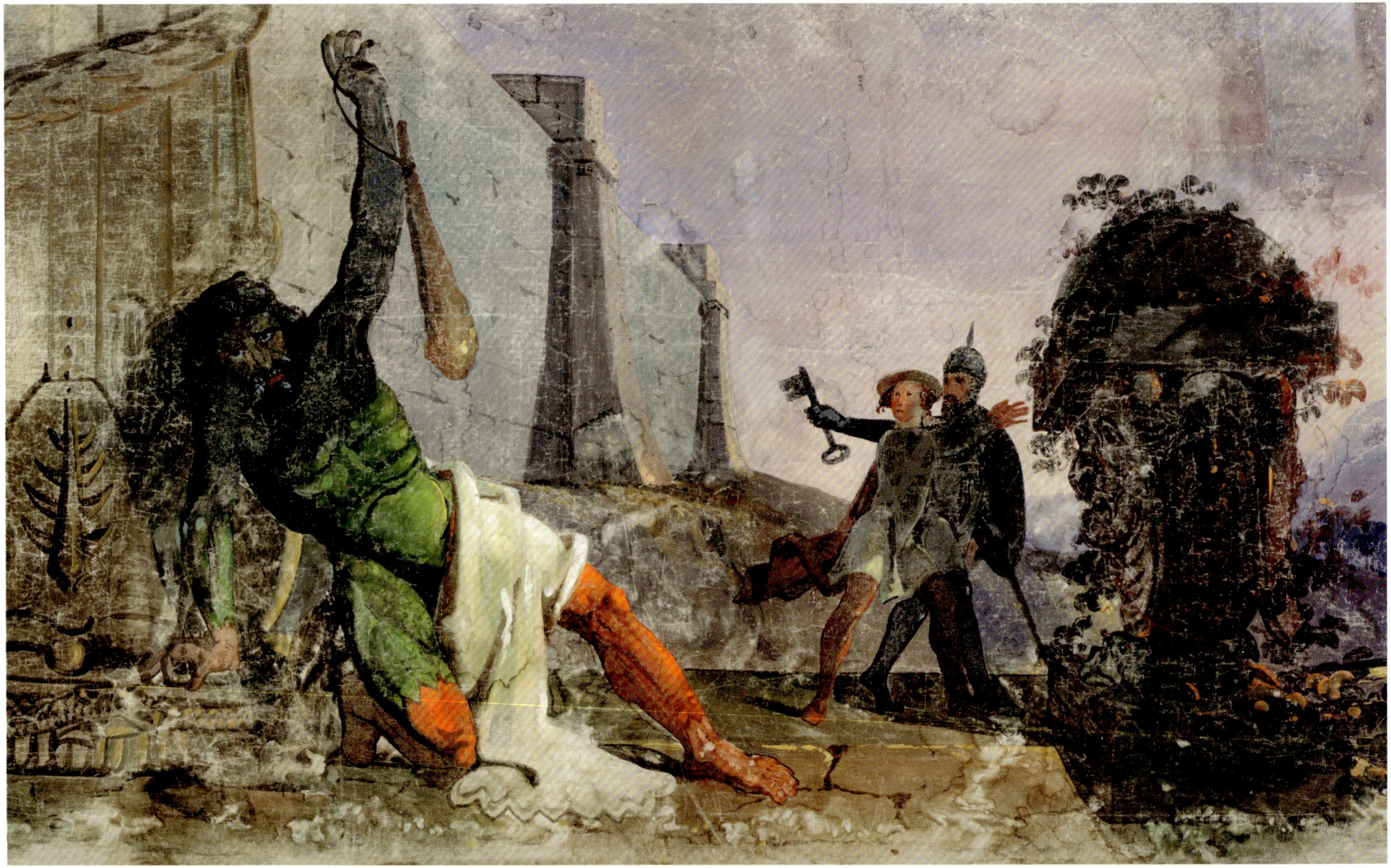

PLATE 24. *The Pilgrims' Escape*, design attributed to Paul Duggan.

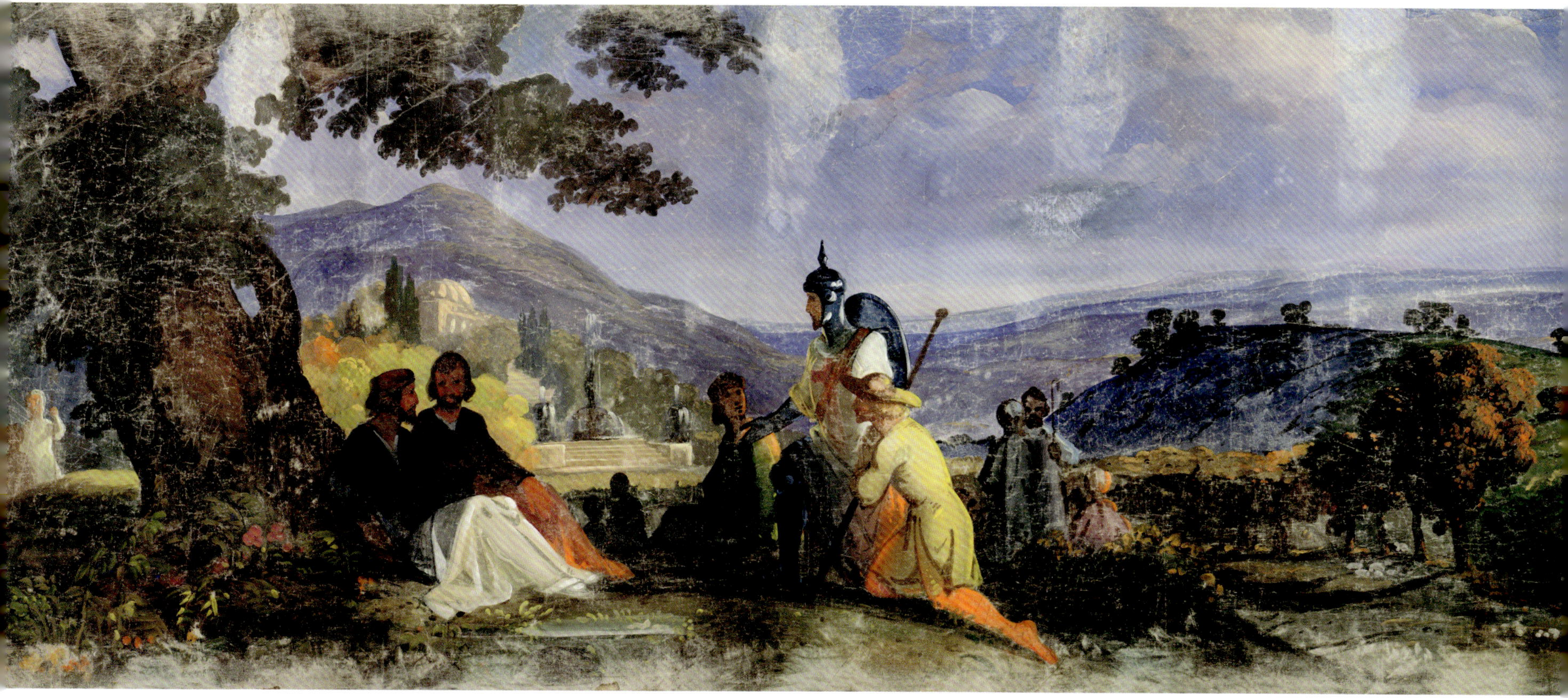

PLATE 25. *They Arrive at the Delectable Mountains*, design attributed to Joseph Kyle and Edward Harrison May.

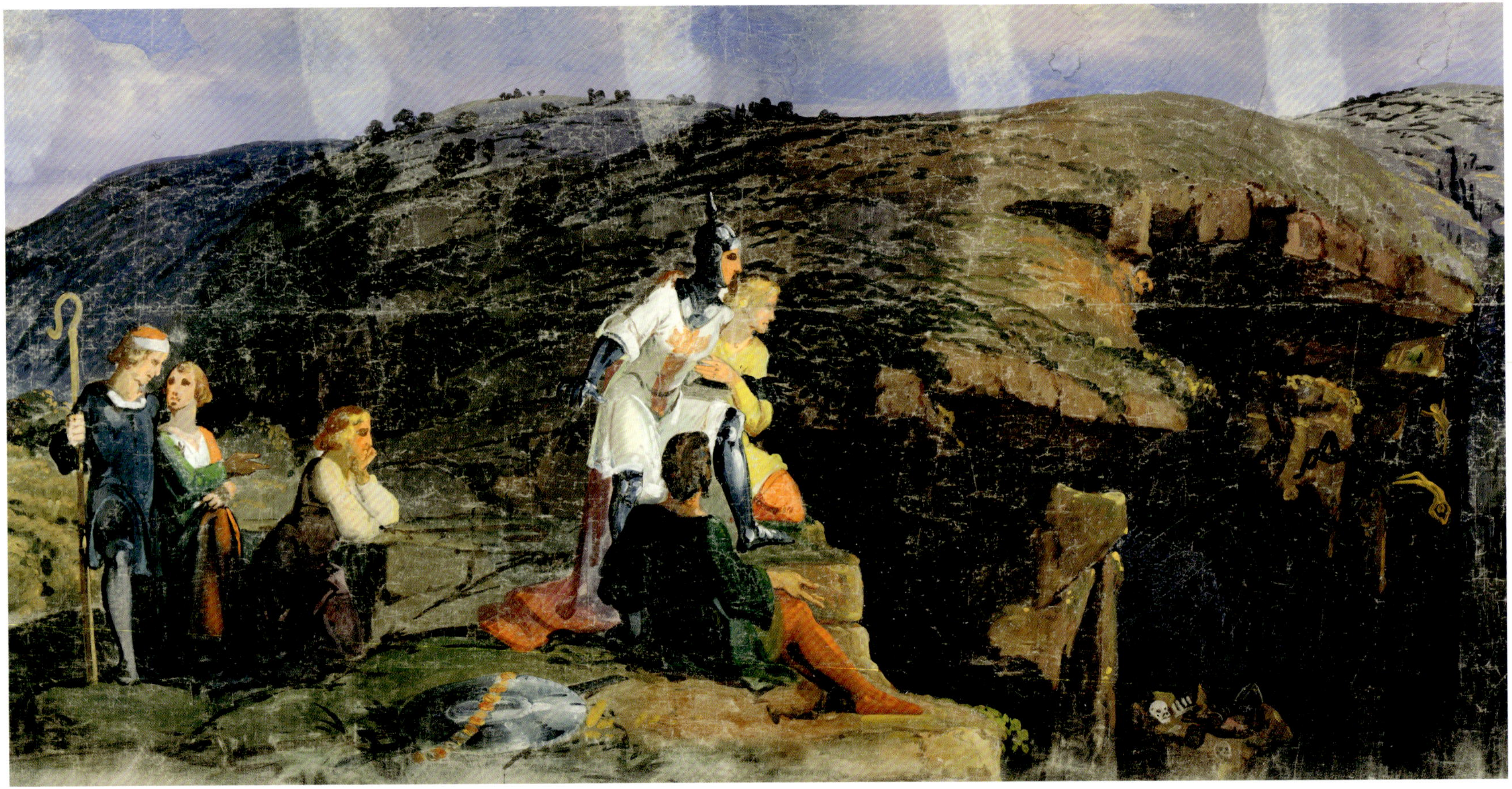

PLATE 26. *They Behold the Fate of Those Who Have Fallen from the Hill of Error*, design attributed to Joseph Kyle and Henry Courtney Selous.

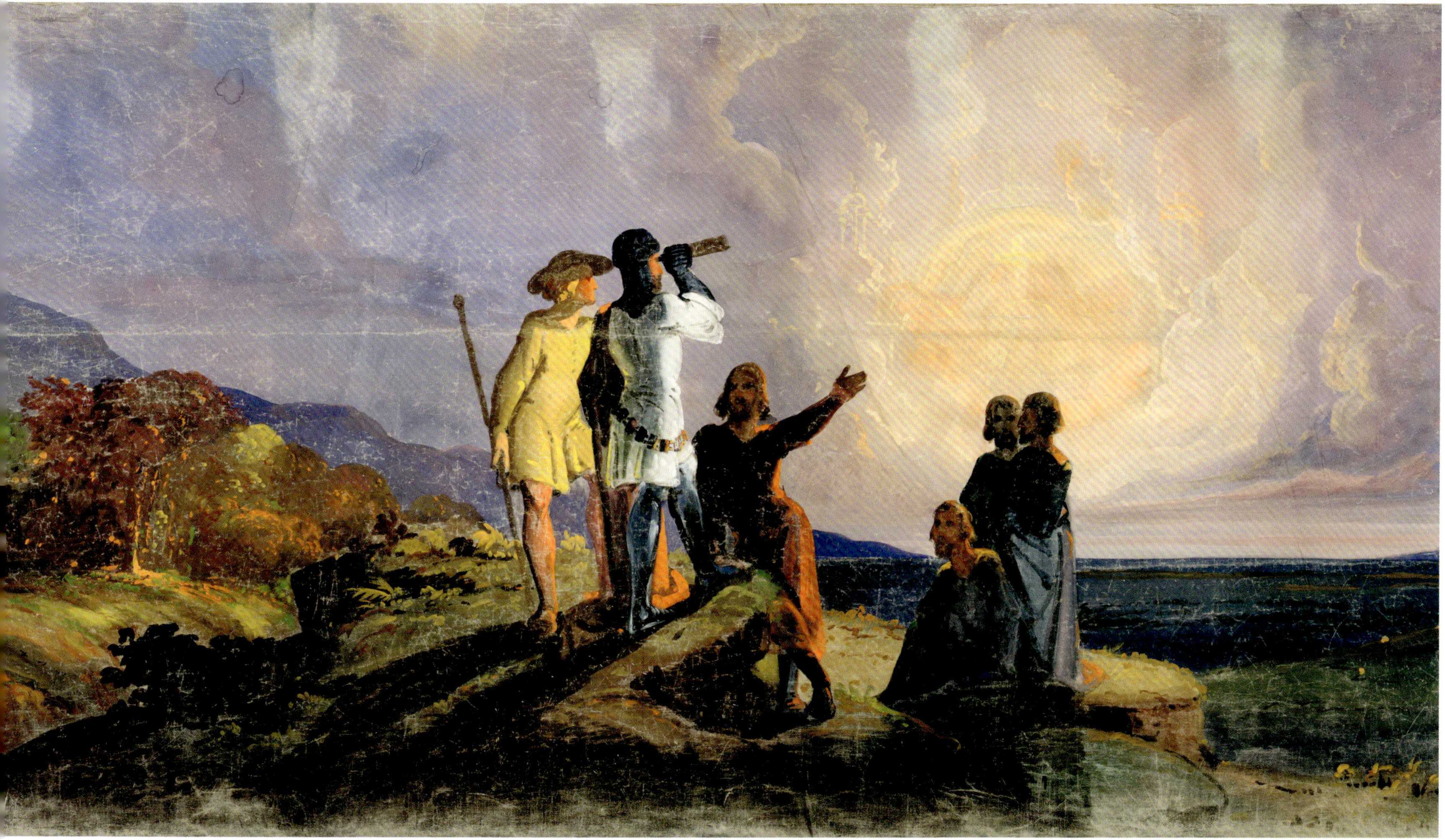

PLATE 27. *The Shepherds Point Out the Gates of the Celestial City from Hill Clear*, design attributed to Joseph Kyle and Edward Harrison May.

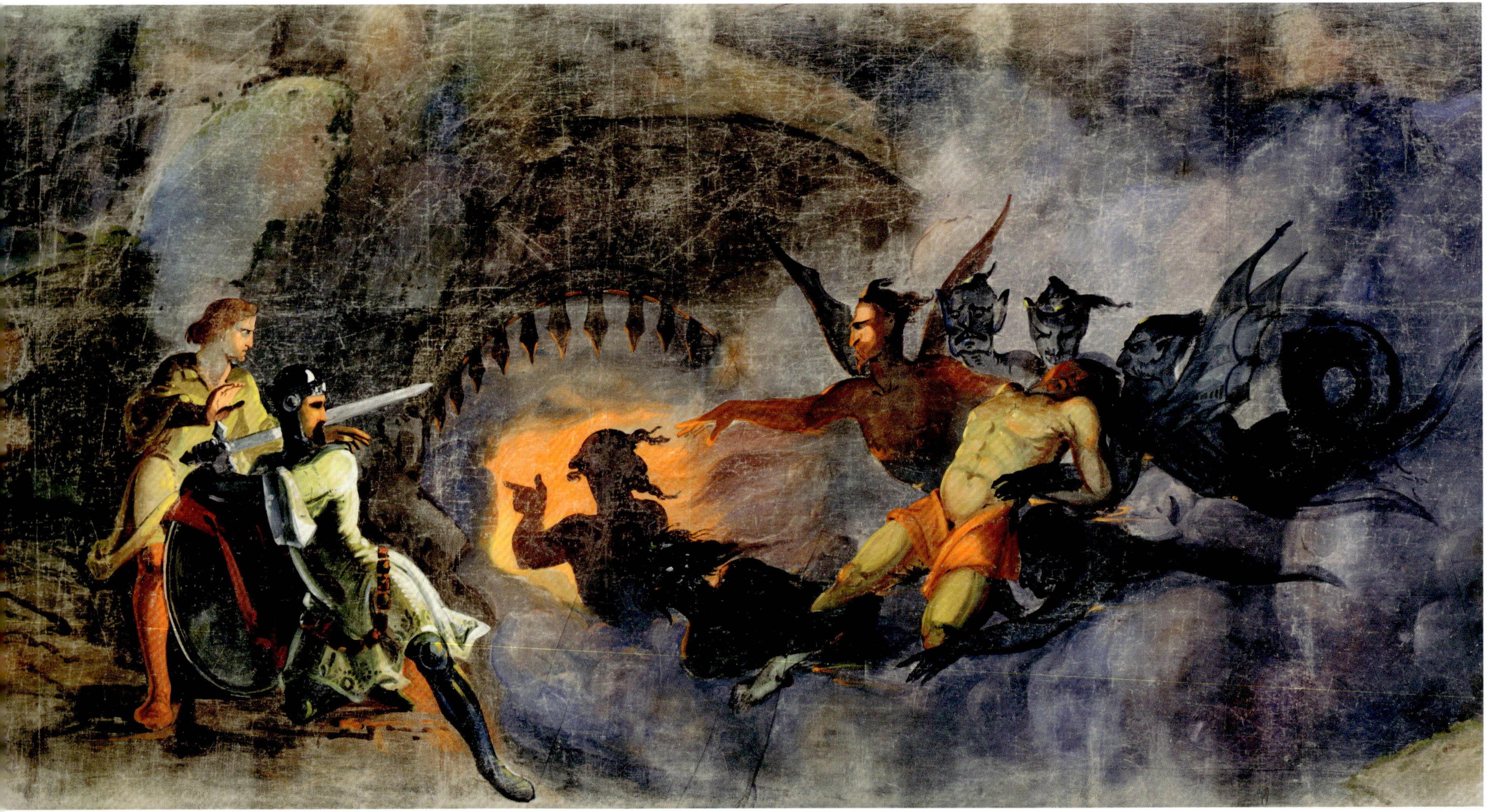

PLATE 28. *They Behold the Fate of the Apostate*, design attributed to Joseph Kyle and Henry Courtney Selous.

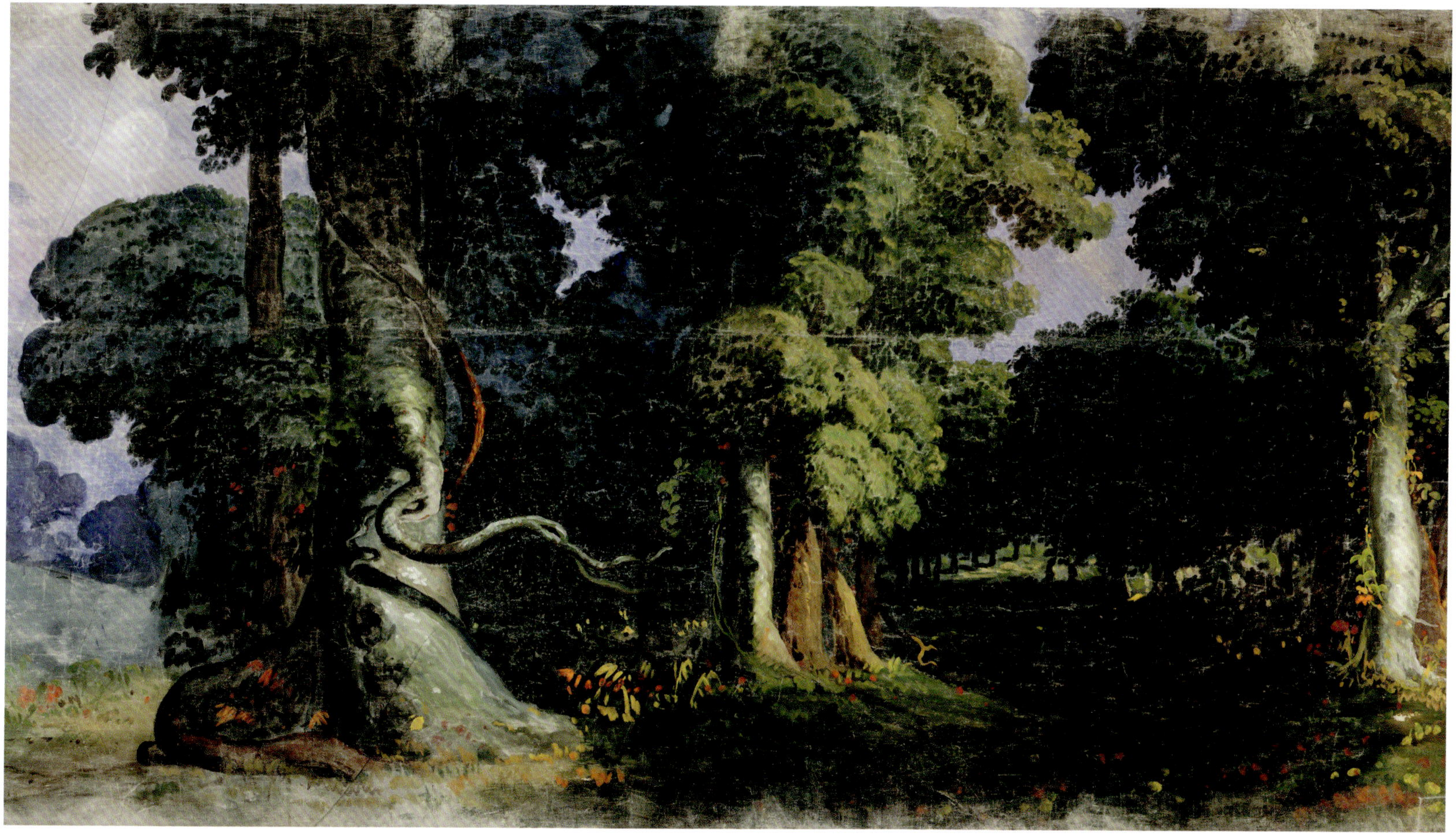

PLATE 29. *Enchanted Ground*, design attributed to Joseph Kyle.

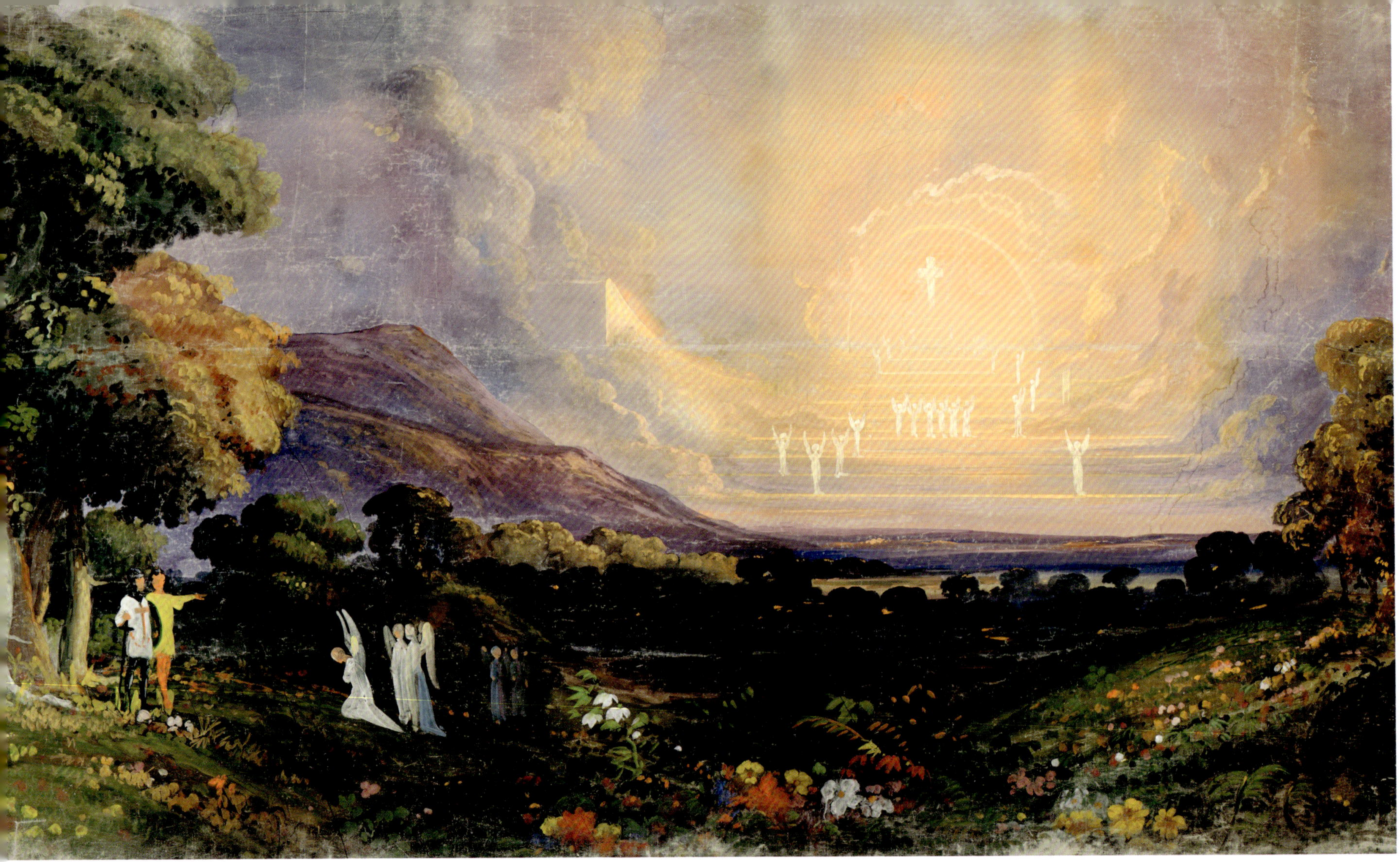

PLATE 30. *Land of Beulah*, design attributed to Jasper Cropsey.

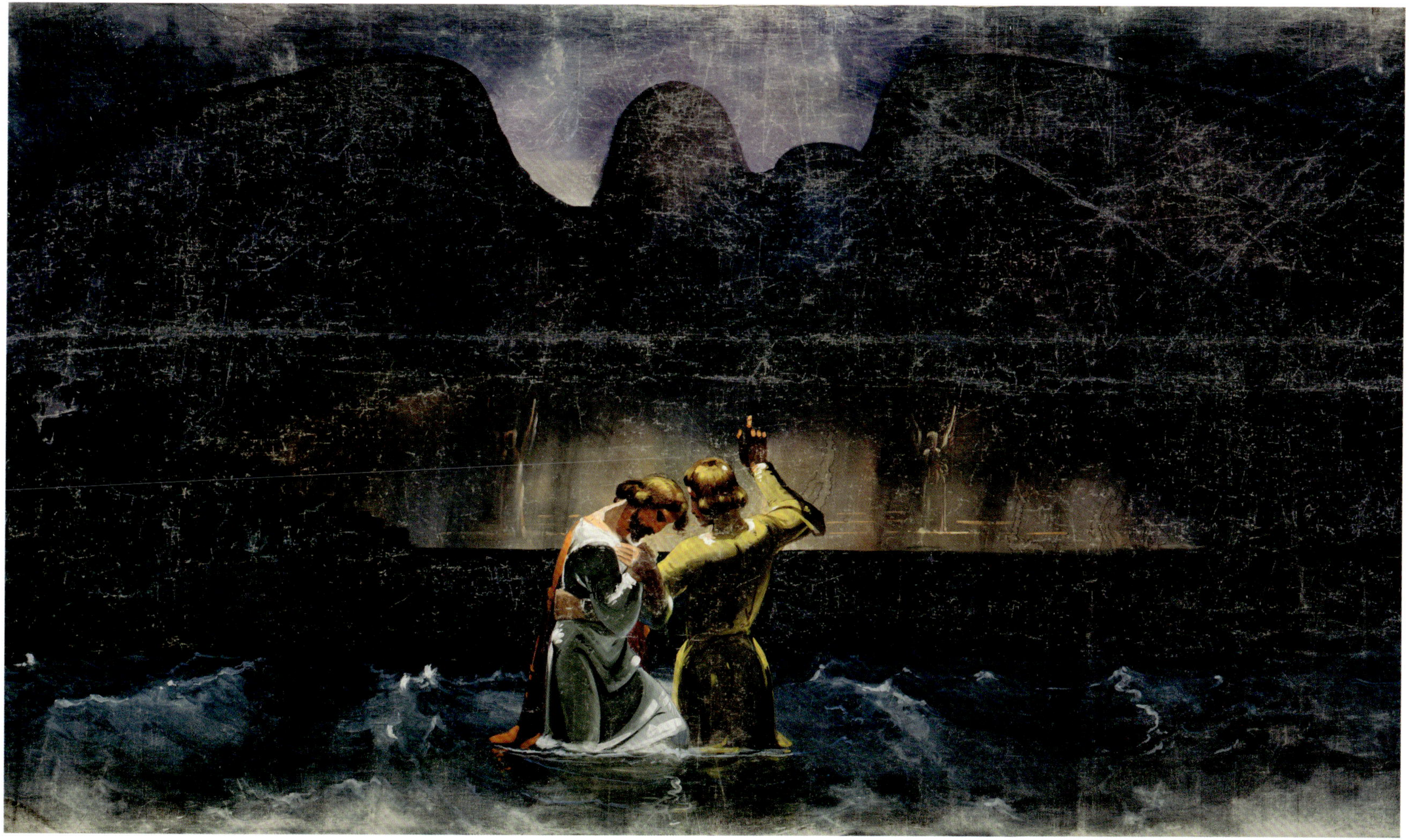

PLATE 31. *Christian and Hopeful Enter the River of Death*, design attributed to Edward Harrison May.

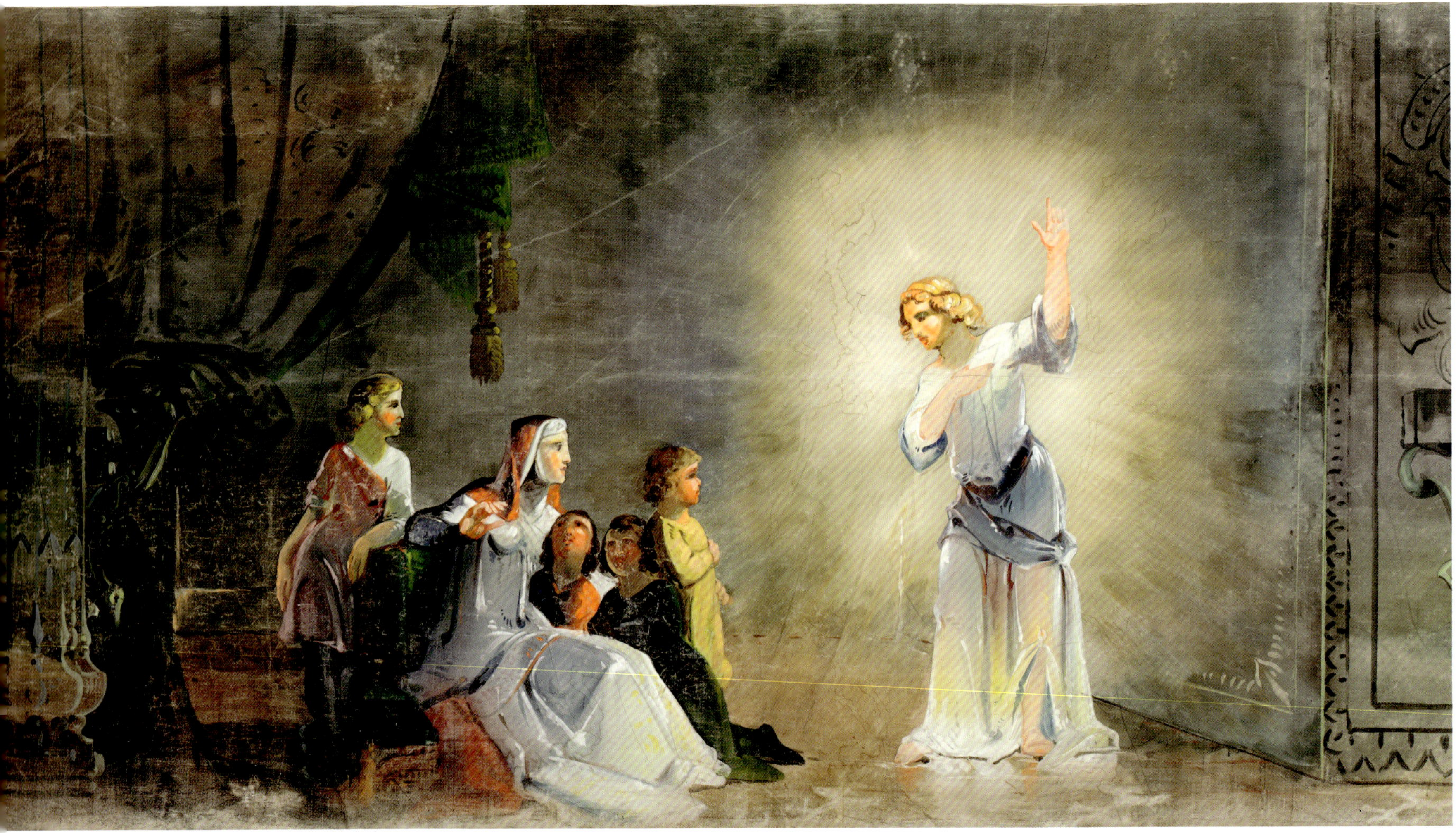

PLATE 32. *Christiana, Her Children, and Secret*, designer unknown.

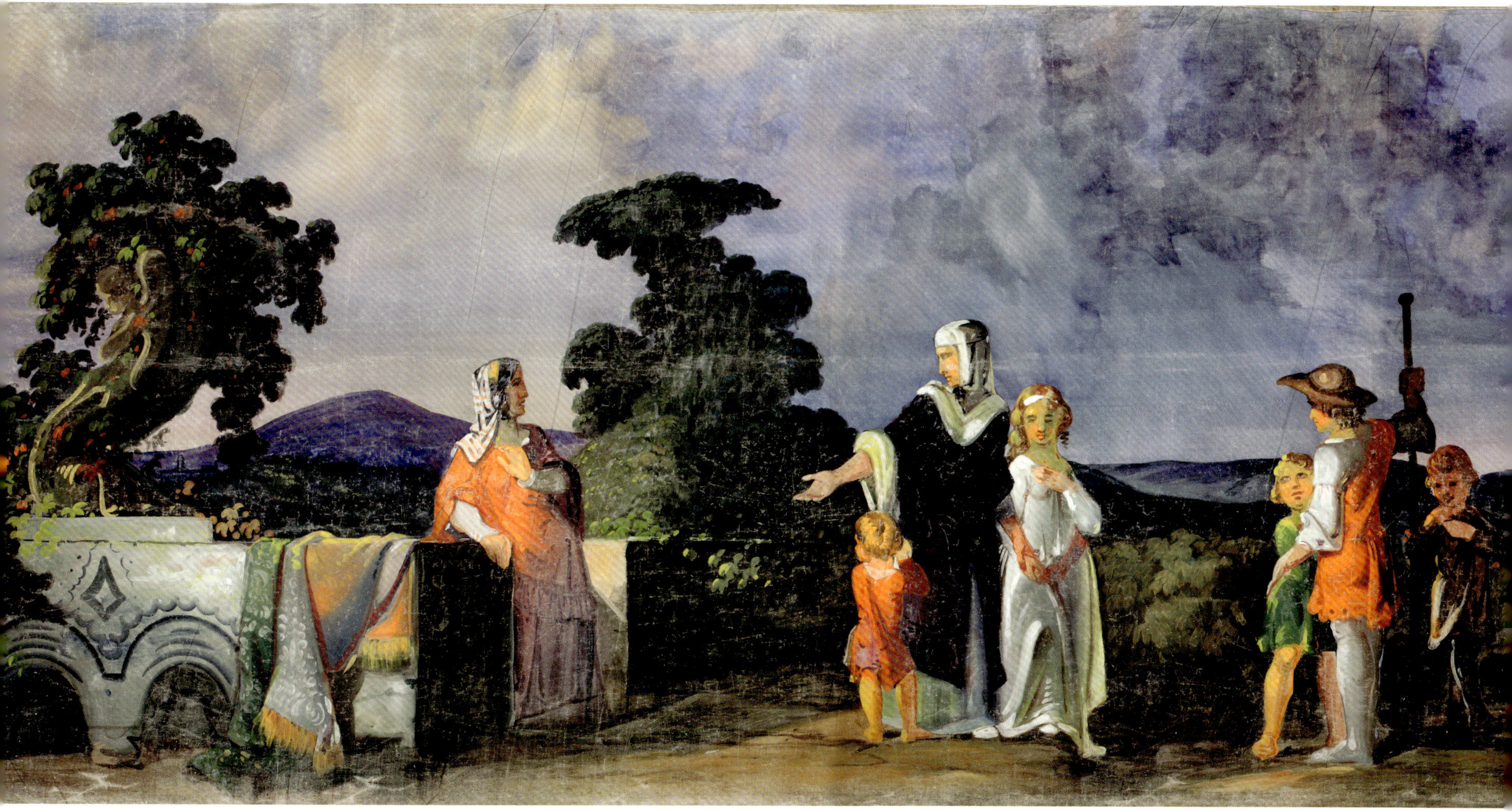

PLATE 33. *Christiana and Her Family Leave the City of Destruction*, designer unknown.

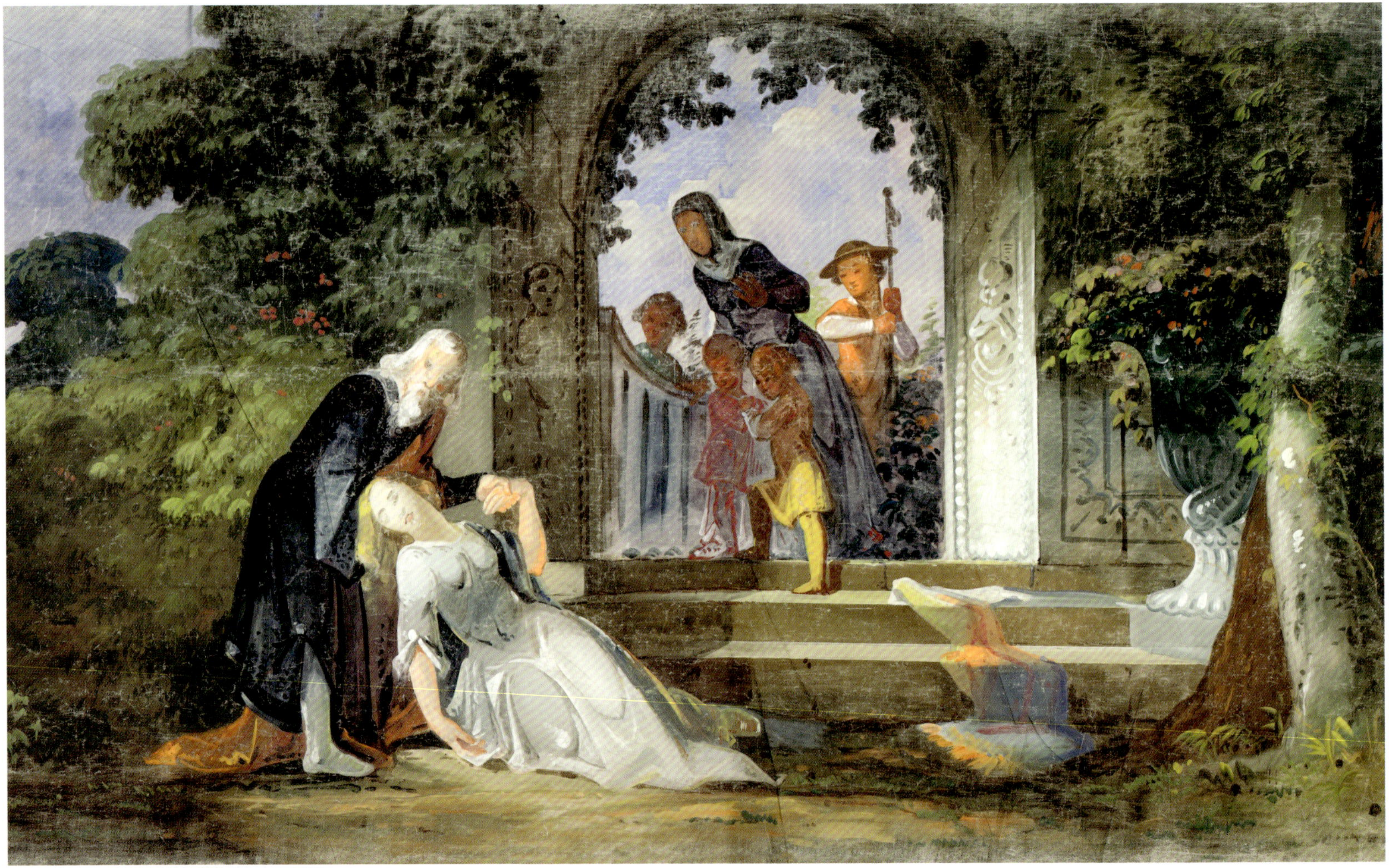

PLATE 34. *Mercy Faints at the Wicket Gate*, design attributed to Edward Harrison May.

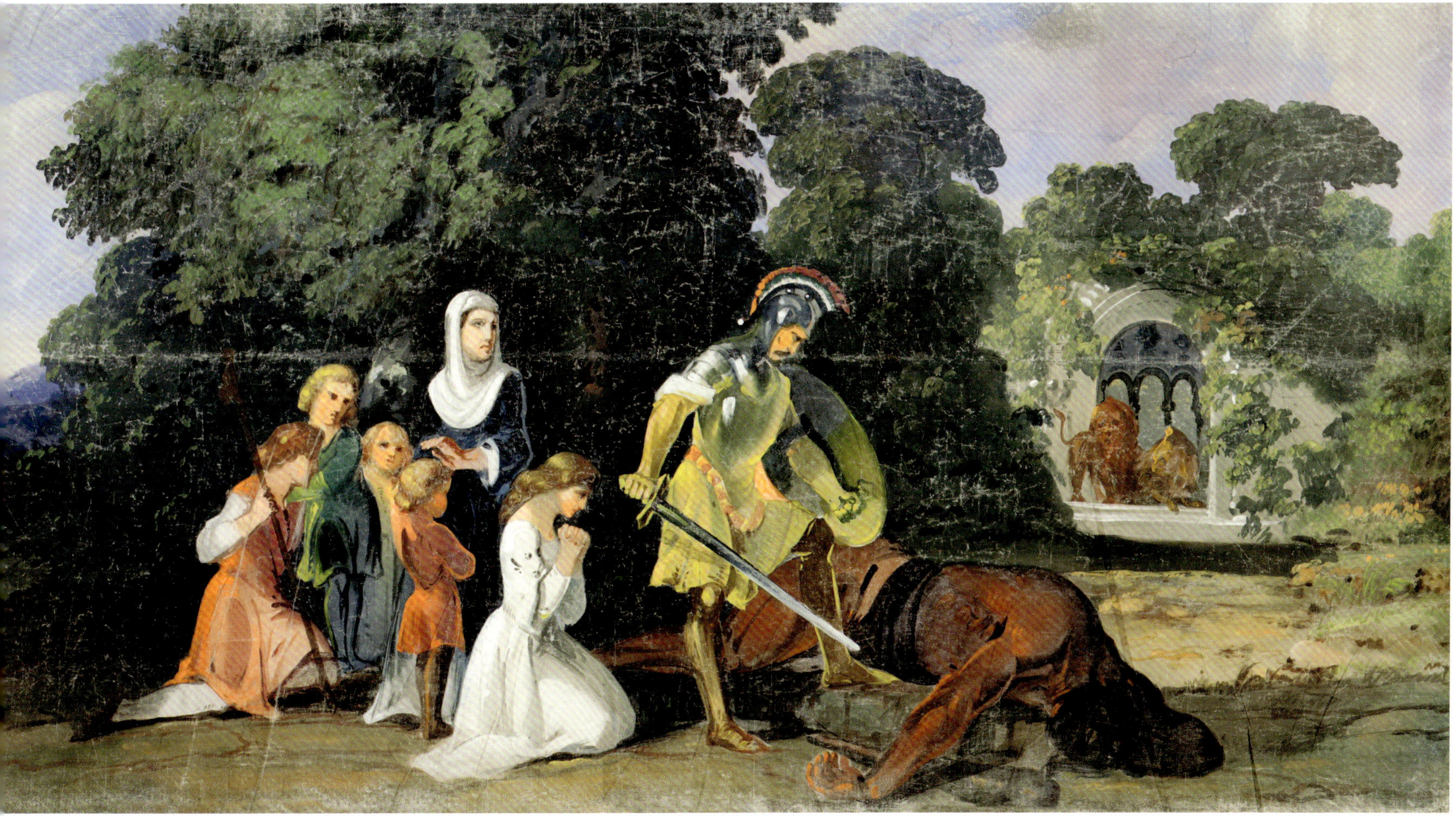

PLATE 35. *Entrance to Temple Beautiful, and Death of Giant Grim*, design attributed to Felix Octavius Carr Darley and Edward Harrison May.

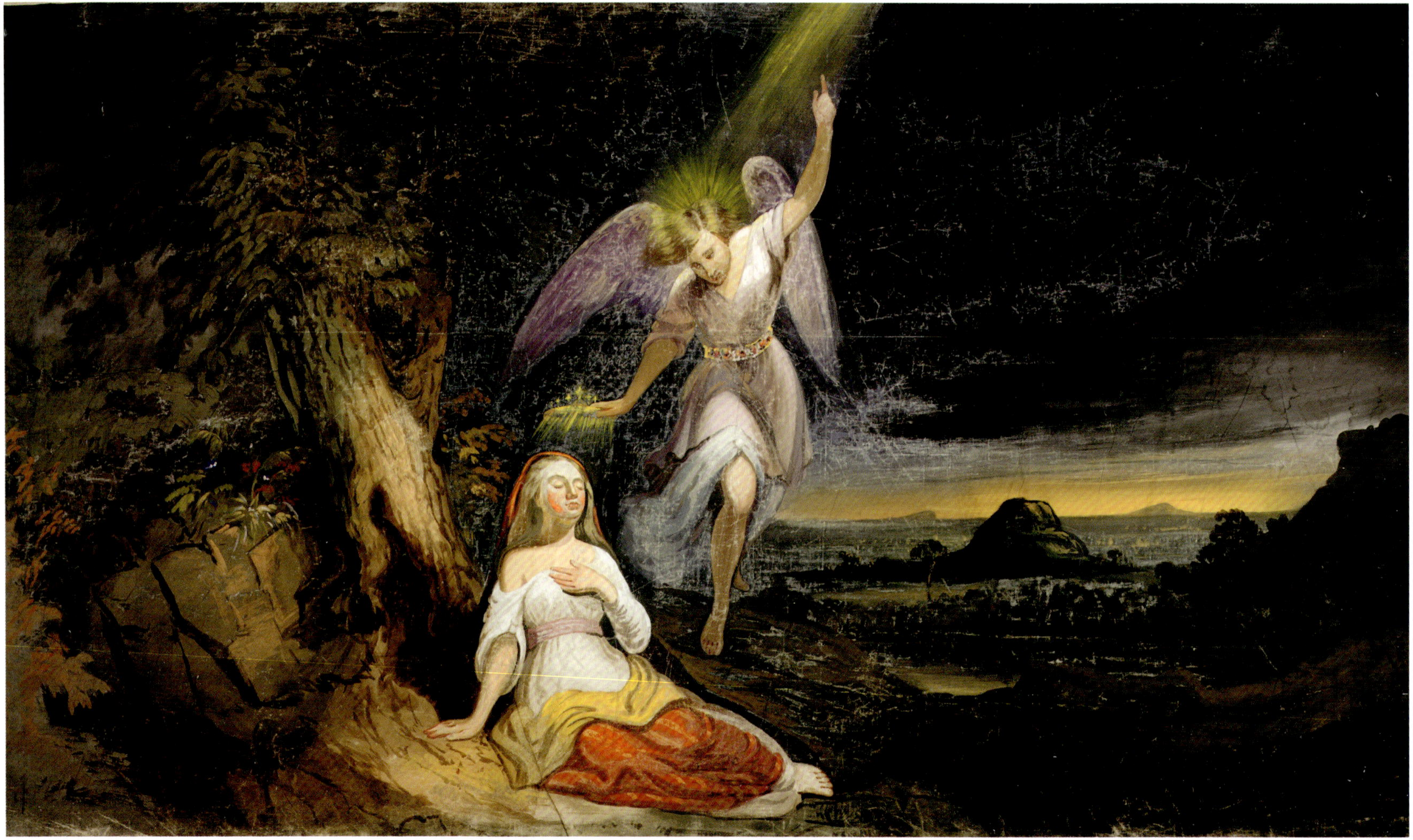

PLATE 36. *Mercy's Dream*, design attributed to Daniel Huntington.

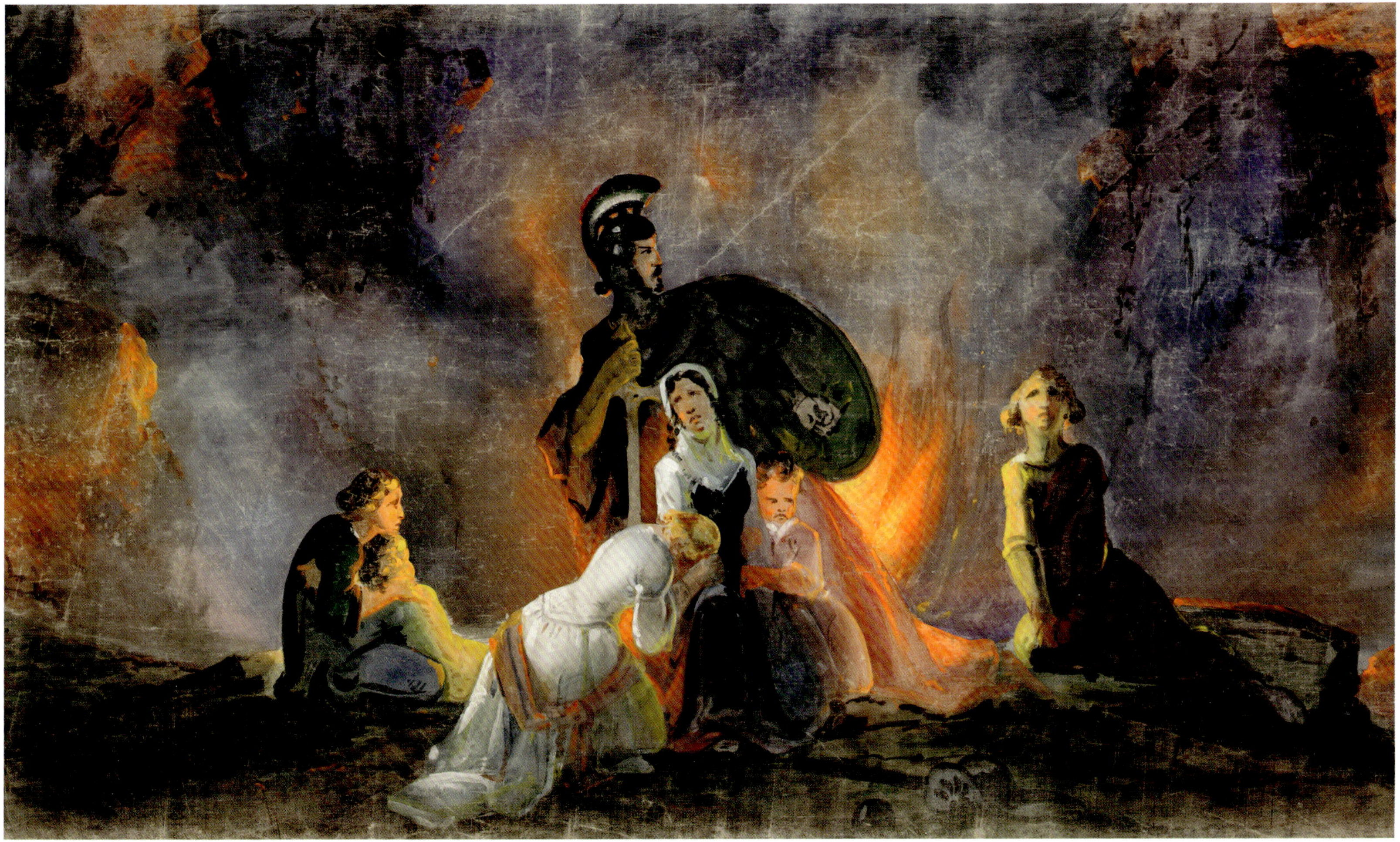

PLATE 37. *They Lost Their Way in the Valley of the Shadow of Death*, design attributed to Daniel Huntington and Joseph Kyle.

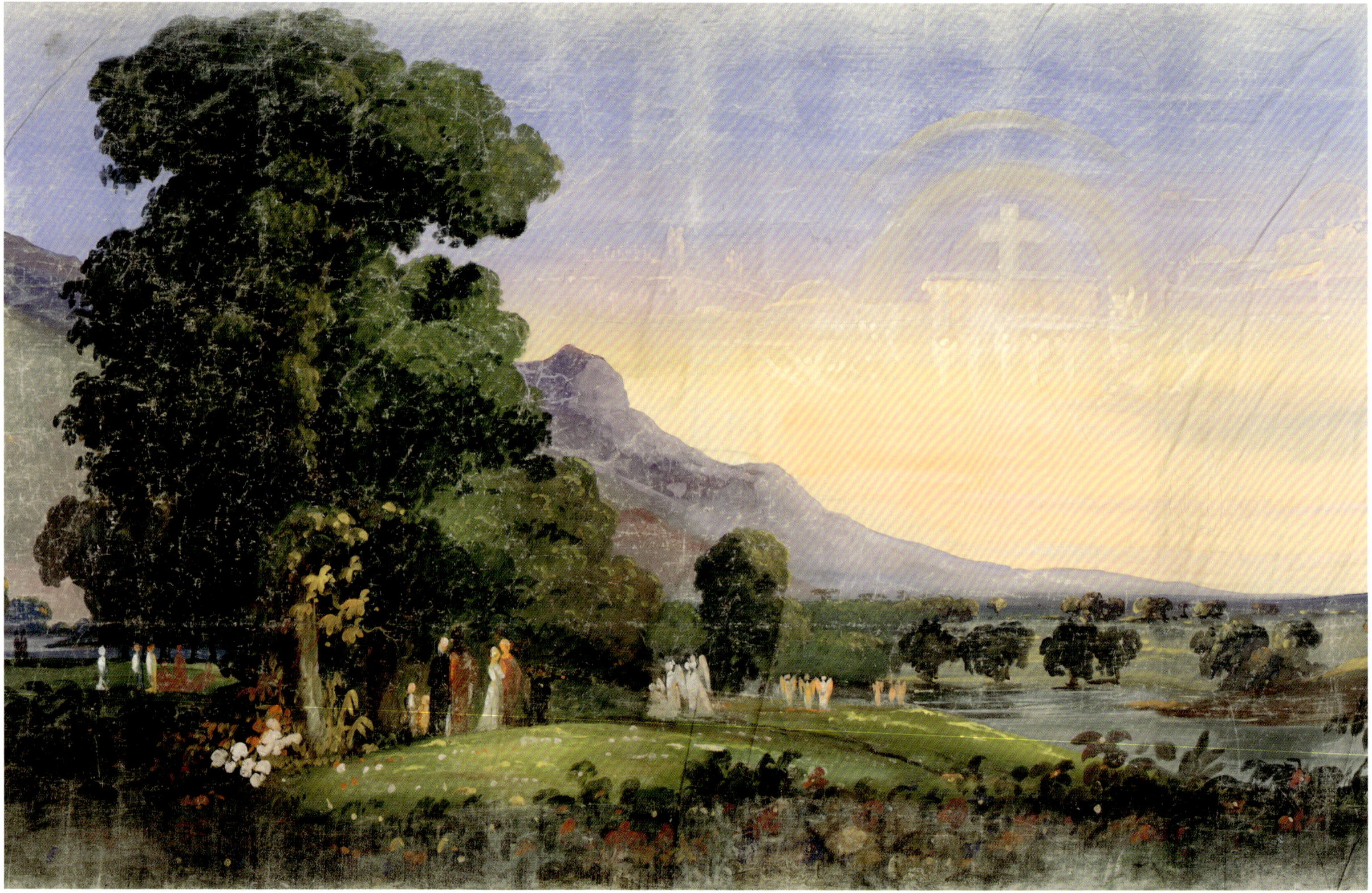

PLATE 38. *Land of Beulah*, design attributed to Joseph Kyle.

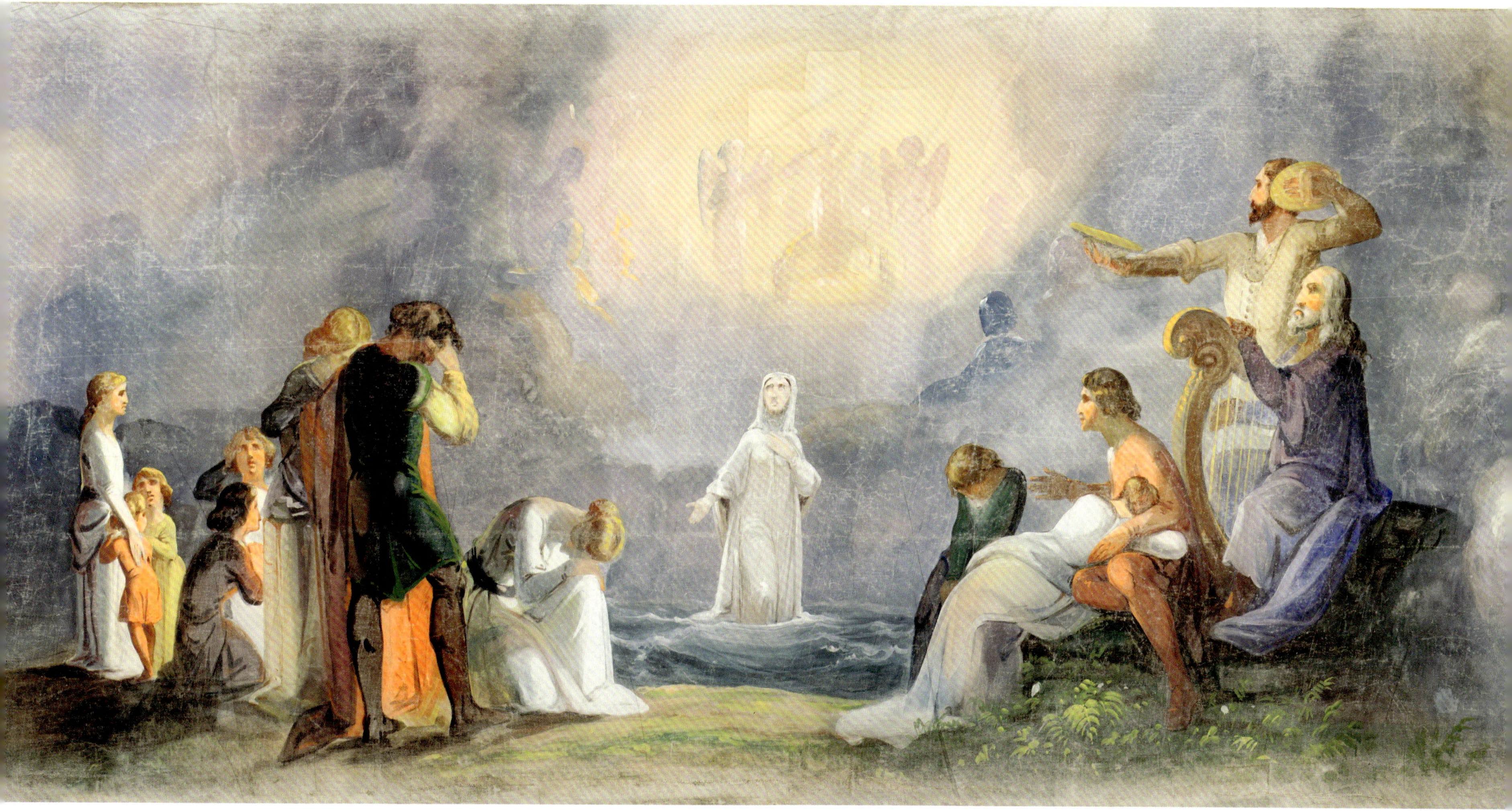

PLATE 39. *Christiana Parts with Her Children*, design attributed to Edward Harrison May.

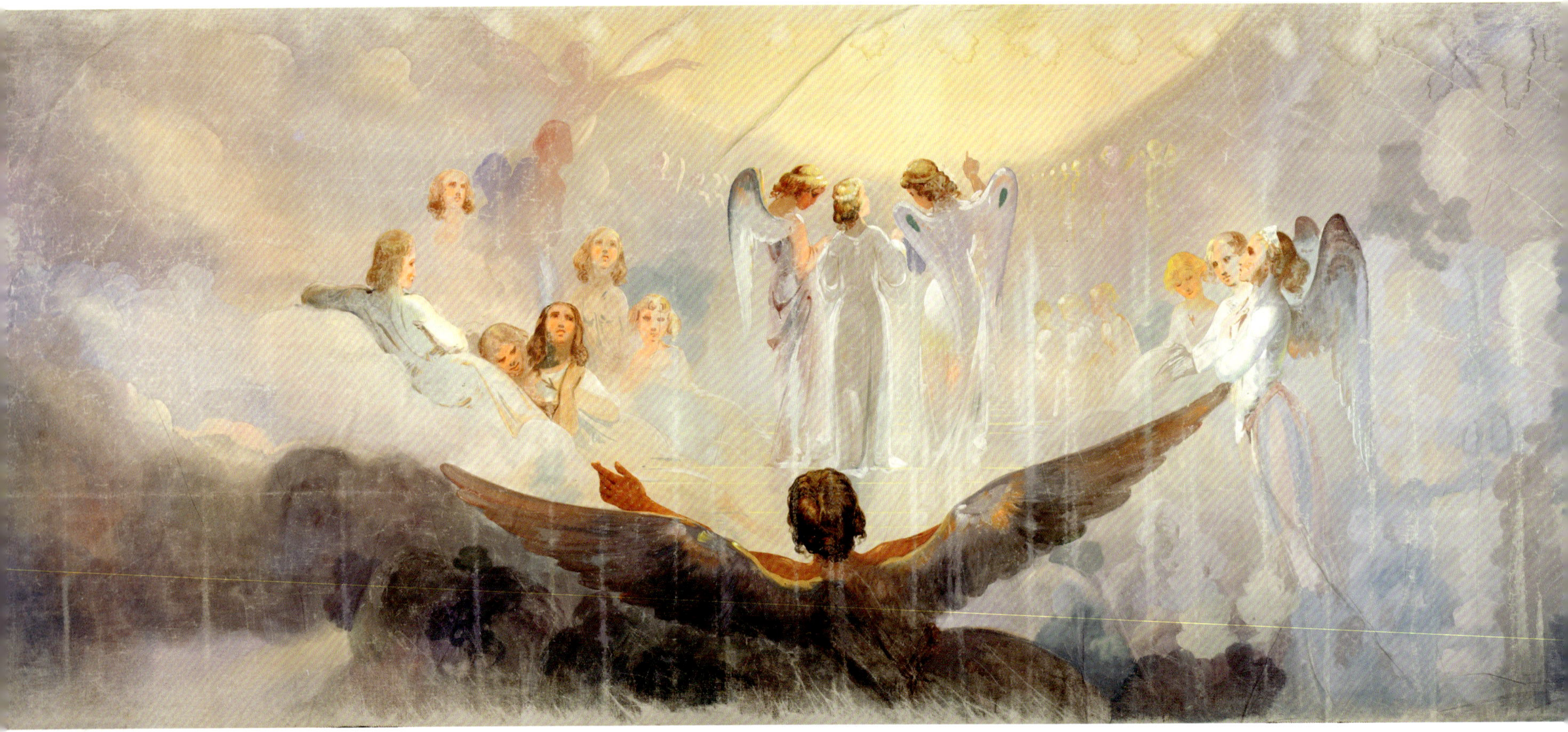

PLATE 40. *Arrival at the Entrance of the Celestial City*, design attributed to Jacob Dallas and Joseph Kyle.

THOMAS HARDIMAN JR.

THE PANORAMA'S PROGRESS

A History of Kyle and Dallas's *Moving Panorama of Pilgrim's Progress*

In October of 1896, the York Institute in Saco, Maine, received a donation of a most unusual painting, an enormous panorama illustrating John Bunyan's allegorical narrative *The Pilgrim's Progress*. As outlined in the preceding essays by Jessica Skwire Routhier and Kevin J. Avery, the painting is the second version of an original conceived in 1848, and it was created by Joseph Kyle and Jacob Dallas in 1850–51, based on the designs of many prominent artists. At the time, the press declared the eight-foot-tall, eight-hundred-foot-long painting a "valuable addition" to the museum's eclectic collection of regional art, colonial relics, and natural history specimens, even though the full history of the huge painting already had been lost.[1]

By the time the gift was made to the Institute, the panorama was nearly half a century old and somewhat of a relic itself, having endured decades of wear and neglect. This was in stark contrast to its initial reception in the early 1850s, when it was a tremendously popular traveling show touring much of North America. Then, into the 1870s, the panorama became a sideshow attraction playing in smaller venues in southern Maine.[2] Aside from the 1896 press notice of the acquisition and an exhibition of part of the panorama at the York Institute the following year,[3] the object was neglected. It was never catalogued or labeled, and the significance of the huge rolls of painted muslin sheeting was soon forgotten. By 1925 the panorama had become so obscure that the local newspaper ran a feature about its regrettable disappearance.[4] Then, in 1996 — a century after the York Institute acquired the panorama — it was rediscovered in the museum's basement. As a result, its remarkable history can now be pieced together.

The *Moving Panorama of Pilgrim's Progress* was a product of the mid-nineteenth-century phenomenon of moving panoramas, detailed in the preceding essay by Kevin J. Avery. The huge stationary panoramas common earlier in the century were supplanted in America by paintings on muslin or sheeting, which were placed on spools and reeled across a stage, simulating movement as if observed from the deck of a ship or the seat of a rolling railroad car. Moving panoramas were more portable than fixed panoramas and did not require a specialized building for exhibition, and so they could benefit from traveling to various audiences. For example, the incredible financial success of John Banvard's moving panorama of the Mississippi River, which toured in America starting in 1846 and England in 1848, inspired many entrepreneurial artists to paint panoramas of their own.[5] In the ensuing decade, hundreds of moving panoramas, depicting myriad voyages, travels, and historical events, were exhibited as traveling entertainments all across the country. Of the scores of panoramas created in this "Age of Panoramas," only a handful survive, because of the damage inflicted by frequent rolling and unrolling. But even if they all had survived, the *Moving Panorama of Pilgrim's Progress* most likely would be the most significant today, both because of its unique connection to popular and fine art (via its association with important artists of the National Academy of Design in New York) and because of its unusual subject matter.

The story of *The Pilgrim's Progress* offered both artists and audiences plenty to sink their teeth into, from Christian's various tests of faith to his final, triumphant arrival at the Celestial City. Early in the story, Christian almost drowns in the murky Slough of Despond, is forced to climb Hill Difficulty on his hands and knees, and survives a battle with the monster Apollyon as well as a passage through the Valley of the Shadow of Death. However, his pilgrimage also induces joyful episodes, such as his visit to the Palace Beautiful. Because of its moral plot, vivid imagery, and appeal to the common person, the book was wildly popular in England and America for centuries.[6] During the Protestant revival of the early nineteenth century, *The Pilgrim's Progress* was regarded as second only to the Bible as the most widely read and translated book of the era.[7]

The original *Moving Panorama of Pilgrim's Progress*, conceived and executed by Edward Harrison May and Joseph Kyle, was not the first attempt to bring Bunyan's allegory to the stage in a panoramic format. A small panorama of fifteen scenes from *The Pilgrim's Progress* toured the Northeast in 1845, and the Italian-trained portraitist Alfred Hart exhibited a panorama of the same subject in Hartford in 1848.[8] Neither of these earlier attempts to break the purely scenic format of most panoramas by illustrating stories from literature seems to have been successful. In contrast, the panorama of *The Pilgrim's Progress* initiated by May and Kyle in 1848 was so successful that it grossed $100,000 in its first six months. Unlike most panoramas, which were created by amateur artists or theatrical scene painters, May and Kyle's

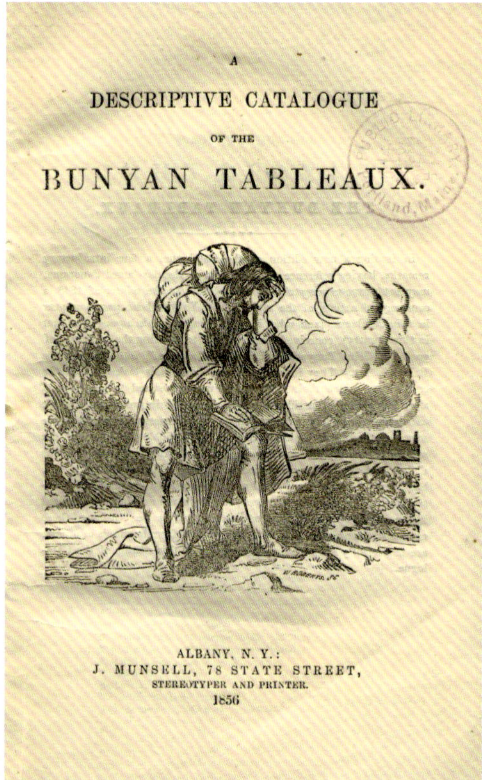

A
DESCRIPTIVE CATALOGUE
OF THE
BUNYAN TABLEAUX.

ALBANY, N. Y.:
J. MUNSELL, 78 STATE STREET,
STEREOTYPER AND PRINTER.
1856

FIGURE 3.1.
A Descriptive Catalogue of the Bunyan Tableaux (Albany, N.Y.: J. Munsell, 1856). Collections of the Dyer Library and Saco Museum, Saco, Maine. Gift of Debra and William Barry.

panorama (also known as "The Bunyan Tableaux") was executed by formally trained artists buoyed by the power and the cachet of America's premier art school, New York's National Academy of Design.

Edward Harrison May (1824–1887) was born in England but came to America as a youth, when his father, a minister in the Dutch Reformed Church, was asked to take a parish in New York City.[9] As a young man, he studied engineering before taking up painting under the National Academician Daniel Huntington. May's Protestant background might have inspired him to illustrate Bunyan's classic Protestant allegory. He would have been familiar with Huntington's easel paintings *Mercy's Dream* (figure 1.20) and *Christiana and Her Family Passing through the Valley of the Shadow of Death* (figure 1.18), which depict scenes in the second part of *The Pilgrim's Progress*. He also would have known Thomas Cole's moralistic *Voyage of Life* (figures 1.6–1.9) and *Cross and the World* series (see figure 1.11), which echo themes in *The Pilgrim's Progress*. May also was part of the rising trend of exhibiting easel compositions based on scenes from Bunyan, detailed by Jessica Skwire Routhier in her preceding essay. An astonishing number of these were produced within a span of only two years. The American Art-Union exhibition of 1847 featured May's *Bunyan Parting with His Blind Daughter* (unlocated) as well as Jesse Talbot's *Christian and the Cross* (figure 1.15). The same year, at the National Academy of Design, Huntington exhibited his *Mercy Fainting at the Wicket Gate* (unlocated), and Frederic Edwin Church exhibited *Christian on the Borders of the Valley of the Shadow of Death* (figure 1.13), which was followed the next year by its companion, *The River of the Water of Life* (unlocated).[10] Each of these subjects informed a scene in the panorama.

May's partner in the panorama project, Joseph Kyle (1809–1863), was a native of Cleremont County, Ohio. He had studied painting in Cincinnati and later in Philadelphia under Thomas Sully and Bass Otis. In 1846 Kyle moved to New York, where he exhibited portraits and still lifes but became best known for his work on panoramas.[11] Between 1848 and 1858, Kyle painted at least nine panoramas, mostly in partnership with his son-in-law, Jacob Dallas (1825–1857), a popular illustrator whose work appeared in *Harper's*, *Leslie's*, and *Putnam's* magazines.[12] When he returned to painting portraits after Dallas's untimely death in 1857, Kyle was described as "among the few of our artists, who were born for another sphere in art. With the lamented Dallas, he wrought those magnificent series of panoramas which have never been, and never may be equaled."[13]

The artistic precedents for the *Moving Panorama of Pilgrim's Progress* in the work of Thomas Cole, Frederic Church, Jasper Cropsey, Daniel Huntington, Paul Duggan, Henry Courtney Selous, and Felix Octavius Carr Darley have been explored thoughtfully in Jessica Skwire Routhier's preceding essay. As she notes, many of those painters had been influenced by the British Romantic artist John Martin's well-known mezzotints illustrating the 1827 edition of Milton's *Paradise Lost*.[14] Additional similarities include May's figure of Apollyon (plate 17), which directly relates to Martin's *Conflict Between Satan and Death*, and the blending of figure and landscape in Cropsey's conception of the *Land of Beulah* (plate 30), which is similar to Martin's compositions for *Adam and Eve: The Morning Hymn* and *The Approach of the Archangel Raphael* from the same series. In a less direct way, the rolling river of fire in *Valley of the Shadow of Death* (whose design was credited to Church; plate 20) is reminiscent of a similar feature in Martin's *Satan on the Lake of Fire*. Martin's *Expulsion of Adam and Eve* is echoed not only in the depictions of the Wicket Gate in the panorama (plates 7 and 34), but also, as Routhier notes, in Thomas Cole's *Expulsion from the Garden of Eden*, which in turn provided inspiration for the panorama artists. Kyle's version of the *Land of Beulah* (plate 38), described as "the landscape gem of the entire Work,"[15] is little more than an elongated copy of Martin's *Celestial City* (figure 1.10), published to illustrate a new edition of *The Pilgrim's Progress* in 1830. Likewise, Darley's design for *Death of Giant Grim* (plate 35), while bearing compositional similarities to an earlier work of Darley's,[16] is also related to an engraving of the same scene by William Harvey in the same edition.

Similar connections can be made to works by the English artist William Blake. Although Blake's illustrations for *The Pilgrim's Progress* were not reproduced or widely seen until the twentieth century, May's designs for *Bunyan Dreaming*, *Christian Meditating in the Field,* and *Giant Despair Visits the Pilgrims in Their Dungeon* (plates 2, 3, and 23) are surprisingly similar to Blake's compositions of the same passages.[17] Like Blake, May dressed Bunyan's characters in long robes or medieval garb, rather than in the seventeenth-century costumes that typically appeared in illustrations of the book. In copying Selous's *The Fate of the Apostate*, Kyle deleted Selous's original figure of the unfortunate Apostate and substituted one more closely resembling Blake's *The Blasphemer* (ca. 1800, Tate Gallery; see plate 28).

The reliance of the panorama painters on preexisting illustrations and paintings probably was part expedience and part necessity. The religious revival of the early nineteenth century led to dozens of illustrated editions of *The Pilgrim's Progress* in England and America. The engravings in these books were generally copies, with minor variations, of archetypal images of specific passages from Bunyan in earlier editions, especially those of Thomas Stothard in 1788.[18] As artists, May and Kyle wanted to execute unique compositions, but as illustrators, they needed to show their audience images that were familiar and recognizable.

The *Moving Panorama of Pilgrim's Progress* made its debut in New York's Washington Hall in November of 1850. In an age when a popular panorama exhibition lasted only six or eight weeks, the *Moving Panorama of Pilgrim's Progress* played to full houses in the same venue in New York for six months straight. Nearly one-third of the city's population — two hundred thousand people — paid fifty cents each for admission.[19] After its extended engagement in New York, the panorama toured through Hartford, Providence, and Boston, and eventually to other eastern cities, including Richmond and Charleston.[20] It was still touring in 1887, when it returned for another six-month run in New York.[21]

In response to the popularity and huge financial success of the panorama, the artist-entrepreneurs crafted a second version of the painting intended to play in cities in the interior of the country while the original toured the Atlantic Coast cities.[22] This second version of the panorama had its debut in New York in April of 1851, then traveled to Newark and Elizabethtown, New Jersey, before making its way to Maine and ultimately, the Saco Museum.

By the time the second version of the panorama was ready for exhibition, Edward Harrison May had left for Paris to study with Thomas Couture[23] and was not credited for his designs.[24] Newspaper accounts attribute the painting to only Dallas, Kyle, and sometimes "Wright," who is probably Charles Washington Wright (1824–1869), an illustrator who worked with Dallas at *Harper's* and *Leslie's* magazines.[25] Later, Daniel Huntington's name was added to the credits, along with William Cogswell's.[26] The creators of the second version insisted that the new panorama was not a direct copy of the first but a "revised edition," also with fifty-three scenes. After its initial showing, the *New York Tribune* reported, "The artists have varied the original design in many parts, and with much success."[27]

Because the original panorama is no longer extant, a comparison of the two versions is difficult, but placing various contemporary sources alongside the Saco Museum's panorama sheds some light on what was done. The two scenes from the original work — *Christian Meditating in the Field* (plate 3) and *Christian Reposing After the Combat* (plate

18) — that appeared as wood engravings in R. J. Greenwood's *Descriptive Catalogue of the Bunyan Tableaux*[28] (figure 3.1) and a surviving handbill[29] (figure 2.1) match scenes in the surviving panorama with only minor differences.[30] Contemporary descriptions of scenes in the original *Moving Panorama of Pilgrim's Progress* fit the same ones in the surviving copy equally well. A comparison of the sequence of scenes in the panorama with Greenwood's *Descriptive Catalogue* indicate that at least three scenes, *Hill Difficulty*, *Pilgrims Leave the Valley of Humiliation*, and *Christiana Crosses the River of Death*, were eliminated from the second version.[31] *Hill Difficulty* had been singled out by at least one critic who noted this as a weak scene in the original,[32] and the two other scenes, depicting Christiana retracing the steps of her husband's journey, may have been seen as unnecessary repetitions of similar scenes in the first part of the panorama. As an added attraction, at least three new scenes were added: *Bunyan Parting with His Blind Daughter*; *Christiana, Her Children, and Secret*; and *Mercy's Dream* (plates 1, 32, and 36).[33] The first of the new scenes is almost certainly the design May exhibited in 1847 and suggests that May was involved in the early stages of the "revised edition." The scene inspired by Daniel Huntington's *Mercy's Dream* is notable in that it is physically inserted into the panorama (having been painted on a separate piece of fabric), sewn in just before *They Lost Their Way in the Valley of the Shadow of Death.* This alteration of the second version is documented in the *Newark Daily Advertiser* of May 29, 1851, which reported "A new scene 'Mercy's Dream' has been added."[34]

Further alterations of the design of the panorama are speculative. One reviewer of the first panorama, critical of the way the scenes ran together (which resulted in the principal characters often being visible in two places as the painting was rolled across the stage), suggested that the artists should have "isolated the scenes more completely, or, at any rate, taken care that the same characters should never be seen twice on the portion of the canvas presented at any one time to the eye" and "introduced . . . large intervals of clouds, covering the picture, and only interrupted by successive scenes, into which the chief points of landscape and incident might have been concentrated."[35] In the extant version, the first ten scenes do tend to run together, but the later scenes are more distinctly separated by billowing clouds, outcroppings of rock, sprays of foliage, and architectural elements. In one instance, the artists eased the transition between the nightmarish *They Lost Their Way in the Valley of the Shadow of Death* (plate 37) and the bucolic *Land of Beulah* (plate 38) by introducing a sublime, dark waterfall that is not part of either scene (figure 3.2). The elongation of the compositions beginning around the tenth scene, *Christian at the Cross*, suggests that alterations were made in response to this criticism.

In a preemptive strike against any criticism that the "revised edition" was inferior, Kyle and Dallas secured a statement from the National Academy of Design, declaring the work "equal if not superior to any work of this class [probably a reference to the moving panorama format] ever exhibited in this country."[36] Thirty-one artists signed the resolution, including John F. Kensett, Jerome Thompson, and Thomas Seir Cummings, along with the noted author Bayard Taylor. Later, the painter Emanuel Leutze wrote a personal letter of endorsement for the second version.[37] Newspaper editors would cite these testimonials for more than a decade as proof of the impeccable artistic pedigree of the panorama. Many echoed the sentiment of the editor of the Concord, New Hampshire, *Independent Democrat* when he remarked, "with all the 'cheap shows' and second-rate exhibitions of the day, we are glad at length to recognize a work of superior artistic merit and of such excellent character."[38]

One reviewer went so far as to say it was "beyond exception the finest work of art ever produced in this country."[39] However, most echoed the narrower remarks of Portland

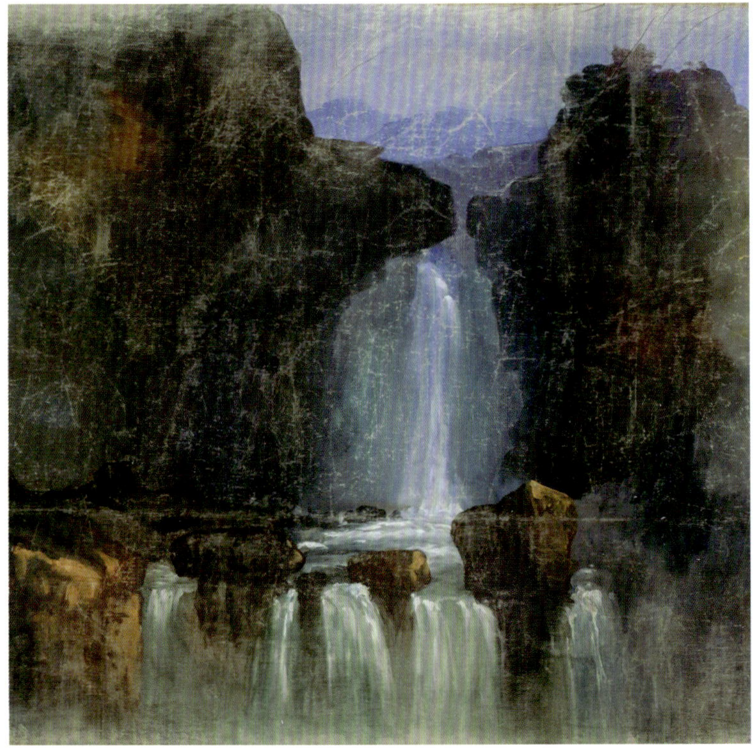

FIGURE 3.2. *Waterfall,* designer unknown, from the *Moving Panorama of Pilgrim's Progress*, 1851, distemper on muslin. Saco Museum, Saco, Maine. Gift of the heirs of Luther Bryant, 1896. Photo by Matthew Hamilton, courtesy Williamstown Art Conservation Center.

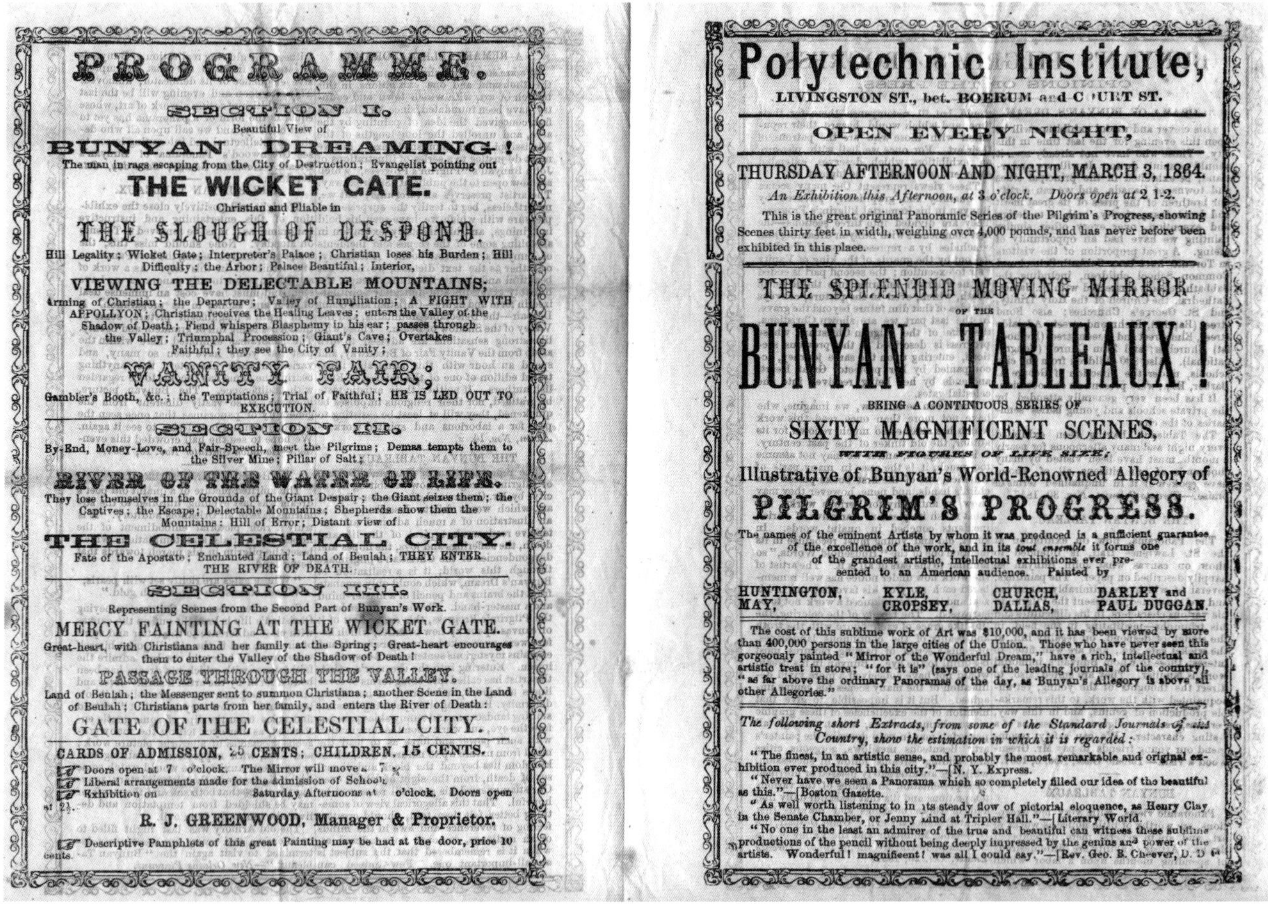
PROGRAMME.

SECTION I.

Beautiful View of

BUNYAN DREAMING!

The man in rags escaping from the City of Destruction; Evangelist pointing out

THE WICKET GATE.

Christian and Pliable in

THE SLOUGH OF DESPOND.

Hill Legality; Wicket Gate; Interpreter's Palace; Christian loses his Burden; Hill Difficulty; the Arbor; Palace Beautiful; Interior,

VIEWING THE DELECTABLE MOUNTAINS;

Arming of Christian; the Departure; Valley of Humiliation; A FIGHT WITH APPOLLYON; Christian receives the Healing Leaves; enters the Valley of the Shadow of Death; Fiend whispers Blasphemy in his ear; passes through the Valley; Triumphal Procession; Giant's Cave; Overtakes Faithful; they see the City of Vanity;

VANITY FAIR;

Gambler's Booth, &c.; the Temptations; Trial of Faithful; HE IS LED OUT TO EXECUTION.

SECTION II.

By-End, Money-Love, and Fair-Speech, meet the Pilgrims; Demas tempts them to the Silver Mine; Pillar of Salt;

RIVER OF THE WATER OF LIFE.

They lose themselves in the Grounds of the Giant Despair; the Giant seizes them; the Captives; the Escape; Delectable Mountains; Shepherds show them the Mountains; Hill of Error; Distant view of

THE CELESTIAL CITY.

Fate of the Apostate; Enchanted Land; Land of Beulah; THEY ENTER THE RIVER OF DEATH.

SECTION III.

Representing Scenes from the Second Part of Bunyan's Work.

MERCY FAINTING AT THE WICKET GATE.

Great-heart, with Christiana and her family at the Spring; Great-heart encourages them to enter the Valley of the Shadow of Death!

PASSAGE THROUGH THE VALLEY.

Land of Beulah; the Messenger sent to summon Christiana; another Scene in the Land of Beulah; Christiana parts from her family, and enters the River of Death:

GATE OF THE CELESTIAL CITY.

CARDS OF ADMISSION, 25 CENTS; CHILDREN, 15 CENTS.

☞ Doors open at 7 o'clock. The Mirror will move at 7 ½
☞ Liberal arrangements made for the admission of Schools
☞ Exhibition on Saturday Afternoons at o'clock. Doors open at 2½.

R. J. GREENWOOD, Manager & Proprietor.

☞ Descriptive Pamphlets of this great Painting may be had at the door, price 10 cents.

Polytechnic Institute,

LIVINGSTON ST., bet. BOERUM and COURT ST.

OPEN EVERY NIGHT,

THURSDAY AFTERNOON AND NIGHT, MARCH 3, 1864.

An Exhibition this Afternoon, at 3 o'clock. Doors open at 2 1-2.

This is the great original Panoramic Series of the Pilgrim's Progress, showing Scenes thirty feet in width, weighing over 4,000 pounds, and has never before been exhibited in this place.

THE SPLENDID MOVING MIRROR OF THE

BUNYAN TABLEAUX!

BEING A CONTINUOUS SERIES OF

SIXTY MAGNIFICENT SCENES,

WITH FIGURES OF LIFE SIZE;

Illustrative of Bunyan's World-Renowned Allegory of

PILGRIM'S PROGRESS.

The names of the eminent Artists by whom it was produced is a sufficient guarantee of the excellence of the work, and in its *tout ensemble* it forms one of the grandest artistic, intellectual exhibitions ever presented to an American audience. Painted by

HUNTINGTON, MAY, KYLE, CROPSEY, CHURCH, DALLAS, DARLEY and PAUL DUGGAN.

The cost of this sublime work of Art was $10,000, and it has been viewed by more than 400,000 persons in the large cities of the Union. Those who have never seen this gorgeously painted "Mirror of the Wonderful Dream," have a rich, intellectual and artistic treat in store; "for it is" (says one of the leading journals of the country), "as far above the ordinary Panoramas of the day, as Bunyan's Allegory is above all other Allegories."

The following short Extracts, from some of the Standard Journals of this Country, show the estimation in which it is regarded:

"The finest, in an artistic sense, and probably the most remarkable and original exhibition ever produced in this city."—[N. Y. Express.

"Never have we seen a Panorama which so completely filled our idea of the beautiful as this."—[Boston Gazette.

"As well worth listening to in its steady flow of pictorial eloquence, as Henry Clay in the Senate Chamber, or Jenny Lind at Tripler Hall."—[Literary World.

"No one in the least an admirer of the true and beautiful can witness these sublime productions of the pencil without being deeply impressed by the genius and power of the artists. Wonderful! magnificent! was all I could say."—[Rev. Geo. B. Cheever, D. D.

FIGURE 3.3.
"The Splendid Moving Mirror of the Bunyan Tableaux!" Polytechnic Institute (location unknown), circa 1857. Collections of the Dyer Library and Saco Museum, Saco, Maine. Gift of Kathleen M. Swaim.

(Maine's) *Eastern Argus*, which stated that it was "superior in execution and design to anything of this kind that has visited our City,"[40] thus comparing it — as had the National Academy of Design — to the standards of contemporary panorama painting. One has only to see other surviving moving panoramas, such as Russell and Purrington's *Whaling Voyage Round the World*, to get the impression that most moving panoramas, while grand in scale and conception, made few pretensions to being fine art. With its huge, heroically posed figures and evocative landscapes composed by academically trained artists, the *Moving Panorama of Pilgrim's Progress* may have been the most sophisticated work of art that typical patrons of panoramas had ever seen. The editor of the *Argus* may have challenged his readers' sense of sophistication by writing, "No person with any pretension to taste can fail to be charmed with its inimitable scenes."[41]

And yet, the *Moving Panorama of Pilgrim's Progress* is very different from the grand studio paintings its designers were producing at the time. It is painted in broad strokes, and the colors verge on garishness in order to be legible from a distance. Some scenes are well finished, but others are sketchy. This is consistent, however, with the way a moving panorama was intended to be exhibited. It was rolled out from one giant spool onto another spool, exposing a few feet of the painting at a time,[42] and was usually accompanied by a lecturer and "the low soft melody of an instrument [typically a pianoforte or an organ] appropriately played."[43] In a typical two-hour presentation, each scene would be visible for several minutes, probably lit by gas footlights, and the viewer might be seated as much as thirty or more feet from the canvas. To finish the scenes like studio oils would have been a waste of effort, given the brief time each scene was on view. Instead, the panoramists created impressions of elaborate historical figure paintings and sublime landscapes.

One of the most universally acclaimed scenes in both versions of the panorama, May's *Christian and Hopeful Enter the River of Death* (plate 31), is one of the least complex in composition and the sketchiest in execution, with the angels on the opposite shore barely articulated in shorthand strokes of yellow paint. Yet a contemporary reviewer summed up the response to this image as it passed across the stage by saying it "is certainly a conception of peculiar power. We know not in all the language of poetic description a combination of figures equal to it."[44] The same writer singled out one of the most finished scenes, *Christiana Parts with Her Children* (plate 39), as being "of equal merit." The bold technique along with the short viewing time of each scene actually enhanced the illustrative and emotional effects of the compositions.

One of the most interesting criticisms of the first version of the *Moving Panorama of Pilgrim's Progress* — a criticism doubtless applicable to the extant second version — appeared in *Literary World*: "We might object to an excess of gaudy color, particularly towards the close of the series and to a want of softness in an occasional scene."[45] Eight years later, the painting was "said to look better than when new, age having a tendency to mellow down and coalesce the tints, and bring out more clearly its artistic beauties."[46] Today, the liberal employment of vivid color is one of the most striking features of the panorama, yet evidently it was even brighter when it was new.

Besides its own remarkable success, the panorama left a substantial legacy in the arts. At the National Academy of Design exhibition of 1851, Paul Duggan displayed a crayon sketch for *The Pilgrim's Progress* that was probably a design from the panorama,[47] and the following year Jasper Cropsey's designs for the panorama were exhibited at the Academy.[48] Another scene, *Hill Difficulty*, was redrawn by Felix O. C. Darley as the frontispiece for a popular edition of Bunyan's book.[49] Henry Courtney Selous published his third set of engravings of *The Pilgrim's Progress*, which, as part of *Cassell's Illustrated Bunyan*, was frequently reprinted through the end of the century.[50] A large engraving illustrating *The Pilgrim's Progress*, designed by the Reverend D. Wright and drawn by Hammett Billings, was published in Boston in 1853 and relates to the panorama by the repeated depiction of the characters in a continuous landscape.[51] Emanuel Leutze, who had endorsed Kyle and Dallas's panorama, contributed to yet another panorama of *The Pilgrim's Progress* that toured in the 1850s and played at New York's "Bunyan Hall" in 1867.[52]

As widely popular as the several panoramas of *The Pilgrim's Progress* were, all of them were quickly forgotten. After its debut in New York and New Jersey in 1851, the second version of Kyle, May, and Dallas's panorama went west and was playing in Detroit in 1853. It returned east for a tour of New England in 1854–55, being "carried from city to city in a beautifully painted cart hauled by two handsome horses."[53] Three years later, it made its second tour through Biddeford, Maine, and never seems to have left the region. It was apparently performed in southern Maine into the 1870s,[54] after which it was shown as a regular feature in an old barn on Hill Street in Biddeford.[55] At some point it became the property of Luther Bryant (1818–1894), a Biddeford real estate agent, whose heirs donated it to the York

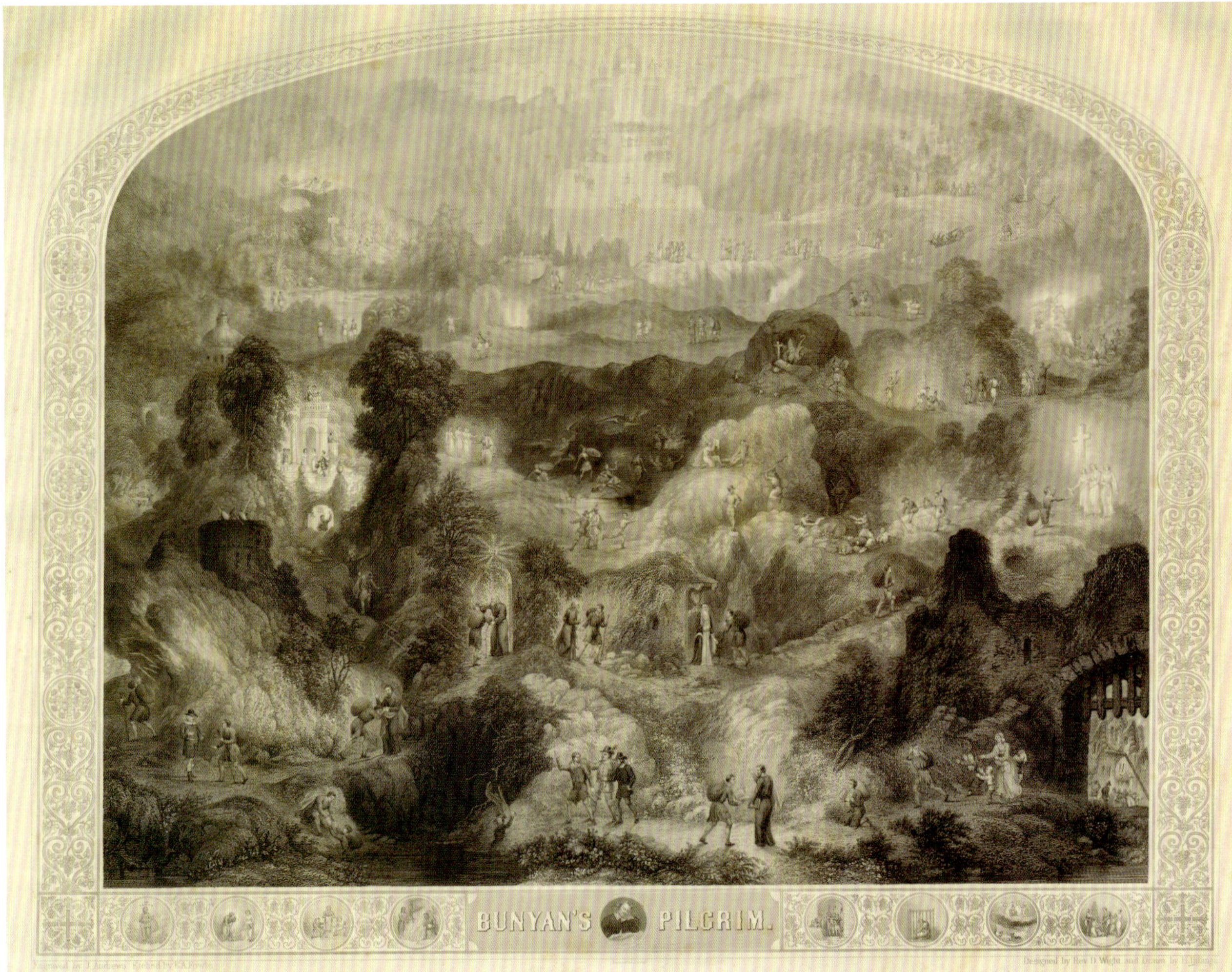

FIGURE 3.4. Hammat Billings (1818–1874), *Bunyan's Pilgrim*, engraving on paper, etched by E. A. Fowles (1818–1874), designed by the Reverend Daniel Wight Jr., and engraved by J. Andrews (1806–1873). Published by John P. Jewett, Boston, 1853. Collections of the Dyer Library and Saco Museum, Saco, Maine. Gift of Maureen McEwen, 2007.

Institute two years after his death. It seems most likely that Bryant acquired the panorama in 1877, when he purchased the Biddeford property of Charles A. Shaw (1831–1909), a millionaire entrepreneur who ran a chain of theaters in Biddeford, Boston, Lowell, and Providence and, according to an 1870 source, was an owner of the panorama.[56] Shaw acted as an agent for all types of performers in the region, including the famous showmen P. T. Barnum, Artemus Ward, Ossian Dodge, and George W. Peck.[57]

By the time the York Institute Museum exhibited the panorama in 1897, extensive portions of the first roll had been overpainted by Erastus H. Thompson (1847–1918), a Biddeford carriage painter who signed his name to the back. Conservators speculate that Thompson is responsible for adding the cartoonish ghoul to the scene of *Dawn of Day over the Valley of the Shadow of Death* (plate 20), whose design is attributed to Frederic Edwin Church.[58] At some point, approximately thirteen scenes were removed from the middle, including a depiction of the gambler's booth in Vanity Fair and Cropsey's *River of the Water of Life*, both regarded as highlights of the original work.[59] Given the loss of pigment and the threadbare condition of the fabric in adjacent scenes, it seems likely that a large part of the panorama became unexhibitable and was discarded.

Despite the losses and damage, it is miraculous that some forty scenes on eight hundred feet of sheeting have survived in salvageable condition. The panorama never was intended to be a lasting work of art in itself. As a document of designs by distinguished American artists, however, the value of the work is inestimable. Equally important is its existence as a rare surviving example of popular entertainment culture. The panorama also gives us insight into the relationship between the fine and popular arts of the nineteenth century. While the first version of the panorama was still in production, one critic noted:

> We like the spirit in which these five or six young men have contributed to this work. It shows that they are superior to the vulgar notion that it is the character of the materials upon which depends the dignity of any undertaking in Art. They know well, it is rather the idea they are to seek to develop which will ennoble their productions, no matter whether they are moulded in earth or carved in marble — whether they are executed in enduring fresco, or, like this panorama, with common house paints on poor thin cotton cloth . . . and we may be sure that Art will make but little progress in our own time, unless she descends from her lofty throne, and bestows

the charm of her influence in the same way upon the every day pursuits and amusements of the people.[60]

To glimpse the figure of Christian, large as life and in lurid color, is to share an experience that was once marveled upon by stoic clerics, country "Jonathans," and worldly-wise artists. It would be difficult to imagine any work of art today that could meet the demands and interests of as broad a spectrum of viewers as those who filled gaslit halls to see the *Moving Panorama of Pilgrim's Progress* and left feeling utterly satisfied.

JESSICA SKWIRE ROUTHIER

EPILOGUE

THE STORY OF THE *Moving Panorama of Pilgrim's Progress* does not end, of course, with its deposit at the York Institute at the end of the nineteenth century, nor with its rediscovery and resurrection in 1996. Nor did media culture, launched in part by the moving panorama phenomenon, leapfrog directly from gaslit auditoriums to IMAX movie theaters. Like all good epic stories, this one has subplots and a satisfying denouement.

Even before the *Moving Panorama of Pilgrim's Progress* came to languish in Luther Bryant's barn in Biddeford, moving panoramas had become so much a part of the American cultural consciousness that, like *The Pilgrim's Progress* before them, they had become prey for humorists. As Kevin Avery notes in his essay in this book, Artemus Ward found an appreciative audience for his parody panoramas, including one in 1864 about the Mormon pioneers, which he presented both in the United States and London. Lest we assume that our own age has cornered the market in media-jaded satire, Ward wittily parroted the language of other promoters to boast that his panorama offered everything from "A Mile of Pictures" to "Sixteen Cubic Feet of Fine Moral Sentiment" and "A Small Black Travelling-Bag Containing Phosphorescent Quips."[1] Just a year later, Mark Twain penned a small sketch entitled "The Entertaining History of the Scriptural Panoramist," focusing on the "wooden-headed old slab" hired to play the piano accompaniment, which was wildly off-kilter with the subject matter.[2] It is noteworthy that these two best-known panorama send-ups both targeted religious-themed panoramas; the self-professed high moral purpose of these entertainments must have made it seem that they and their audiences were in particular need of raillery. The growing view of panoramas as laughable relics becomes even more topical for our purposes with the 1912 novel *Watch Yourself Go By*,[3] which describes (and illustrates!) an ill-fated performance of a moving panorama of *The Pilgrim's Progress*.

As media scholar Erkki Huhtamo explains in his remarkable book on the moving panorama tradition, *Illusions in Motion*, the Civil War changed things for moving panoramas just as it changed every other aspect of American life.[4] While audiences welcomed war themes and showmen were eager to capitalize, their promotional language either avoided or improved upon the word *panorama* — perhaps seeking to combat the perception of superficiality that critics had come to associate with the term. Moving panoramas continued, but generally as only a part of a larger evening's entertainment, and they were now often described as "dioramas" (a resurrected term from the earlier nineteenth century; not to be confused with the three-dimensional models popular later with museums and hobbyists) or with perplexing hybrid terms such as "pano-diorama."[5]

Photography, too, became a larger part of American life at this time, with Matthew Brady's battlefield shots demonstrating the new medium's power to transport a viewer to a specific time and place. Soon stereoviews and photographically produced magic lantern shows arose as new kinds of immersive entertainment experiences; *The Pilgrim's Progress* was a favorite subject for both.[6] These innovations intersected with panoramas in entertainments dubbed "stereoramas" and "panstereoramas" and in the vogue for "dissolving views,"[7] in which a specialized magic lantern or "stereopticon" used two or more projection lenses to overlay and shift among images and enhance a sense of narrative. Such novelties, with their ghostly illusions, provided new opportunities for capitalizing on a Victorian taste for the paranormal.

Phantasmagorias, Spectrascopes, and Phantoscopes, along with myriad other variations, all promised viewers direct contact with spectral presences.[8]

It is easy to understand how these undefinable and often otherworldly spectacles — their workings cloaked in secrecy then as they are to some degree now — drew attention away from moving panoramas, which no matter how impressive were still clearly just painted cloth on rollers. Photography-based formats like magic lantern shows would ultimately prevail, but the victory was not immediate. The last quarter of the nineteenth century saw direct and heated competition for audiences between stereoscopists and panoramists.[9] For the latter, reworkings such as the "Myriorama," which added special effects and featured performances to the traditional matrix,[10] extended the moving panorama's life into the early twentieth century, although its popularity was much reduced. In the end, economics were at play: magic lantern shows were less expensive to produce and perform, and they could be duplicated, franchised, and presented across the country in a way that an original artwork like a panorama could not.[11] Even the cynical saw the potential payday of such a format. In 1891 Mark Twain, who had lampooned panoramas in the past, soberly debated the economics of a "stereopticon panorama" — presumably some sort of hybrid

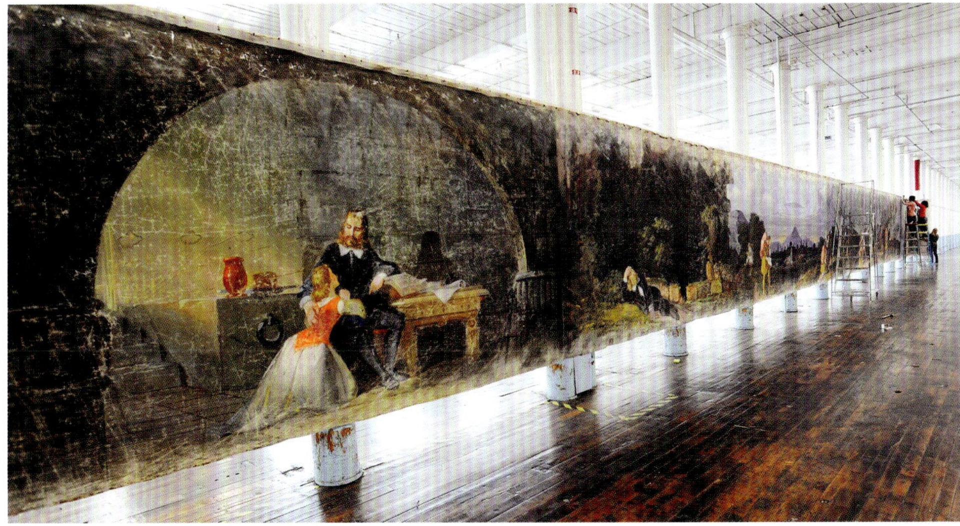

FIGURE 4.1. The *Moving Panorama of Pilgrim's Progress* on view in Building 13 of the Pepperell Mill Campus, Biddeford, Maine, June 18, 2012. Photo by Shawn Patrick Ouellette, courtesy *Portland Press Herald/Maine Sunday Telegram.*

of the two media — that "could be exhibited in all countries at the same time & would clear a fortune in a year."[12] The subject he proposed was *The Pilgrim's Progress.*

Twain's interest is evidence that, even after their heyday had passed, panoramic formats persisted in the use of religious instruction. Initially, as with the *Moving Panorama of Pilgrim's Progress* and other moving panoramas depicting the Holy Lands or biblical themes, there was little distinction between public entertainment and spiritual teaching. But as the proprietors of religious-themed panoramas sought to distinguish their productions as morally and intellectually superior to other entertainment options, and as secular panoramas became ever more a sideshow attraction, the religious community increasingly "embraced the ideology of the object lesson."[13] Brigham Young University's remarkable *Mormon Panorama*, one of the few moving panoramas still in existence today, toured the western interior of the United States through the 1880s.[14] Beginning in 1896, a hand-cranked, desktop, printed panorama called *The Royal Scroll* was used by Sunday schools and missionaries internationally.[15] And in his chapter entitled "The Cranking God: Panoramas and the Religious Imagination," Huhtamo also discusses how similar panoramic tools and metaphors were used to parse contemporary debates about creation versus evolution.[16]

It was probably in the general interest of such instruction and inquiry that the trustees of the York Institute — then as much a lyceum and a museum of natural history as anything else[17] — agreed to accept the *Moving Panorama of Pilgrim's Progress* as a gift from the heirs of Luther Bryant in 1896.[18] Internal records show that the panorama was shown the following year, or at least there was a stated intention to show it,[19] but there is no information about the manner in which it was displayed — in part or in its entirety? static or in motion? onstage or on a wall? with a lecture or music? — nor about whether the thirteen lost scenes were then a part of it. There is also no indication that anyone remembered that the panorama was associated with major American artists — not even Frederic Edwin Church, who was still very much alive at the time and widely revered as a living patriarch of American landscape painting.

Whether it was seen in 1897 or not, the panorama certainly was not seen again for many, many years after that. Twenty-eight years later, no one in town remembered any longer what had happened to it, though surely it was still housed somewhere in the York Institute's building in Saco's Sweetser block. A newspaper article of November 17, 1925, stated that its "last known owner was the late Nehemiah Day" — no mention of Luther Bryant or the York Institute.[20] The collective amnesia persisted a year later as the York Institute moved into a new building at 371 Main Street in Saco, the current location of the Saco Museum. Although the panorama must have been among the artifacts relocated during that move, no one seems to have been aware of what it was or to have made any record of its existence or location. The same thing must have happened in or around 1969, when a new wing was added to the Main Street building, including the storage basement where the panorama apparently was moved and lay, unused and unidentified, for another twenty-seven years. Whatever purpose the 1896 trustees originally had in mind for it, for a full century it had done nothing but gather dust.

Curator Thomas Hardiman's rediscovery and subsequent identification of the panorama in 1996 cast it into the limelight once again. Together, he and trustee Peter Morelli connected with Kevin J. Avery, whose 1995 dissertation featured a meticulously researched discussion of the *Moving Panorama of Pilgrim's Progress* (presumed lost at the time of his writing) and who was, at the time, a curator at The Metropolitan Museum of Art in New York and also involved with the Montclair Art Museum in New Jersey. In just three short years,[21] the York Institute and the Montclair Art Museum worked together to finance and organize a major exhibition that opened in Montclair and then traveled to the Portland Museum of Art in Maine and the Edwin A. Ulrich Museum of Art at Wichita State University in Kansas. Avery and Hardiman wrote essays for the accompanying catalogue,[22] both of which are reprinted here. In preparation for the 1999 exhibition, about half of the panorama (it was found in two pieces in 1996) was conserved by the staff of the Williamstown Art Conservation Center in Massachusetts, but because the center's facility lacked the space necessary to work on such a massive canvas, they set up work in a recently restored, nineteenth-century mill in nearby North

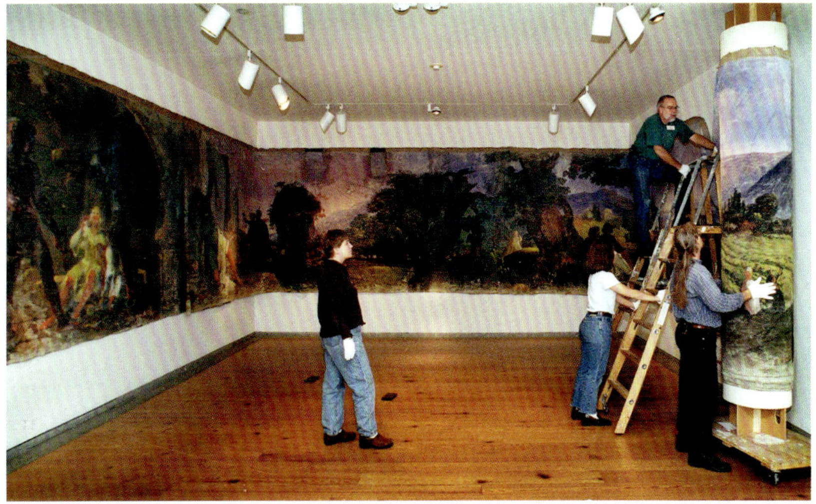

FIGURE 4.2. Museum staff installs the *Moving Panorama of Pilgrim's Progress* in the galleries of the Portland Museum of Art, Portland, Maine, October 29, 1999. Holding the ladder is the author of this essay. Photo by Gordon Chibroski, courtesy *Portland Press Herald/Maine Sunday Telegram.*

Adams.[23] That space has since become the central gallery of the Massachusetts Museum of Contemporary Art, better known as MASS MoCA.

As impactful as those efforts were, much was still left undone. In order to make handling the panorama easier and safer, Williamstown's conservators had divided the half that they treated into half once again, and staff at the York Institute ultimately did the same with the section that remained at the museum. Constraints of budget and available exhibition space had limited the 1990s treatment campaign to only two of those four sections, leaving two sections — the most damaged ones — still in poor condition, though safely stored in newly designed crates fabricated according to Williamstown's specifications. Through subsequent staff changes at the York Institute, Peter Morelli remained committed to finding a way to restore the complete panorama, to display it in its entirety, and ideally to recreate in some way the dynamic viewing experience that nineteenth-century audiences had enjoyed.

In the early 2000s, he began conversations with Andy Graham, the owner of Portland Color, a design and printing firm based in Maine and New York,[24] about using new digital photography and printing methods to create a replica of the panorama on modern, synthetic fabric that could withstand the stresses of performance. A test sample proved promising, but the technology still had not quite caught up with the ambitions of the project. Costs would be prohibitive both for photography and for printing at such a large scale. In the meantime, the two restored sections of the panorama were displayed at the Saco Museum in 2004. Because the museum's galleries are much too small to display so many running feet of canvas, the panorama was folded and doubled over strategically in order to display only a few of the major scenes. Viewers still weren't seeing the whole story.

When I became the director of the Saco Museum in 2008, I was very aware of the *Moving Panorama of Pilgrim's Progress*, having been on staff at the Portland Museum of Art when part of it was displayed there in 1999 (see figure 4.2). My ambitions for the Saco Museum dovetailed with Peter's dreams for the panorama, and together we crafted a grant proposal for Save America's Treasures to complete the conservation, create a life-size replica for performances, and produce a web-based film that would allow scholars from all over the world to experience the panorama in motion, as it was originally intended to be seen. In December 2009, we learned that the proposal had been approved, effectively kick-starting the final chapter of the project begun some thirteen years earlier. The panorama was one of the last proj-

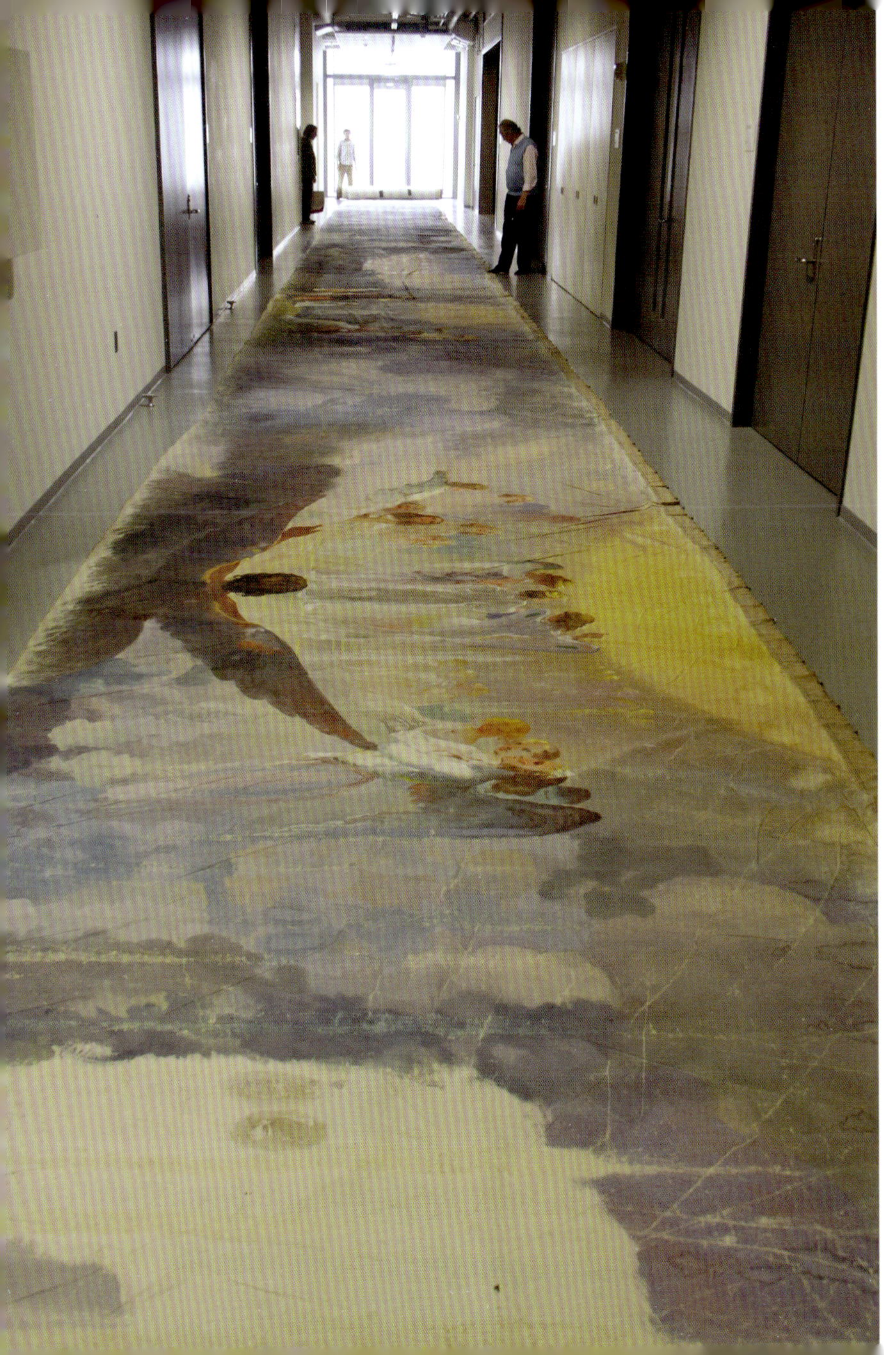

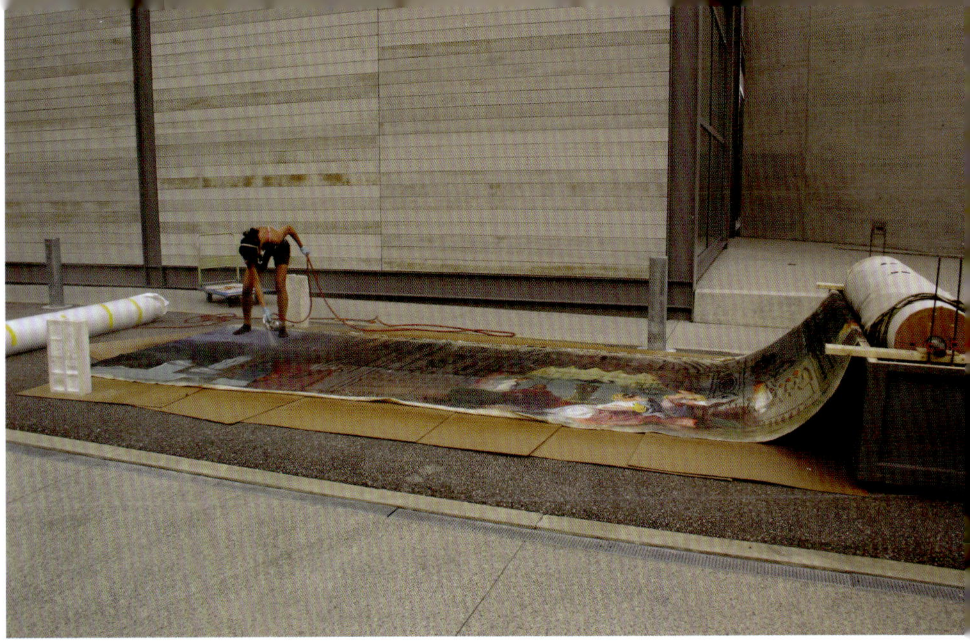

left:

FIGURE 4.3. The *Moving Panorama of Pilgrim's Progress* at the Williamstown Art Conservation Center, Williamstown, Massachusetts, 2011. WACC director Tom Branchick (right) supplies a sense of scale. Photo by Matthew Hamilton, courtesy Williamstown Art Conservation Center.

top:

FIGURE 4.4. Conservator Gabriel Dunn sprays consolidant over the surface of the panorama at the Williamstown Art Conservation Center in 2011. Photo by Matthew Hamilton, courtesy Williamstown Art Conservation Center.

ects to receive funding through this landmark federal grant program, which was discontinued in 2011. Up until that time it had helped to preserve objects and buildings of national significance, from the Star-Spangled Banner to Rosa Parks's bus.

Through 2010 and much of 2011, the panorama was once again in Williamstown, being treated in its entirety at the Center's new Tadeo Ando–designed building, whose capacious hallways now offered plenty of room for 64,000 square feet of fabric (see figures 4.3 and 4.4). Ultra-high-resolution photography accompanied every phase of conservation and became the bedrock for the interpretive tools. Some 150 individual captures by Williamstown photographer Matthew Hamilton were spliced together in Portland Color's studios to create a continuous image that could be printed on fabric at full scale and digitally animated for the film, produced by Back Lot Films in Fremont, New Hampshire. The first half of 2012 was dedicated to completing these tools — including a mechanism that could actually make the printed replica move, no trivial endeavor — in time for a June kickoff of all things panorama.

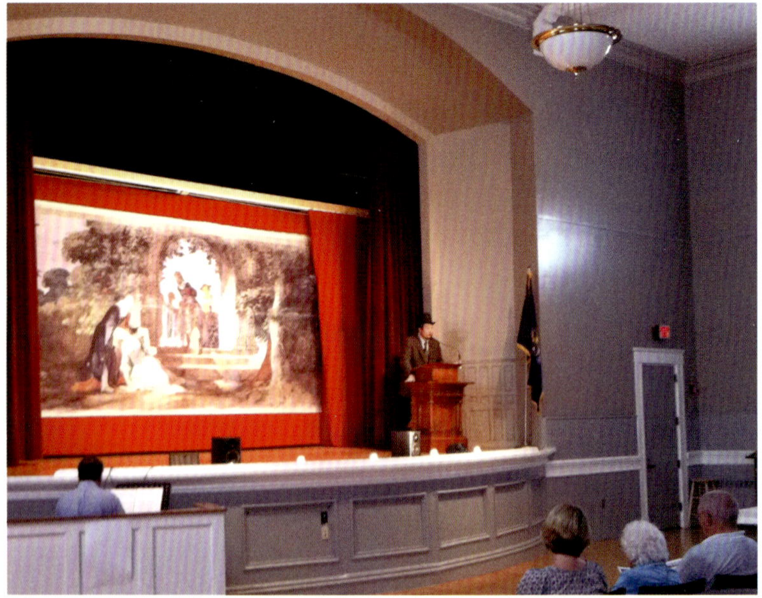

FIGURE 4.5. The full-scale replica of the panorama midperformance at Saco City Hall, Saco, Maine, 2012.

Friday, June 23, 2012, saw the first live performance of the *Moving Panorama of Pilgrim's Progress* in as many as 148 years, as the modern replica debuted onstage at Saco City Hall's historic auditorium. Some one hundred people watched the story of *The Pilgrim's Progress* pass before their eyes, "Life sized!" and "In Color!" just as the 1850s broadsides had proclaimed. A piano accompaniment and live narration, with a script derived from the extant "Descriptive Catalogues" and informed stylistically by the script for *The*

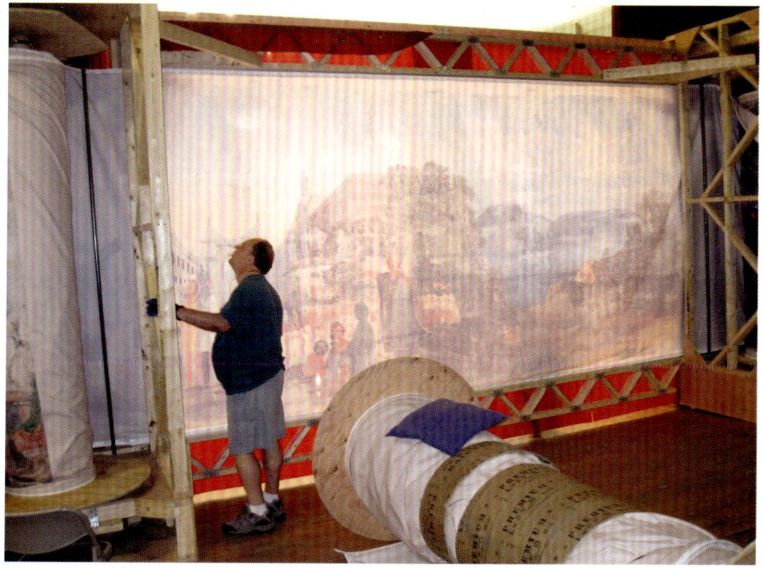

FIGURE 4.6. Peter Morelli inspects the machinery that animates the full-scale replica. Photo courtesy Jeff Rapsis.

Grand Moving Mirror of California,[25] completed the historic recreation, illuminated by footlights. Performances were repeated on a monthly basis throughout 2012,[26] giving some seven hundred people the chance to see something that no one alive had ever seen before.

Just a week after the replica's debut, on June 29, history once again repeated itself when the entire, original *Moving Panorama of Pilgrim's Progress* opened for public view in two locations: the Saco Museum, displaying one of the four sections, or about two hundred feet, and the Pepperell Mill Campus in downtown Biddeford, just a half mile away, exhibiting the other three sections, or six hundred feet. Pepperell Mills' soaring, nineteenth-century industrial space — evoking the unknown mill in which the fabric for the panorama must have been woven, as well as the North Adams mill in which it was conserved in the 1990s — provided a poignant setting for "Part One" of the panorama, illustrating the full scope of Christian's journey to the Celestial City. Though we always had considered it something of a disadvantage that the historic, 1851 panorama could no longer be seen in motion, as it was intended to be, it was nevertheless a powerful thing to be able to take it all in with one sweeping — panoramic, if you will — glance in its place at the mill. And at the Saco Museum, visitors could see the entirety of "Part Two" of the panorama, Christiana's journey, alongside books, prints, and ephemera related both to *The Pilgrim's Progress* and to the strange, vanished world of the moving panorama.

This book represents the culmination of the efforts begun with the Save America's Treasures award in 2009. Like everything else related to the panorama, it has been

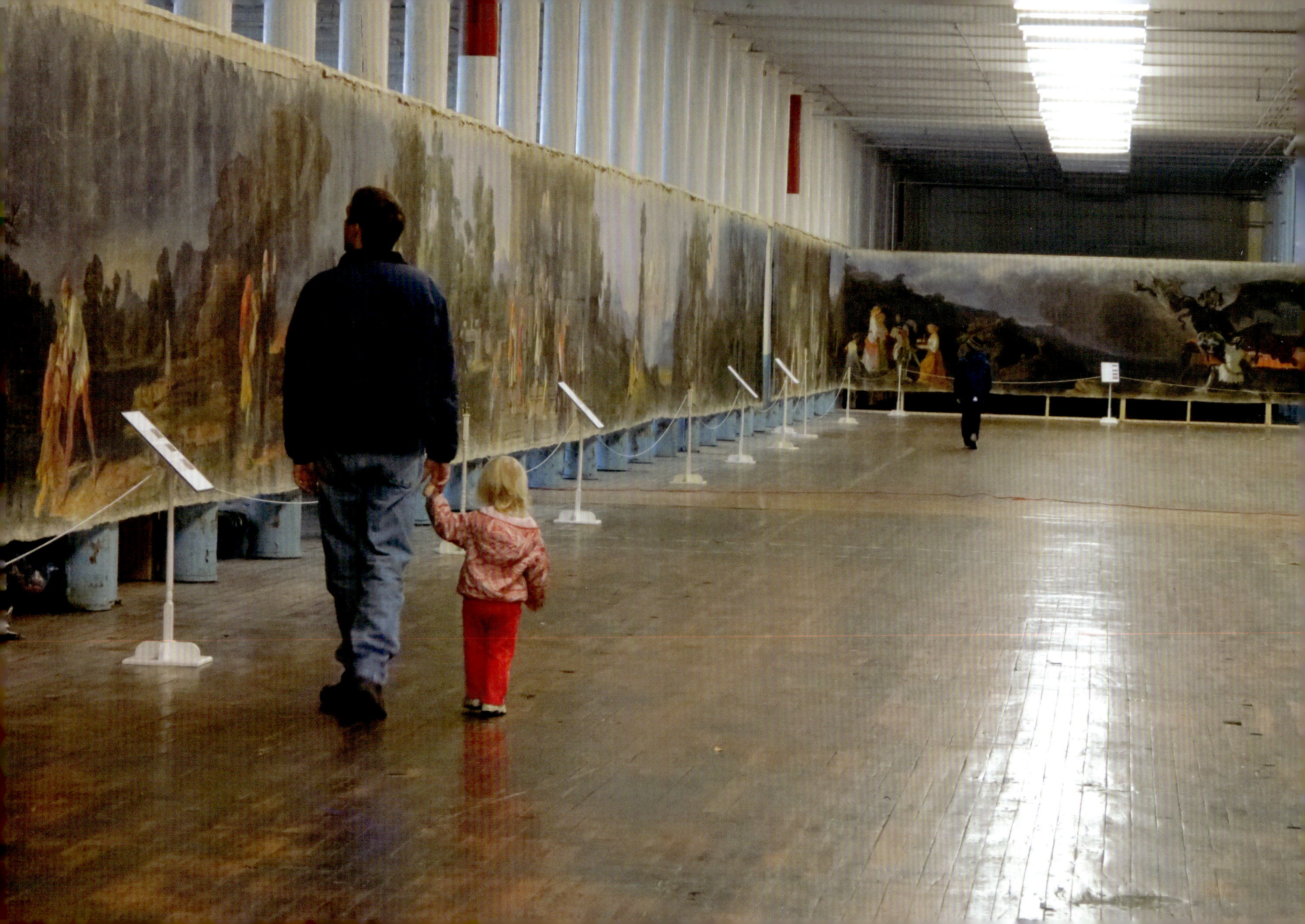

characterized by stops and starts, but also like the panorama, it is here nevertheless: a real and tangible object in today's world, despite the counterflow of technology. But it is not the end of the story, either. Now that the panorama is restored, reanimated, and documented — in these pages and under the stewardship of the Saco Museum — it is finally fully accessible to scholars from a wide variety of disciplines: religious studies, art history, theater, film, literature, and more. With the promise of their future attention and inquiry, it is poised to regain its place within the canon of American art, history, and culture.

opposite:
FIGURE 4.7. Museum visitors of all ages enjoyed the panorama's major exhibition in 2012. Photo by Peter Morelli.

NOTES

"A MORE PERFECT VIEW THEREOF"

This essay relies heavily upon previous scholars' examinations of the *Moving Panorama of Pilgrim's Progress*, notably Kevin J. Avery, Thomas Hardiman Jr., and Peter and Julia Morelli. They have my appreciation and gratitude, as well as that of the Dyer Library/Saco Museum and panorama scholars worldwide, for their disciplined research in unraveling the panorama's mysteries and for guidance and support of this project. Thanks also are due to Leslie Rounds and David Skwire for their review of and suggestions of sources for early versions of this essay.

1 The York Institute merged with the Dyer Library, which serves as Saco's public library, in the 1970s to form the Dyer Library Association. The York Institute's name was changed to the Saco Museum in 2000.

2 *New Hampshire Crossroads*, New Hampshire Public Television, Durham, 1996.

3 Two versions of the *Moving Panorama of Pilgrim's Progress* were produced; the Saco Museum's panorama is the second version, created in 1851. Among the many references to the panorama in art-historical scholarship, before its rediscovery in 1996, are Kevin J. Avery's dissertation *The Panorama and Its Manifestation in American Landscape Painting, 1795–1870*, Columbia University, 1995 (Ann Arbor: UMI Company, 1995), which included a chapter entitled "The Artists' Panorama," 234–68, dedicated to the lost *Moving Panorama of Pilgrim's Progress*.

4 For an overview of moving panoramas in American cultural life, see Kevin J. Avery, "Movies for Manifest Destiny," in this book, originally published in *The Grand Moving Panorama of Pilgrim's Progress* (Montclair, N.J.: Montclair Art Museum, 1999), 1–12. Banvard's panorama is also addressed in John Francis McDermott, *The Lost Panoramas of the Mississippi* (Chicago: University of Chicago Press, 1958), and Joseph Earl Arrington, "John Banvard's Moving Panorama of the Mississippi, Missouri, and Ohio Rivers," *Filson Club Historical Quarterly* 32 (July 1958), 207–40.

5 A list of extant moving panoramas may be found in Erkki Huhtamo, *Illusions in Motion: Media Archaeology of the Moving Panorama and Related Spectacles* (Cambridge, Mass.: MIT Press, 2012). This volume is the most extensive treatment to date on the moving panorama phenomenon.

6 The panorama's history is detailed in Thomas Hardiman Jr., "The Panorama's Progress: The History of Kyle and Dallas's Moving Panorama of Pilgrim's Progress" in this volume, originally published in *The Grand Moving Panorama of Pilgrim's Progress*, 13–24. The genesis of the panorama, as cited by Hardiman, is detailed in the *Bulletin of the American Art-Union* 3, no. 5 (August 1850): 82. An overview of the artists who contributed to the panorama is provided by Peter and Julia Morelli in "The Moving Panorama of Pilgrim's Progress: The Hudson River School's Moving Exhibition," in *The Panorama in the Old World and the New*, ed. Gabriele Koller (Amberg, Germany: International Panorama Council, 2010), 58–62. Hardiman and the Morellis relied heavily on Avery's "The Artists' Panorama."

7 See Hardiman, "The Panorama's Progress," 92. A biographical sketch of May is in David Bernard Dearinger, *Paintings and Sculpture in the Collection of the National Academy of Design: 1826-1925* (New York: Hudson Hills Press, 2004), 383. For titles of some of May's paintings preceding the panorama see Mary Bartlett Cowdrey's *American Academy of Fine Arts and American Art-Union Exhibition Record 1816-1852* (New York: New-York Historical Society, 1953) and her *National Academy of Design Exhibition Record, 1826-1860*, vol. 2 (New York: New-York Historical Society, 1943), 20.

8 He also worked on *Colonel Fremont's Overland Route*, depicting the American West, shortly before collaborating on the *Moving Panorama of Pilgrim's Progress*. See Avery, "Movies for Manifest Destiny," 41. A biographical sketch of Kyle is in Dearinger, *Paintings and Sculpture in the Collection of the National Academy of Design,* 339. For more about Kyle's biography and involvement in the panorama, see also Hardiman, "The Panorama's Progress," 92.

9 Dearinger, *Paintings and Sculpture in the Collection of the National Academy of Design,* 339.

10 *Bulletin of the American Art-Union* 3, no. 5 (August 1850): 82.

11 For more about the panorama's debut, see Hardiman, "The Panorama's Progress," 94.

12 Like Kyle, Dallas had studied in Philadelphia under the portraitist Bass Otis. See Dearinger, *Paintings and Sculpture in the Collection of the National Academy of Design*, 339–40.

13 See Hardiman, "The Panorama's Progress," 94–96, for a full analysis of the changes between the first version and the second.

14 For more on the critical reception of the second version of the panorama, see Hardiman, "The Panorama's Progress," 95 ff.

15 A reviewer from the *Hamilton Spectator* wrote on November 10, 1857: "The panoramas exhibited here within the past few years have been so many, and varied in their character, that anything bearing the name has become to be regarded with indifference. The Bunyan picture is so vastly different from the

generality of panoramas that once seen the beholder cannot but desire to see it again." Quoted in the handbill "The Splendid Moving Mirror of the Bunyan Tableaux!" Polytechnic Institute [location unknown], circa 1857. Collections of the Dyer Library and Saco Museum, Saco, Maine.

16 In the words of a reviewer from the *Hamilton Banner*, October 10, 1857, quoted in "The Splendid Moving Mirror of the Bunyan Tableaux!"

17 The price tag of $10,000 is frequently cited in contemporary reviews, the equivalent of about $280,000 in 2013 dollars. See "The Splendid Moving Mirror of the Bunyan Tableaux!"

18 *Toronto Leader*, October 20, 1857, quoted in "The Splendid Moving Mirror of the Bunyan Tableaux!" (emphasis added).

19 A compelling overview of the book's relevance to American discourse is found in Galen K. Johnson, "*The Pilgrim's Progress* in the History of American Public Discourse," *LATCH* 4 (2011): 1–31.

20 Judging by the numbers of editions in print, *The Pilgrim's Progress* enjoyed two distinct peaks of popularity in nineteenth-century America: from 1800 to 1820, and then again from 1840 to 1850, coinciding with the creation of the panorama. David E. Smith, "Publication of John Bunyan's Works in America," *Bulletin of the New York Public Library* 66 (1962): 632.

21 Hawthorne, *The Celestial Railroad*, 1843. A reprint was published in 1844 by the American Sunday School Union, Philadelphia, under the title *A Visit to the Celestial City*.

22 Johnson, "*The Pilgrim's Progress* in the History of American Public Discourse," 12. The print was copyrighted in 1844 by James Baillie.

23 The artist/printer is unknown; it was probably published in Philadelphia in 1848, according to the Library of Congress.

24 For more on the history of illustrations for *The Pilgrim's Progress,* see Hardiman, "The Panorama's Progress," 93–94, and David E. Smith, "Illustrations of American Editions of Pilgrim's Progress to 1870," *Princeton University Library Chronicle* 26, no. 1 (Autumn 1964): 16–26.

25 A small, rolled paper panorama version of *The Pilgrim's Progress*, designed by Ralph Hudson and published by J. Hudson, London, in 1820, is in the collection of Jacqueline and Jonathan Gestetner. Regarding metamorphoses, see Johnson, "*The Pilgrim's Progress* in the History of American Public Discourse," 5–6.

26 See Hardiman, "The Panorama's Progress," 91.

27 John Martin's portrait engraving of John Bunyan and illustrations of *The Valley of the Shadow of Death* and *The Celestial City* appear in the edition published by J. Murray and J. Major (see n. 37). Henry Courtney Selous's line drawings of *The Pilgrim's Progress* were issued by the London Art-Union in 1844 and republished with text and a second set of illustrations later that year by M. M. Holloway of London (see n. 87). William Blake also made watercolor illustrations for *The Pilgrim's Progress* beginning around 1824, though they were not published in his lifetime; they were reproduced in a Limited Editions Club volume in 1941. For more on Martin and Blake's influence on the

panorama artists, see Hardiman, "The Panorama's Progress," 93.

28 Examples include panoramas of London and John Vanderlyn's famous panorama of Versailles (1819), in the collections of The Metropolitan Museum of Art. See Avery, "Movies for Manifest Destiny," 36–37.

29 See Avery, "Movies for Manifest Destiny," 38–42, for an overview of Mississippi River panoramas. The Grand Panorama of a Whaling Voyage Round the World (1847–1848) by Benjamin Russell (1804–1885) and Caleb Pierce Purrington (1812–1876) is in the collections of the New Bedford Whaling Museum, Massachusetts. See Michael Dyer, "Revisiting the Content and Context of Russell and Purrington's 'Grand Panorama of a Whaling Voyage Round the World'" in Koller, *The Panorama in the Old World and the New*, 52–57, and Kevin J. Avery, "Whaling Voyage Round the World: Russell and Purrington's Moving Panorama and Herman Melville's 'Mighty Book,'" *American Art Journal* 22, no. 1 (Spring 1990): 50–78.

30 Alan Wallach, "Making a Picture of the View from Mount Holyoke," in *American Iconology*, ed. David C. Miller (New Haven and London: Yale University Press, 1993), 82. The connection between panoramas and nineteenth-century landscape painting has also been explored by Avery, *The Panorama and Its Manifestation in American Landscape Painting* and by Angela Miller, *The Imperial Republic: Narratives of National Expansion in American Art, 1820-1860* (Ph.D. diss, Yale University, 1985).

31 The importance of meaningful "associations" for all branches of art, including painting and literature, was a popular theory propounded by Scotsman Archibald Alison. See Alison, *Essays on the Nature and Principles of Taste* (Edinburgh: 1811; reprint: Boston: Cummings and Hillard, 1812). The importance of Alison's theories to early American landscape painting is discussed in Ralph N. Miller, "Thomas Cole and Alison's Essays on Taste," *New York History* 37 (1956): 281–99, and also in Edward J. Nygren, ed., *Views and Visions: American Landscape before 1830* (Washington, D.C.: Corcoran Gallery of Art, 1986), esp. p. 206.

32 For more on the early development of American landscape painting, see Nygren, *Views and Visions.*

33 John Neal, "Fine Arts," in *First Exhibition and Fair of the Maine Charitable Mechanic Association* (Portland: Board of Managers, Maine Charitable Mechanic Association: 1839), 39.

34 "I will now conclude, in the hope that, though feebly urged, the importance of cultivating a taste for scenery will not be forgotten. Nature has spread for us a rich and delightful banquet. Shall we turn from it? We are still in Eden; the wall that shuts us out of the garden is our own ignorance and folly." Thomas Cole, "Essay on American Scenery," *American Monthly Magazine* 1 (January 1836).

35 A complete history of the original four-painting series (several later versions and copies exist) can be found in Paul D. Schweizer, "The Voyage of Life: A Chronology," in *Thomas Cole's Voyage of Life* (Utica, N.Y.: Munson-Williams-Proctor

Institute, 1985). Of the fall and winter from 1839 to 1840, Schweizer notes, "Among the books that Cole was reading at this time was John Bunyan's *Pilgrim's Progress*."

36 Martin's easel painting of *Belshazzar's Feast* provided the source imagery, not entirely to Martin's satisfaction, for a panorama on the same subject. See Ralph Hyde, *Panoramania! The Art and Entertainment of the "All-Embracing" View* (London: Trefoil Publications and Barbican Art Gallery, 1988), 123, as well as Avery, "Movies for Manifest Destiny," 37.

37 John Bunyan, *The Pilgrim's Progress*, with an essay on the "Life of Bunyan" by Robert Southey, Esq., and illustrations by John Martin (London: J. Murray and J. Major, 1830). Collections of the Dyer Library and Saco Museum, Saco, Maine.

38 Quoted in Schweizer, "The Voyage of Life," 48.

39 Taken when three paintings from the uncompleted series were exhibited at the Brooklyn Art Association in 1872, the photographs are reproduced in Ellwood C. Parry, *The Art of Thomas Cole: Ambition and Imagination* (Wilmington: University of Delaware Press, 1988).

40 Though it bears noting that in the Land of Beulah scene for Part II of the panorama (plate 38), there is a prominent cross at the entrance to the city. Intriguingly, it seems possible to pinpoint a moment in Cole's career when his perception of the "city-in-the-sky" changed from a heavenly ideal to a worldly one. In his career-long notebook of painting ideas, housed in the New York State Library in Albany, he dedicates considerable space to a description of a series called "Human Life — An Allegory," clearly an early title for what would become *The Voyage of Life*. In his plan, the final scene would have shown the guardian angel leading the aged pilgrim toward a "city dazzling with golden light"; in the final series, however, the pilgrim is led toward only an unarticulated blaze of light in the clouds. The dazzling, golden city-in-the-sky appears instead in the scene dedicated to *Youth*, where it represents more worldly adolescent dreams and aspirations, clearly indicating a change of outlook on Cole's part between when he articulated his theme in words (probably around 1837, according to Schweizer in "The Voyage of Life") and illustrated it in paint on his easel. See Earl A. Powell, *Thomas Cole* (New York: Harry N. Abrams, 1990), 135.

41 Mark Twain, *The Innocents Abroad, or The New Pilgrims' Progress* (Hartford, Conn.: American Publishing Company, 1869; facsimile ed.: New York: Hippocrene Books). I am grateful to Craig Hotchkiss of the Mark Twain House Museum for bringing this comparison to my attention.

42 William Cullen Bryant, "A Funeral Oration, Occasioned by the Death of Thomas Cole, Delivered before the National Academy of Design, New-York, May 4, 1848" (New York: D. Appleton, 1848), 3–4.

43 Kevin J. Avery has suggested that the incomplete state of Cole's *Cross and the World* also may have provided an incentive for the panorama's creation. Correspondence with the author, February 2012.

44 *A Descriptive Catalogue of the Panorama of Bunyan's Pilgrim's*

Progress (New York: R. Craighead, 1851). Catalogues dated 1854, 1856, and 1867 — which give the author as R. J. Greenwood and are titled *A Descriptive Catalogue of the Bunyan Tableaux* (Albany, N.Y.: J. Munsell) — also were produced. A copy of the 1856 catalogue is in the collections of the Dyer Library and Saco Museum, Saco, Maine.

45 The painting, like the panorama, was thought lost for many years until its rediscovery and the confirmation of its attribution in 1980 (though it was well known during its original period of creation). See J. Gray Sweeney, "'Endued with Rare Genius": Frederic Edwin Church's 'To the Memory of Cole,'" *Smithsonian Studies in American Art* 2, no. 1 (Winter 1988): 44–71.

46 Sweeney, "'Endued with Rare Genius," 49.

47 The painting is praised in *The Knickerbocker, or New-York Monthly Magazine* 29 (June 1847): 571. Talbot also exhibited a painting entitled *The Departure of Christian from the Palace, Called Beautiful*, in 1849. For more about Talbot, see Dearinger, *Paintings and Sculpture in the Collection of the National Academy of Design,* 382–83.

48 Cropsey to his wife, July 7, 1850, quoted in "'The Brushes He Painted with That Last Day Are There . . .': Jasper F. Cropsey's Letter to His Wife, Describing Thomas Cole's Home and Studio, July, 1850," *American Art Journal* 16 (Summer 1984): 81.

49 It bears noting that there are notable differences, as well as similarities, between *Ideal Landscape* and Cropsey's *Land of Beulah.* This could suggest that *Ideal Landscape* is actually the study for *The Water of the River of Life*, the other panorama scene designed by Cropsey, now lost. Complicating this hypothesis is the fact that the poem by Alfred B. Street that serves as an eyewitness description of *The Water of the River of Life* (see p. 21) does not resonate particularly well with *Ideal Landscape.* For the purposes of this essay, I have elected to accept the Newington-Cropsey Foundation's position that *Ideal Landscape* is a study for *Land of Beulah.* See the entries for "Ideal Landscape: Homage to Thomas Cole" in Newington-Cropsey Foundation, *Jasper Francis Cropsey: Catalogue Raisonné,* vol. 1, 1842–1863 (Hastings-on-Hudson, N.Y.: Newington-Cropsey Foundation, 2013) as well as Barbara Novak, ed., *The Thyssen-Bornemisza Collection: Nineteenth-Century American Painting* (1986; reprint: New York, London, and Paris: Abbeville Press, Artabras, 1991).

50 In an e-mail to the author dated June 14, 2011, Anthony Speiser of the Newington-Cropsey Foundation wrote, "It has been our view that Cropsey was asked to be involved in the panorama due to his status as a leading American artist and probably his connections in the NY art organizations."

51 The complex relationship between nature, religion, and art — and how it intersected with religious and secular rhetoric in America during this time — is the subject of the chapter entitled "The Final Tribute" in Neil Harris, *The Artist in American Society: The Formative Years, 1790–1860* (Chicago: University of Chicago Press, 1966; reprint, 1982), 300–16. See also

the chapter entitled "Millennium/Apocalypse: The Ambiguous Mode" in Angela Miller's *The Empire of the Eye: Landscape Representation and American Cultural Politics, 1825–1875* (Ithaca and London: Cornell University Press, 1993), 107–36.

52 The remarks of the Reverend Samuel Osgood at the opening of an American Art-Union exhibition are quoted in *Literary World* 9 (September 27, 1851): 252, cited in Harris, *The Artist in American Society*, 305.

53 *Puritan Recorder*, undated, quoted in the broadside *The Story in Color!! Bunyan's Pilgrim's Progress*, 1851, Connecticut Historical Society, Hartford, Connecticut.

54 Robert S. Duncanson to the Reverend James Francis Conover, December 30, 1854, cited in Joseph D. Ketner II, "An Enclave of African American Artists in Antebellum Cincinnati: James P. Ball and Robert S. Duncanson" (lecture presented at the Ira Wallach Art Gallery, Columbia University, N.Y., September 13, 2012). Ketner goes on to say that the resulting painting, four by six feet in its completed state and exhibited in 1856, is now lost.

55 Ketner says that it is likely Duncanson saw the panorama in Detroit in February 1853 (ibid.). He also notes that "it is reasonable to assume that Duncanson saw the panorama when it was in Cincinnati in 1853. The comparison of his drawing to the scene in the Saco panorama is too close to be coincidence. In addition, one of his patrons, William Brisbane (an abolitionist), wrote in his diary for January 7, 1853, 'This evening (having free tickets) I took my family to see the Panorama of Bunyan's Dream & to hear the Baker family sing.'" E-mail correspondence with the author, August 18, 2013.

56 The reviewer for the *Bulletin of the American Art-Union* makes reference to the "views of the *Water of Life* (from designs of Church, we believe)" suggesting that Cropsey's panorama scene was influenced by an earlier work by Church. *Bulletin of the American Art-Union* 3, no. 9 (December 1850): 156.

57 Cropsey's journal is in the collections of the Newington-Cropsey Foundation; I am grateful to Anthony Speiser for providing this citation.

58 *The Poems of Alfred B. Street*, vol. 2 (New York: Hurd and Houghton, 1867), 200–201. Collections of the Dyer Library and Saco Museum, Saco, Maine.

59 The British artist Henry Melville published a print with the same title through Fisher, Son & Co. in 1845; its landscape forms seem analogous to American landscape painting of the time and may have informed Church's painting or Cropsey's panorama scene or both. See also n. 49 for a discussion of whether Cropsey's easel painting *Ideal Landscape* may give some clue as to this scene's appearance.

60 Cropsey to Fletcher Williams, October 1855, Newington-Cropsey Foundation, cited in William S. Talbot, *Jasper F. Cropsey, 1823–1900* (Washington, D.C.: Smithsonian Institution Press, 1970), 29 n. 39. That letter from Cropsey to Williams was followed by another dated January 8, 1856 (Newington-Cropsey Foundation), in which Cropsey describes the planned series in detail — including scenes of Vanity Fair, the Valley of

the Shadow of Death, and the Celestial City — making explicit the connection to Bunyan. There is no evidence that the series was ever completed.

61 Cropsey's religious ideals as related to his artistic ambitions are explored in Anthony Speiser, "Jasper F. Cropsey: Painter of Faith," the introduction to Newington-Cropsey Foundation, *Jasper Francis Cropsey: Catalogue Raisonné,* vol. 1, 1842–1863.

62 *Bulletin of the American Art-Union* 3, no. 5 (August 1850): 82.

63 This aspect of Huntington's work is fully explored in Wendy Greenhouse, "Daniel Huntington and the Ideal of Christian Art," *Winterthur Portfolio* 31, no. 2/3 (Summer/Autumn 1996): 103–140.

64 William H. Gerdts gleans this from Huntington's 1851 lecture on Christian art, in the collections of the Winterthur Library. William H. Gerdts, "Daniel Huntington's *Mercy's Dream*: A Pilgrimage through Bunyanesque Imagery," *Winterthur Portfolio* 14, no. 2 (Summer 1979): 173 (entire article 171–94). Huntington mentions Bunyan by name on page 11 of the transcribed lecture, provided by Winterthur Library: Daniel Huntington, *Lecture on Christian Art Read at the National Academy of Design*, New York, July 1851, Winterthur Library, Winterthur, Del., manuscript collections, doc. 519. Huntington's concept "of his own artistic career as a kind of visual ministry" is also expanded in Greenhouse, "Daniel Huntington and the Ideal of Christian Art," 114–15.

65 "The well loved Overbeck is but one instance (though surely a marked one) of those Pilgrims in art, who have kept their eyes steadily fixed on the Heavenly city, and who if they have looked back — it has only been to take lessons from the monuments which former pilgrims have left along the way, and not to be distracted by the follies and madness of the crowds that press around them." Huntington, *Lecture on Christian Art*, 30.

66 Greenhouse, "Daniel Huntington and the Ideal of Christian Art," 111–12.

67 *Newark Daily Advertiser*, April 30, 1851.

68 Greenhouse, "Daniel Huntington and the Ideal of Christian Art," 125.

69 *Bulletin of the American Art-Union* 3, no. 5 (August 1850): 82.

70 An iconic example is Piero della Francesca's *Madonna della Misericordia* (1462, Pinacoteca Comunale, Sansepolcro, Italy).

71 Cole's biographer, Louis Legrand Noble, dedicated a page and a half to a discussion of the painting. Louis Legrand Noble, *The Life and Works of Thomas Cole*, 3rd ed. (New York: Sheldon, Blakeman, 1856), 349–50.

72 *American Repertory of Artists, Sciences and Manufactures* 3, no. 5 (June 1841): 356, cited in Gerdts, "Daniel Huntington's *Mercy's Dream*," 180.

73 He also returned to Mercy as a subject in 1847, with *Mercy Fainting at the Wicket Gate*. See *Catalogue of Paintings by Daniel Huntington, N.A., Exhibiting at the Art Union Buildings* (New York: Snowden, 1850), 31.

74 See Gerdts, "Daniel Huntington's *Mercy's Dream*," 183–87.

75 As Hardiman notes in "The Panorama's Progress," 95, "This alteration of the second version is documented in the *Newark*

Daily Advertiser of May 29, 1851, which reported 'A new scene 'Mercy's Dream' has been added.'"

76 Gianlorenzo Bernini's marble *The Ecstasy of St. Theresa* (1652, Santa Maria della Vittoria, Rome) is a familiar example. For more on this tradition in the visual arts, see Robert T. Petersson, *The Art of Ecstasy: Teresa, Bernini, and Crashaw* (New York: Athenaeum, 1974).

77 Huntington also uses similar landscape motifs in his 1850 canvas *In the Mountain Fastness* (University of Michigan Museum of Art). Greenhouse ("Daniel Huntington and the Ideal of Christian Art," 114) and the UMMA website (http://quod.lib.umich.edu/m/musart/x-1916.1/1916.1.jpg) both claim that the title of this work is taken from a line in *The Pilgrim's Progress*; however, I can find no evidence of the phrase "mountain fastness" in Bunyan's text. While the mountaintop setting is suggestive of several passages in Bunyan's narrative, including Legality Hill, Mount Sinai, and more, nothing in the composition supports a specific connection to the story.

78 Or is it a sun*set?* In his article about Church's *To the Memory of Cole,* J. Gray Sweeney has some interesting things to say about identifying glowing red skies as either early- or late-day effects, including the possibility that some paintings of this era are intentionally ambiguous. Sweeney, "'Endued with Rare Genius,'" 54, 57, and 64.

79 "That living picture, the plodding dust-loving multitude saw it not — But there was one, who gazed long and wistfully at it — on whose soul all its beauty is impressed forever — the humble landscape painter; and he will perpetuate it in colors, if not so bright, at least more enduring, and shall it not be for the Glory of the Creator?" Daniel Huntington, *Lecture on Christian Art*, 9. Greenhouse also cites the lecture's advocacy of landscape painting in "Daniel Huntington and the Ideal of Christian Art," 114. A painted manifestation of Huntington's ambitions for landscape painting can be found in his *In the Mountain Fastness* (ibid., n. 77).

80 *Home Journal*, November 23, 1851, quoted in Greenwood, *A Descriptive Catalogue of the Bunyan Tableaux*, 1856, 44 (emphasis added).

81 "Entering into the dreamer's spirit, the artist has called into being forms of loveliness and grace, and demons of horrifying deformity. Frowning cliffs, yawning chasms, smiling landscapes and sunny skies pass before the eye, and work upon the imagination with such power and force as to lead the mind from nature up to nature's God, whose kingdom lies beyond the black and dismal sea of death, from the sight of which even Christian averted his gaze till reassured by hopeful." *Hamilton Banner*, Saturday, October 10, 1857, quoted in the handbill "The Splendid Moving Mirror of the Bunyan Tableaux!" (emphasis added).

82 Ibid.

83 Information about Duggan and his painting *Lazar House in the Tropics* is gleaned from his entry in Dearinger, *Paintings and Sculpture in the Collection of the National Academy of Design,* 167–68. The painting is also explored in Gail E. Husch, *Some-*

thing Coming: Apocalyptic Expectation and Mid-Nineteenth-Century American Painting (Hanover, N.H.: University Press of New England, 2000), 79.

84 "... all maladies / Of ghastly spasm or racking tortures, qualms / Of heart-sick agony, all feverous kinds / Demoniac phrenzy, moping melancholy, / and moon-struck madness, pining atrophy, / Maramus, and wide wresting pestilence, / Dire was the tossing and deep the groans, despair / Tending the sick, busiest from couch to couch." Quoted in Dearinger, *Paintings and Sculpture in the Collection of the National Academy of Design,* 168.

85 Kevin Avery has observed a marked similarity between the figure of Giant Despair and Samuel F. B. Morse's *Dying Hercules* of 1812. Correspondence with the author, May 2012.

86 A thorough examination of Selous's life and work can be found online on *The Victorian Web: Literature, History, and Culture in the Age of Victoria*: www.victorianweb.org/art/illustration/selous.

87 John Bunyan, *Pilgrim's Progress Illustrated*, ill. Henry Courtney Selous (London: M. M. Holloway, 1844). Collections of the Dyer Library and Saco Museum, Saco, Maine.

88 *The Victorian Web* cites Selous's involvement in the stationary panorama *Description of Summer and Winter Views of the Polar Regions* (1850).

89 See n. 81.

90 Though he was also a painter, exhibiting work at the National Academy from the mid-1840s on. He became an honorary "professional" member in 1852 and was a full-fledged member from 1853 until his death in 1888. A chronology of Darley's career can be found in Christine Anne Hahler, . . . *Illustrated by Darley* (Wilmington: Delaware Art Museum, 1978), 1–2. This volume, the catalogue for a 1978 exhibition, is the only substantive published source on Darley's life and career; all subsequent details about Darley are gleaned from it.

91 Then called the "Century Association."

92 Catlin published his illustrated, multivolume *Letters and Notes on the Manners, Customs, and Conditions of the North American Tribes* in 1841. For a thoughtful and substantive discussion of the buffalo hunter theme in Darley's work, including Catlin's influence, see Martin E. Peterson, "On the Nature of the Horse of the American West in Nineteenth Century Art," *Great Plains Quarterly* 7 (Winter 1986): 39–42. See also Paul Chadbourne Mills, *The Buffalo Hunter and Other Related Versions of the Subject in Nineteenth-Century American Art and Literature* (Santa Barbara: Santa Barbara Museum of Art, 1973).

93 Such as Albert Bierstadt, *The Last of the Buffalo*, 1888 (Corcoran Gallery of Art).

94 Hahler, . . . *Illustrated by Darley,* 66.

95 For more on panoramas' contributions to the origins of "media culture," see the chapter entitled "From Panoramas to Media Culture" in Huhtamo, *Illusions in Motion: Media Archaeology of the Moving Panorama and Related Spectacles*, 361–69.

MOVIES FOR MANIFEST DESTINY

This essay was written for the catalogue *The Grand Moving Panorama of Pilgrim's Progress* (ISBN 0-936489-57-X), which accompanied the exhibition of the same title that premiered January 31, 1999, at the Montclair Art Museum and toured to two other venues. The exhibition was organized by the Montclair Art Museum. The essay is reprinted here, with minimal revisions, with the permission of the Montclair Art Museum.

1 Erkki Huhtamo's *Illusions in Motion: Media Archaeology of the Moving Panorama and Related Spectacles* (Cambridge, Mass.: MIT Press, 2012) is the most substantive treatment of moving panoramas to date. Prior to the publication of Huhtamo's book, moving panoramas were generally treated in the context of the larger panorama phenomenon of the nineteenth century. Probably the most comprehensive and analytical of those is Stefan Oettermann, *The Panorama; History of a Mass Medium,* translated by Deborah Lucas Schneider (Reprint: New York: Zone Books, 1997), esp. 323–44. See also Ralph Hyde, *Panoramania!* (London: Barbican Art Gallery, 1988), esp. 131–68. Perhaps the most entertaining account of moving panoramas is in Richard D. Altick, *The Shows of London* (Cambridge, Mass.: Harvard University Press, Belknap Press, 1978), 198–210.

2 The length of moving panoramas is addressed with reference to those of the Mississippi River in John Francis McDermott, *The Lost Panoramas of the Mississippi* (Chicago: University of Chicago Press, 1958), 165–67.

3 The invention of the panorama is described in Oettermann, *The Panorama*, 99–115.

4 Quoted in Oettermann, *The Panorama*, 101, 103.

5 Ibid., 7; for panoramic precursors of the movies, see C. W. Ceram, *Archaeology of the Cinema* (London: Hudson and Thames, 1965) and the chapter entitled "From Panoramas to Media Culture" in Huhtamo, *Illusions in Motion*, 361–69.

6 The history of Vanderlyn's panorama is described in detail in Kevin J. Avery and Peter M. Fodera, *John Vanderlyn's Panoramic View of the Palace and Gardens of Versailles* (New York: Metropolitan Museum of Art, 1988).

7 For the invention and spread of the diorama, see Oettermann, *The Panorama*, 74–82.

8 Martin's direct influence on silent movie epics such as D. W. Griffith's *Intolerance* (1916) is discussed in William Feaver, *John Martin* (Oxford: Clarendon Press, 1975), 212–13.

9 Altick, *The Shows of London*, 414–415; see also Hyde, *Panoramania!*, 123.

10 For the influence of panoramas and dioramas on Cole, see Ellwood C. Parry III, *The Art of Thomas Cole* (Newark: University of Delaware Press, 1988), 174–76, 212, 246.

11 The career of Banvard (and of other Mississippi River panoramists) is described at length in McDermott, *The Lost Panoramas of the Mississippi*, esp. 19–46; see also Joseph Earl Arrington, "John Banvard's Moving Panorama of the Mississippi, Missouri, and Ohio Rivers," *Filson Club Historical Quarterly* 32 (July 1958), 207–40.

12 A blurb attributed to the American statesman Edward Everett, that Banvard was "the first projector of this highly instructive class of paintings," was printed on the London editions of the panorama program, and it was reprinted as fact in a review of the panorama from an unidentified newspaper in Bath, England. This and other reviews of his panorama were clipped and saved by Banvard in a scrapbook now in the Minnesota Historical Society. See Kevin J. Avery, "The Panorama and Its Manifestation in American Landscape Painting, 1795–1870" (Ph.D. diss., Columbia University, 1995), 121.

13 For the origins of the moving panorama in Britain, see Altick, *The Shows of London*, 198–204.

14 For the Hudson River panorama, see Altick, *The Shows of London*, 204; George C. D. Odell, *Annals of the New York Stage*, vol. 3 (New York: Columbia University Press, 1928), 407–8; William Dunlap, *A Trip to Niagara* (New York: E. B. Clayton, 1830); and Oral S. Coad, *William Dunlap* (1917; reprint: New York: Russell and Russell, 1962), 107–8.

15 Banvard's exploits on the Mississippi are amusingly retold by him in "Adventures of an Artist," in *Description of Banvard's Panorama of the Mississippi River* (Boston: Putnam, 1847), 4–5.

16 McDermott, *The Lost Panoramas of the Mississippi*, 49–50.

17 "Lewis's Panorama of the Mississippi River," *Western Journal* 3 (October 1849): 70.

18 Arrington, "John Banvard's Moving Panorama of the Mississippi," 210–14.

19 Quoted from a caption to a broadside illustration of Banvard exhibiting his panorama to Queen Victoria and her entourage at Windsor Castle, printed for a performance in North Shields, Leeds, England, about 1851, Banvard Scrapbook, Minnesota Historical Society, St. Paul.

20 Clipping of undated review in the *Times* (London), Banvard Scrapbook, Minnesota Historical Society, St. Paul, 17.

21 "Banvard's Panorama of the Mississippi and Missouri Rivers," *Illustrated London News*, December 9, 1848, quoted in McDermott, *The Lost Panoramas of the Mississippi*, 43.

22 All described in McDermott, *The Lost Panoramas of the Mississippi*, 47ff.

23 John Francis McDermott, "Gold Rush Movies," *California Historical Society Quarterly* 33 (March 1954): 29–31.

24 John C. Fremont, *Report of the Exploring Expedition to the Rocky Mountains in the Year 1842, and to Oregon and North California in the Years 1843–44* (Washington, D.C.: Gales and Seaton, 1845). For the panorama, see Joseph Earl Arrington, "Skirving Moving Panorama: Colonel Fremont's Western Expedition Pictorialized," *Oregon Historical Quarterly* 45 (June 1964): 139–43.

25 "Diorama of Fremont's Overland-Route to Oregon, Texas [*sic*], and California," *Athenaeum* (London: April 27, 1850): 457.

26 Curtis Dahl, "Artemus Ward: Comic Panoramist," *New England Quarterly* 32 (March 1959): 476–78; T. W. Robertson and E. P. Hingston, eds., *Artemus Ward's Lecture* (New York: G. W Carleton, 1869).

27 Elisha Kent Kane, *Arctic Explorations: The Second Grinnell Expedition in Search of Sir John Franklin,* 2 vols. (1856; reprint: London: T. Nelson and Sons, 1861); for the panorama, see [William Morton], *Dr. Kane's Arctic Voyages: Explanatory of a Pictorial Illustration of the Second Grinnell Expedition* (New York: n.p., 1857).

28 "T. F. Meagher's Illustrated Narrative of Central America," *New York Herald*, November 9, 1858, p. 5; Meagher's lecture was formalized in an article, including illustrations, entitled "Holidays in Costa Rica," *Harper's New Monthly Magazine* 20 (December 1859): 18–38; (January 1860): 145–64; (February 1860): 304–25.

29 Altick, *The Shows of London*, 207–8.

30 Kevin J. Avery, "Whaling Voyage Round the World: Russell and Purrington's Moving Panorama and Herman Melville's 'Mighty Book,'" *American Art Journal* 22 (1990): 78.

31 Joseph Earl Arrington, "Godfrey N. Frankenstein's Moving Panorama of Niagara Falls," *New York History* 49 (April 1968): 169–99.

32 For the relationship of American and British painting exhibitions to panoramic exhibitions, see Kevin J. Avery, "*The Heart of the Andes* Exhibited: Frederic E. Church's Window on the Equatorial World," *American Art Journal* 18, no. 1 (1986): 52–72.

33 See Joseph Earl Arrington, "William Burr's Moving Panorama of the Great Lakes, the Niagara, St. Lawrence, and Saguenay Rivers," *Ontario History* 51 (Summer 1959): 141–62.

34 *Italia: A Hand-Book Descriptive of the New Series of Italian Views* (1855; reprint: Philadelphia: n.p., 1867).

35 Arrington, "John Banvard's Moving Panorama of the Mississippi," 233–37.

THE PANORAMA'S PROGRESS

This essay was originally written for the catalogue *The Grand Moving Panorama of Pilgrim's Progress* (ISBN 0-936489-57-X), which accompanied the exhibition of the same title that premiered January 31, 1999, at the Montclair Art Museum and toured to two other venues. The exhibition was organized by the Montclair Art Museum. A revised version of the essay is reprinted here with the permission of the Montclair Art Museum.

1 *Biddeford* [Maine] *Record*, October 12, 1896.

2 Notices in the *Portland Daily Press* of February 21, 1872, and July 2, 1875, indicate that it was shown in a venue known as the "Music Hall."

3 The York Institute records from January 5, 1897, read: "The president was authorized to use the hall to exhibit the panorama of Pilgrim's Progress." Dyer Library/Saco Museum, Saco, Maine, museum archives.

4 "What Do You Know about Biddeford?" unidentified newspaper clipping, November 17, 1925. Dyer Library/Saco Museum, Saco, Maine, Dyer Library Archives, Andrews Scrap Book no. 2, p. 108, col. 4.

5 John Hanners, "John Banvard's Mississippi Panorama," *American History Illustrated* 17, no. 7 (1982): 30–39. For a more thorough treatment of the influence of panoramas in American art and society, see Kevin J. Avery, "Movies for Manifest Destiny" in this book, originally published in *The Grand Moving Panorama of Pilgrim's Progress* (Montclair, N.J.: Montclair Art Museum, 1999), 1–12, and his *The Panorama and Its Manifestation in American Landscape Painting, 1795–1870* (Ph.D. diss.: Columbia University, New York, 1995). The chapter entitled "The Artists' Panorama" deals specifically with the *Moving Panorama of Pilgrim's Progress*.

6 It was already in its tenth edition by 1685. S. Austin Attibone, *A Critical Dictionary of English Literature and British and American Authors* (Philadelphia, 1858; reprint: Detroit: Gale Research, 1965), 283.

7 Ibid., 284.

8 *The Union* [Saco, Maine], December 3, 1845, and June 3, 1846; George C. Groce and David H. Wallace, *The New York Historical Society's Dictionary of Artists in America 1564–1860* (New Haven and London: Yale University Press, 1975), 296.

9 James G. Wilson and John Fiske, eds., *Appleton's Cyclopedia of American Biography* (New York: D. Appleton, 1888), 272.

10 Mary Bartlett Cowdrey, *American Academy of Fine Arts and American Art-Union Exhibition Record 1816–1852* (New York: New-York Historical Society, 1953), and Mary Bartlett Cowdrey, *National Academy of Design Exhibition Record, 1826–1860* (New York: New-York Historical Society, 1943). In the panorama, the designs for *Christian at the Cross* and *Mercy Faints at the Wicket Gate* were by Edward Harrison May, and the design for *The River of the Water of Life* was by Jasper Cropsey.

11 Correspondence from Robert Kyle McCord to the author, June 20, 1997; Joseph Earl Arrington, "William Burr's Moving Panorama of the Great Lakes, the Niagara, St. Lawrence, and Saguenay Rivers," *Ontario History* 51, no. 3 (1959): 2–4.

12 Ibid. After the *Moving Panorama of Pilgrim's Progress*, Kyle and Dallas went on to collaborate on a Mississippi River panorama in 1852, traveling together to New Orleans to research it. They also exhibited a related painting, to which they both contributed, at the National Academy in 1854. The same exhibition also included three solo compositions by Dallas that were clearly derived from the trip to New Orleans they made to research this later panorama. See Bernard Dearinger, *Paintings and Sculpture in the Collection of the National Academy of Design: 1826–1925* (New York: Hudson Hills Press, 2004), 339–40.

13 *Home Journal*, March 20, 1858, cited in Arrington, "William Burr's Moving Panorama of the Great Lakes."

14 Martin had a direct influence on panorama artist Henry Courtney Selous as his teacher and mentor. For a discussion of John Martin's influence on diorama exhibitions and Selous's panorama based on Martin's engraving of Milton's *Pandemonium* (1827), see Ralph Hyde, *Panoramania!* (London: Trefoil Publications in association with Barbican Art Gallery, 1988), 74 and 123.

15 *Literary World,* December 7, 1850.

16 See Jessica Skwire Routhier, "'A More Perfect View Thereof': Landscape, Religion, and the Artistic Underpinnings of the Panorama" in this book, 31.

17 Henry Wemyss, "Blake Watercolors from the Frick Collection," *Sotheby's Preview* (November 1996): 18–19.

18 David E. Smith, "Illustrations of American Editions of *Pilgrim's Progress* to 1870," *Princeton University Library Chronicle* 26, no 1 (Autumn 1964): 16–26.

19 [Biddeford, Maine] *Union and Journal*, October 22, 1858.

20 For an extensive discussion of the panorama's tour and reception in the press, see Avery, "The Artists' Panorama," 234–49.

21 Ibid., 246.

22 *Bulletin of the American Art-Union* (June 1851): 48. Duplicate copies of successful panoramas were not uncommon. Kyle painted two copies of his panorama of the St. Lawrence River in 1848 (Arrington, "William Burr's Moving Panorama of the Great Lakes," 25). The Saco Museum's panorama is documented as the second May and Kyle panorama in contemporary advertisements and by Jacob Dallas's signature embedded in the scene entitled *Christian Reposing After the Combat*. The "JD" next to the jug in front of Christian's shield matches the way that Dallas signed his wood engravings. The distinction between the two panoramas is outlined in the *Newark Daily Advertiser* of April 30, 1851.

23 *Bulletin of the American Art-Union* (June 1851): 50.

24 For example, the notice in the *Newark Daily Advertiser* of April 30, 1851, analyzes the differences between the two versions but never mentions May. All subsequent advertisements for this version credit Kyle and Dallas, and sometimes Wright, but never May.

25 Groce and Wallace, *The New York Historical Society's Dictionary*, 704.

26 See, for example, *Salem Register*, January 29, 1855.

27 "Another Pilgrim's Progress," *New York Tribune*, April 30, 1851, p. 5. I am grateful to Dr. Kevin Avery for this reference.

28 See R. J. Greenwood, *Descriptive Catalogue of the Bunyan Tableaux* (Albany: Joel Munsell, 1856), Collections of the Dyer Library and Saco Museum, Saco, Maine. Catalogues dated 1851 (titled *A Descriptive Catalogue of the Panorama of Bunyan's Pilgrim's Progress;* New York: R. Craighead), 1854, and 1867 also were produced.

29 *The Story in Color!! Bunyan's Pilgrim's Progress* (New York: George F. Nesbitt, circa 1851–1854). Olana State Historic Site, Hudson, New York.

30 These include the addition of Dallas's monogram in the latter scene; see n. 22.

31 Some amount of confusion remains over changes between the first version and the second. *The Arming of Christian* seems to appear in a different sequence in the second version, which could indicate alternatively that the scene that originally preceded it, *Virgins Pointing Out the Delectable Mountains*, was among those omitted in the second version, and the scene currently identified as such is merely transitional landscape of

the kind described in the passage quoted in n. 35. (One also could argue that the scene currently identified as *The Interpreter's House* is more likely a transitional scene, and that a more substantive view of the exterior of the Interpreter's House was omitted between the first version of the panorama and the second.) Similar ambiguity exists around *Mercy Faints at the Wicket Gate*; either the scene preceding it is *Christiana and Her Family at the Spring*, a scene from the original version of the panorama, which would place the scenes rather dramatically out of sequence with Bunyan's story, or it is a new scene by an unknown designer showing Christiana and her fellow travelers taking leave of Mrs. Timorous and the City of Destruction. This book, based on Jessica Skwire Routhier's recent scholarship, supports the latter thesis as more harmonious with Bunyan's narrative and with the panorama designers' presumed intent.

32 "We are perhaps least pleased with the design of [the] Pilgrim ascending the 'Hill Difficulty.' It is too much like a hunter climbing rocks." *Commercial Advertiser* quoted in Greenwood, *A Descriptive Catalogue of the Bunyan Tableaux*, 1856, 30.

33 And also possibly *Christiana and Her Family Leave the City of Destruction*; see n. 31. It is also possible, of course, that new scenes were added into the portion of the panorama that is now missing (see n. 59).

34 I am grateful to Dr. Kevin Avery for this reference.

35 *Bulletin of the American Art-Union* (December 1850): 155–56.

36 *Newark Daily Advertiser*, May 3, 1851. I am grateful to Dr. Kevin Avery for this reference.

37 *Portsmouth Morning Chronicle*, February 9, 1855.

38 [Concord, N.H.] *Independent Democrat*, March 15, 1855.

39 *Picayune*, quoted in Greenwood, *A Descriptive Catalogue of the Bunyan Tableaux*, 1856, 31.

40 *Eastern Argus* [Portland, Maine], September 25, 1855.

41 Ibid.

42 Fifteen feet, in the case of the *Moving Panorama of Pilgrim's Progress*. This measurement was confirmed when a full-scale replica of the panorama was created and performed on the stage of Saco City Hall Auditorium throughout the second half of 2012. The proscenium was designed with a fifteen-foot window in order to accommodate the average width of the panorama's scenes.

43 *Home Journal*, quoted in Greenwood, *A Descriptive Catalogue of the Bunyan Tableaux*, 1856, 30–31.

44 *St. Louis Intelligencer*, quoted in the handbill "The Splendid Moving Mirror of the Bunyan Tableaux!" St. Lawrence Hall, Toronto, October 22, 1857, Metropolitan Toronto Library, Canadian History Department. Ottawa: Canadian Institute for Historical Microreproductions, 1987.

45 *Literary World*, November 23, 1850, 411.

46 *Union and Journal* [Biddeford, Maine], October 22, 1858.

47 *Bulletin of the American Art-Union* (June 1851).

48 The designs are documented in Cropsey's account book for September 15, 1850: "for two designs for Panorama 40.00,"

cited in William S. Talbot, *Jasper F. Cropsey 1823–1900* (New York and London: Garland Publishing, 1977), 311. I am grateful to Kenneth Maddox for this reference. A painting in the Thyssen-Bornemisza collection is thought to be a study for the *Land of Beulah*. See Routhier, "A More Perfect View Thereof," 18–20, as well as the entries for "Ideal Landscape: Hommage to Thomas Cole," in *The Thyssen-Bornemisza Collection: Nineteenth-Century American Painting,* ed. Barbara Novak (1986; reprint: New York, London, and Paris: Abbeville Press, Artabras, 1991) and Newington-Cropsey Foundation. *Jasper Francis Cropsey: Catalogue Raisonné Volume 1, 1842–1863*. Hastings-on-Hudson, N.Y.: Newington-Cropsey Foundation, 2013.

49 *The Pilgrim's Progress* (New York: American Tract Society), n.d. Collections of the Dyer Library and Saco Museum, Saco, Maine, gift of Thomas Hardiman.

50 John Bunyan, *The Pilgrim's Progress: Cassell's Illustrated Bunyan*, ill. Henry Courtney Selous and M. Paolo Priolo (London: Cassell, Petter and Galpin, n.d.; circa 1870). The Dyer Library and Saco Museum owns an American edition: John Bunyan, *The Pilgrim's Progress*, ill. Henry Courtney Selous and M. Paolo Priolo (Boston and St. Louis: I. N. Richardson, 1870). Collections of the Dyer Library and Saco Museum, Saco, Maine, museum purchase.

51 For more on Hammatt Billings, see James F. O'Gorman, *Accomplished in All Departments of Art: Hammatt Billings of Boston, 1818–1874* (Amherst: University of Massachusetts Press, 1998). The *Pilgrim's Progress* print is discussed and illustrated on p. 97.

52 Smith, "Illustrations of American editions of *Pilgrim's Progress* to 1870," 24; also see Avery, "The Artists' Panorama," 247.

53 "What Do You Know about Biddeford?"

54 *Portland Daily Press*, February 21, 1872, and July 2, 1875. The clippings promote performances of a panorama of *The Pilgrim's Progress*, "endorsed by a very large number of clergymen in all parts of the country" (1872) and "highly recommended by Rev. Dr. Cuyler of Brooklyn, and other well-known clergymen, as well as by the leading newspapers of the country" (1875), at Portland's Music Hall. The suggestion of a national reputation for this panorama — added to the fact that we know that Kyle and Dallas's panorama ended up in southern Maine — suggests that it was the Saco Museum's *Moving Panorama of Pilgrim's Progress*. The 1872 listing also indicates that the same panorama "was exhibited in this city about four years since," thus documenting an 1868 performance of the panorama, though the specific venue is unknown.

55 "What Do You Know about Biddeford?"

56 "The celebrated Panorama of Bunyan's Pilgrim's Progress, the most successful and best known exhibition of the kind which ever traveled, was also for many years owned though not exhibited by him personally." George Presbury Rowell & Co., "Charles A. Shaw," in *The Men Who Advertise: An Account of Successful Advertisers Together with Hints on the Methods of Advertising* (New York: Nelson Chesman, 1870), 64.

57 *York County Independent*, June 7, 1877, and Edwin Emery, *History of Sanford, Maine* (Fall River: William Morrell Emery, 1901), 502–6.

58 Thompson signed the back of the panorama with black pigment applied with the same brush width as the black paint that outlines many of the figures in the first scenes of the panorama. Conservators at the Williamstown Art Conservation Center confirmed, in the late 1990s conservation campaign, that both the outlines and the ghoul are overpaint and not part of the original design.

59 The *Newark Daily Advertiser* for November 22, 1850, cites both of these scenes among "the principal ones distinguished in the panorama for their beauty." Consulting Greenwood's *Descriptive Catalogue of the Bunyan Tableaux*, 1856, the full list of missing scenes may be identified: *Triumphal Procession Entering the Town of Vanity*, *Christian and Faithful Passing Through the Fair*, *King of the Place Offers Them Worldly Honors*, *Trial of Christian and Faithful*, *Martyrdom of Faithful*, *Final Scene* (this is the last scene before what is identified as part 2, indicating an intermission in the performance at this point as the panorama operators changed reels), *Christian and Hopeful Meet By-Ends*, *Demas Entices hem to the Silver Mine*, *The Pilgrim's* [*sic*] *Behold the Fate of Lot's Wife*, *They Approach the River of the Water of Life*, *The River of the Water of Life*, *By-Path Meadows*, and *Giant Despair Catches the Pilgrims Asleep on His Grounds.*

60 *Bulletin of the American Art-Union* 3, no. 5 (August 1850): 82.

EPILOGUE

1 Ward's program leaflet is quoted in Erkki Huhtamo, *Illusions in Motion: Media Archaeology of the Moving Panorama and Related Spectacles* (Cambridge and London: MIT Press, 2012), 246.

2 Ibid., 247. The quote comes from the earliest appearance of the story in the November 18, 1865, issue of *The Californian*. It appeared there within a larger story entitled *"Mark Twain" on the Launch of the Steamer "Capital"*; the two parts of that story are entitled "I Get Mr. Muff Nickerson to Go with Me and Assist in Reporting the Great Steamboat Launch. He Relates the Interesting History of the Travelling Panoramist" and "The Entertaining History of the Scriptural Panoramist," which is told in the voice of the forementioned Nickerson. Twain later revised and reprinted the story in several other formats.

3 A copy is in the collections of the Dyer Library and Saco Museum, Saco, Maine; gift of Peter Morelli.

4 See Huhtamo, *Illusions in Motion,* 264–67.

5 A broadside in the collections of the Kennebec Historical Society in Augusta, Maine, promotes "The Gigantic Moving Pano-Diorama: Atlantic Cable!!" Huhtamo also notes the existence of the Miratorium, Polemorama, Polyorama, Stratopateticon, Pantechnoptemon, and Zographicon, among others. Stationary panoramas, the predecessor of the moving panorama, also had a renaissance in the last quarter of the nineteenth century. Their proprietors, too, avoided the term and dubbed their works "cy-

cloramas" or "cosmoramas"; a notable example is the Gettysburg Cyclorama (1883), a later version of which is featured at the Gettysburg National Military Park, Pennyslvania.

6 Stereoviews by F. G. Weller (1877) are in the collections of the Dyer Library and Saco Museum, as are glass lantern slides from around the same period (gift of Peter Morelli). Joseph Boggs Beale also produced a popular set of lantern slides based on *The Pilgrim's Progress*, probably in the 1880s or 1890s (see n. 26).

7 For more on dissolving views, see Huhtamo, *Illusions in Motion,* 293 and 267–73.

8 Ibid., 268.

9 Ibid., 276–80.

10 Ibid., 292. Huhtamo outlines the complete history of the Myriorama in his chapter entitled "A Medium's Final Fanfares," 287–96.

11 Ibid., 280

12 Twain's notebook is quoted in Huhtamo, *Illusions in Motion,* 280.

13 Ibid., 342. It should be noted that magic lantern shows and stereoviews also were common tools in religious instruction.

14 This is according to texts for the Brigham Young University Museum of Art exhibition *On the Road with C.C.A. Christensen: Utah Panorama Paintings* (2003), retrieved online at www.tfaoi.com/aa/3aa/3aa452.htm on November 3, 2013.

15 Huhtamo, *Illusions in Motion,* 342–44.

16 Ibid. Tabletop panoramas were also popular educational toys in the late nineteenth century. Milton Bradley's *Historiscope*, providing an overview of American history, and *Myriopticon*, depicting the American Civil War, are in the collections of Richard Balzer, as is a toy panorama version of *Rip Van Winkle* manufactured by McLoughlin Bros. and Co. For more on toy panoramas, see Huhtamo, *Illusions in Motion*, 367–68.

17 See Kerry A. O'Brien, "Science-Art-History: The Early Years of the York Institute, Saco, Maine, 1866–1971," *Maine Historical Society Quarterly* 26, no. 4 (Spring 1987).

18 The brief mention of the gift in the *Biddeford Evening Record* of October 12, 1896, states that the gift "is valuable in more than one way to the institution."

19 York Institute records from January 5, 1897, read: "The president was authorized to use the hall to exhibit the panorama of Pilgrim's Progress." Dyer Library/Saco Museum, Saco, Maine, museum archives.

20 "What Do You Know about Biddeford?" unidentified newspaper clipping, November 17, 1925. Dyer Library Archives, Andrews Scrap Book no. 2, p. 108, col. 4. The Biddeford City Directory of 1870 lists Day as an auctioneer and purveyor of secondhand furniture; the last entry for Day is 1875. Dyer Library/Saco Museum, Saco, Maine, museum archives. Thanks to Tom Hardiman for these citations.

21 Though, in fact, a piece of the panorama *was* exhibited before three years had elapsed. Peter Morelli remembers, "The York Institute exhibited a large portion of the panorama in 1997. It was going to open without our really knowing what it was, but

I found the descriptive catalog in the Harvard card catalog. Tom got it faxed and rewrote most of his wall text." Correspondence with the author, February 10, 2014.

22 Ellen S. Harris, Kevin J. Avery, and Thomas Hardiman Jr., *The Grand Moving Panorama of Pilgrim's Progress* (Montclair, N.J.: Montclair Art Museum, 1999).

23 A photograph of the panorama unrolled in that space and being worked on by conservators is on p. 22 of Harris et al., *The Grand Moving Panorama of Pilgrim's Progress.*

24 Purchased by Designtex, a global design firm, in 2012.

25 The circa 1853 script for a now-lost panorama known as *The Grand Moving Mirror of California* is in the collections of the Maine Historical Society in Portland, bound together with the showman L. E. Emerson's journal and record book. The Velaslavasay Panorama Theater in Los Angeles used the script in 2010 as the inspiration to create and perform a new moving panorama with the help of local artists.

26 The September 21 performance was presented in conjunction with *Panoramas in Motion: A Public Symposium,* organized by the Dyer Library and Saco Museum and hosted by Saco City Hall, September 21–22, 2012. The performance at the symposium was a twin bill, with Terry Borton of the American Magic Lantern Theater serving as the narrator or "delineator" for the panorama show and also presenting a magic lantern show based on the *Pilgrim's Progress* slides of Joseph Boggs Beale.

SELECTED BIBLIOGRAPHY

Alison, Archibald. *Essays on the Nature and Principles of Taste.* Edinburgh: 1811; reprint, Boston: Cummings and Hillard, 1812.

Altick, Richard D. *The Shows of London.* Cambridge, Mass.: Harvard University Press, Belknap Press, 1978.

"Another Pilgrim's Progress." *New York Tribune*, April 30, 1851, p. 5.

Arrington, Joseph Earl. "Godfrey N. Frankenstein's Moving Panorama of Niagara Falls." *New York History* 49 (April 1968): 169–99.

———. "John Banvard's Moving Panorama of the Mississippi, Missouri, and Ohio Rivers." *Filson Club Historical Quarterly* 32 (July 1958): 207–40.

———. "Skirving Moving Panorama: Colonel Fremont's Western Expedition Pictorialized." *Oregon Historical Quarterly* 45 (June 1964): 139–43.

———. "William Burr's Moving Panorama of the Great Lakes, the Niagara, St. Lawrence, and Saguenay Rivers." *Ontario History* 51 (Summer 1959): 141–62.

Avery, Kevin J. "*The Heart of the Andes* Exhibited: Frederic E. Church's Window on the Equatorial World." *American Art Journal* 18, no. 1 (1986): 52–72.

———. *The Panorama and Its Manifestation in American Landscape Painting, 1795-1870.* Ph.D. diss., Columbia University, 1995. Ann Arbor, Mich.: UMI Company, 1995.

———. "Whaling Voyage Round the World: Russell and Purrington's Moving Panorama and Herman Melville's 'Mighty Book.'" *American Art Journal* 22 (1990): 78.

Avery, Kevin J., and Peter M. Fodera. *John Vanderlyn's Panoramic View of the Palace and Gardens of Versailles.* New York: Metropolitan Museum of Art, 1988.

Banvard, John. "Adventures of an Artist." *Description of Banvard's Panorama of the Mississippi River.* Boston: Putnam, 1847.

Bryant, William Cullen. "A Funeral Oration, Occasioned by the Death of Thomas Cole, Delivered before the National Academy of Design, New-York, May 4, 1848." New York: D. Appleton, 1848.

Bulletin of the American Art-Union. August 1850, December 1850, and June 1851.

Bunyan, John. *The Pilgrim's Progress*. Ed. W. R. Owens. London: Oxford World's Classics, 2008.

———. *The Pilgrim's Progress*, with an Essay on the "Life of Bunyan" by Robert Southey, Esq. London: J. Murray and J. Major, 1830.

———. *Pilgrim's Progress Illustrated*. Ill. Henry Courtney Selous. London: M. M. Holloway, 1844.

Catalogue of Paintings by Daniel Huntington, N.A., Exhibiting at the Art Union Buildings. New York: Snowden, 1850.

Ceram, C. W. *Archaeology of the Cinema*. London: Hudson and Thames, 1965.

Cole, Thomas. "Essay on American Scenery." *American Monthly Magazine* 1 (January 1836).

Cowdrey, Mary Bartlett. *American Academy of Fine Arts and American Art-Union Exhibition Record 1816–1852*. New York: New-York Historical Society, 1953.

———. *National Academy of Design Exhibition Record, 1826–1860*. Vol. 2. New York: New-York Historical Society, 1943.

Dahl, Curtis. "Artemus Ward: Comic Panoramist." *New England Quarterly* 32 (March 1959): 476–78.

Dearinger, David Bernard. *Paintings and Sculpture in the Collection of the National Academy of Design: 1826–1925*. New York: Hudson Hills Press, 2004.

A Descriptive Catalogue of the Panorama of Bunyan's Pilgrim's Progress, A. New York: R. Craighead, 1851.

Feaver, William. *John Martin*. Oxford: Clarendon Press, 1975.

Gerdts, William H. "Daniel Huntington's *Mercy's Dream*: A Pilgrimage Through Bunyanesque Imagery." *Winterthur Portfolio* 14, no. 2 (summer 1979): 171–94.

Greenhouse, Wendy. "Daniel Huntington and the Ideal of Christian Art." *Winterthur Portfolio* 31, no. 2/3 (summer/autumn 1996): 103–40.

Greenwood, R. J. *A Descriptive Catalogue of the Bunyan Tableaux*. Albany, N.Y.: Joel Munsell, 1854.

———. *A Descriptive Catalogue of the Bunyan Tableaux*. Albany, N.Y.: J. Munsell, 1856. Collections of the Dyer Library and Saco Museum, Saco, Maine.

———. *A Descriptive Catalogue of the Bunyan Tableaux*. Albany, N.Y.: J. Munsell, 1867.

Groce, George C., and David H. Wallace. *The New York Historical Society's Dictionary of Artists in America 1564–1860*. New Haven and London: Yale University Press, 1975.

Hahler, Christine Anne. . . . *Illustrated by Darley*. Wilmington: Delaware Art Museum, 1978.

Hanners, John. "John Banvard's Mississippi Panorama." *American History Illustrated* 17, no. 7 (1982): 30–39.

Harris, Ellen S., Kevin J. Avery, and Thomas Hardiman Jr. *The Grand Moving Panorama of Pilgrim's Progress*. Montclair, N.J.: Montclair Art Museum, 1999.

Harris, Neil. *The Artist in American Society: The Formative Years, 1790–1860*. New York: George Braziller, 1966; reprint, Chicago: University of Chicago Press, 1982.

Huhtamo, Erkki. *Illusions in Motion: Media Archaeology of the Moving Panorama and Related Spectacles.* Cambridge, Mass.: MIT Press, 2012.

Huntington, Daniel. "Lecture on Christian Art Read at the National Academy of Design." New York City, July 1851. Winterthur Library, Wilmington, Delaware, Joseph Downs Collection and the Winterthur Archives, doc. 519.

Hyde, Ralph. *Panoramania! The Art and Entertainment of the "All-Embracing" View.* London: Trefoil Publications in association with Barbican Art Gallery, 1988.

Johnson, Galen K. "*The Pilgrim's Progress* in the History of American Public Discourse." *LATCH* 4 (2011): 1–31.

Ketner, Joseph D. II. "An Enclave of African American Artists in Antebellum Cincinnati: James P. Ball and Robert S. Duncanson." Lecture presented on September 13, 2012, at the Ira Wallach Art Gallery, Columbia University, New York.

Koller, Gabriele, ed. *The Panorama in the Old World and the New.* Amberg, Germany: International Panorama Council, 2010.

Literary World, November 23, 1850, p. 411.

McDermott, John Francis. *The Lost Panoramas of the Mississippi.* Chicago: University of Chicago Press, 1958.

Miller, Angela. *The Empire of the Eye: Landscape Representation and American Cultural Politics, 1825–1875.* Ithaca, N.Y., and London: Cornell University Press, 1993.

———. *The Imperial Republic: Narratives of National Expansion in American Art, 1820–1860* (Ph.D. diss., Yale University, 1985).

Miller, Ralph N. "Thomas Cole and Alison's Essays on Taste." *New York History* 37 (1956): 281–99.

Mills, Paul Chadbourne. *The Buffalo Hunter and Other Related Versions of the Subject in Nineteenth-century American Art and Literature.* Santa Barbara, Calif.: Santa Barbara Museum of Art, 1973.

Morelli, Peter and Julia. "The *Moving Panorama of Pilgrim's Progress:* The Hudson River School's Moving Exhibition" in *The Panorama in the Old World and the New*, ed. Gabriele Koller. Amberg, Germany: International Panorama Council, 2010.

Newark Daily Advertiser, November 22, 1850 and April 30, 1851.

Newington-Cropsey Foundation. *Jasper Francis Cropsey: Catalogue Raisonné.* Vol. 1, 1842–1863. Hastings-on-Hudson, N.Y.: Newington-Cropsey Foundation, 2013.

Noble, Louis Legrand. *The Life and Works of Thomas Cole.* 3rd ed. New York: Sheldon, Blakeman, 1856.

Novak, Barbara, ed. *The Thyssen-Bornemisza Collection: Nineteenth-Century American Painting.* New York, London, and Paris: Artabras, Abbeville Press, 1986; reprint, 1991.

Nygren, Edward J., ed. *Views and Visions: American Landscape Before 1830.* Washington, D.C.: Corcoran Gallery of Art, 1986.

Odell, George C. D. *Annals of the New York Stage.* New York: Columbia University Press, 1928.

Oettermann, Stefan. *The Panorama; History of a Mass Medium.*

Trans. Deborah Lucas Schneider. Reprint, New York: Zone Books, 1997.
O'Gorman, James F. *Accomplished in All Departments of Art: Hammatt Billings of Boston, 1818–1874*. Amherst: University of Massachusetts Press, 1998.
Oliver, Christopher C. "Antebellum Moving Panoramas of the Mississippi: Land, Commerce, and Race," presented to the McNeil Center for Early American Studies Seminar Series, Winterthur Museum, Wilmington, Delaware, March 18, 2011.
Parry, Ellwood C. *The Art of Thomas Cole: Ambition and Imagination*. Wilmington: University of Delaware Press, 1988.
Peterson, Martin E. "On the Nature of the Horse of the American West in Nineteenth Century Art." *Great Plains Quarterly* 7 (Winter 1986): 39–42.
Powell, Earl A. *Thomas Cole*. New York: Harry N. Abrams, 1990.
Schweizer, Paul D. "The Voyage of Life: A Chronology" in *Thomas Cole's Voyage of Life*. Utica: Munson-Williams-Proctor Institute, 1985.
Smith, David E. "Illustrations of American Editions of *Pilgrim's Progress* to 1870." *Princeton University Library Chronicle* 26, no. 1 (Autumn 1964): 16–26.
———. "Publication of John Bunyan's Works in America." *Bulletin of the New York Public Library* 66 (1962): 632.
Speiser, Anthony. "Jasper F. Cropsey: Painter of Faith" in Newington-Cropsey Foundation, *Jasper Francis Cropsey: Catalogue Raisonné*, vol. 1, 1842–1863.
"The Splendid Moving Mirror of the Bunyan Tableaux!" Polytechnic Institute [location unknown], circa 1857. Dyer Library/Saco Museum, Saco, Maine, museum archives.
"The Splendid Moving Mirror of the Bunyan Tableaux!" St. Lawrence Hall, Toronto, October 22, 1857. Metropolitan Toronto Library, Canadian History Department. Ottawa: Canadian Institute for Historical Microreproductions, 1987.
The Story in Color!! Bunyan's Pilgrim's Progress. New York: George F. Nesbitt, circa 1851–1854. Olana State Historic Site, Hudson, New York.
Sweeney, J. Gray. "'Endued with Rare Genius": Frederic Edwin Church's 'To the Memory of Cole.'" *Smithsonian Studies in American Art* 2, no. 1 (Winter 1988): 44–71.
Talbot, William S. *Jasper F. Cropsey, 1823–1900*. Washington, D.C.: Smithsonian Institution Press, 1970.
Wallach, Alan. "Making a Picture of the View from Mount Holyoke." In *American Iconology*, edited by David C. Miller. New Haven and London: Yale University Press, 1993.

INDEX

Page numbers in *italic* refer to illustrations.

ABOUT THE AUTHORS

KEVIN J. AVERY is a retired associate curator of American Paintings and Sculpture at the Metropolitan Museum of Art, New York, where he is now a senior research scholar. Dr. Avery also is an adjunct professor of art history at Hunter College of the City University of New York. With Peter Fodera, he is co-author of *John Vanderlyn's Panoramic View of the Palace and Gardens of Versailles*, 1988; and, with Franklin Kelly, of *Hudson River School Visions: The Landscapes of Sanford R. Gifford*, 2003. Dr. Avery is author of *Church's Great Picture: The Heart of the Andes*, 1993; and *Treasures from Olana: Landscapes by Frederic Edwin Church*, 2005. A chapter of Dr. Avery's 1995 doctoral dissertation for Columbia University is dedicated to the *Moving Panorama of Pilgrim's Progress*, then thought to be lost.

THOMAS HARDIMAN JR. is the keeper of the Portsmouth Athenaeum, New Hampshire, and the former curator of the Saco Museum. He is credited with rescuing the panorama and connecting it to the panorama of Dr. Avery's earlier research. Hardiman has written and lectured extensively about the art and material culture of northern New England, including an influential *Antiques* magazine article establishing a body of work for southern Maine cabinetmakers Joshua Cumston and David Buckminster.

JESSICA SKWIRE ROUTHIER, former director of the Saco Museum, led a major project to preserve and interpret the *Moving Panorama of Pilgrim's Progress* in 2012. She has written extensively on regional artistic traditions in Maine, including dedicated publications on landscape painters Charles Codman and Harrison Bird Brown and articles in *Antiques* and *Antiques and Fine Art* magazines, among others. Ms. Routhier also has worked in the curatorial departments of the Museum of Fine Arts, Boston, and the Portland Museum of Art, Maine, and has served as president of Maine Archives and Museums, dedicated to supporting and promoting Maine's collecting institutions. She is a writer, editor, and independent museum professional.

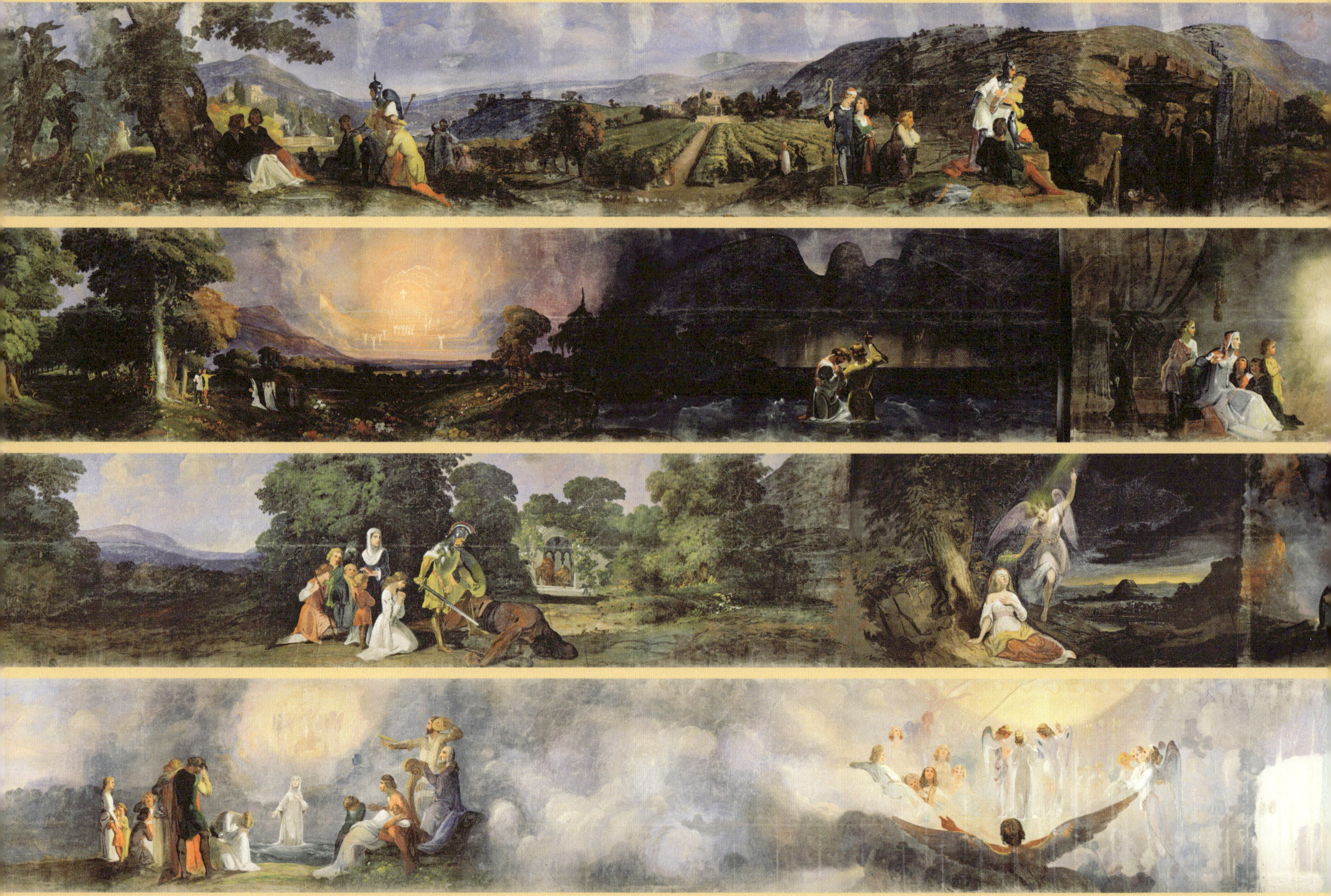